THE ZOMBIE SHOOTING GUIDE

THE ZOMBIE SHOOTING GUIDE

SURVIVAL TRAINING FOR THE WORST-CASE SCENARIO

MARK GREENMAN

Photographs by SAM GOLDENBERG

OODA
MEDIA GROUP

LOS ANGELES

Published by OODA Media Group, Los Angeles, California

For permission to reproduce selections from this book, write to:
3940 Laurel Canyon Blvd #488, Los Angeles, CA 91604
or info@OODAmediagroup.com

Book Design: Laurie Young

Cover Design: Alex Saskalidis

Library of Congress Control Number: 2013911073

ISBN 978-0-9895945-0-9

To YiaYia and Pappou,
Who Make All Things Possible

CONTENTS

INTRODUCTION

YOU'RE PROBABLY GOING to die in the Zombie Apocalypse.

That's not because you're not a survivor. And it's not because Zombies are "the ultimate threat." It's because pretty much everything you've learned from popular culture will get you killed. The Zombie films, TV shows, books, comics, and games that we all know and love are doing us a tremendous disservice when it comes to preparing us for a real-life Zombie Outbreak.

Almost all Z fiction focuses on long-term survival, where the big issues are finding food, shelter and ammunition as the world is consumed by a relentless, shuffling hoard of the Undead. The problem here is that before you can worry about the luxury of long-term survival, you have to survive the initial Outbreak. Which, if you were to apply many of the commonly espoused tactics, is simply not going to happen.

For instance, the recommendation that we fight Zombies with hand-to-hand weapons is suicidal. The chief threat in a Zombie Outbreak is *the Zombie Virus.* So going Hotel Rwanda on a Z's skull with a machete is going to cover you in highly infectious blood — about as good for your long-term survival as cracking open a piñata full of smallpox. Yet, virtually every Zombie reference I have come across advocates this deadly tactic "to conserve ammunition."

Further, Z fiction constantly portrays groups of survivors scavenging for supplies. This is a bad idea. When disaster strikes, you should not be scavenging for anything. Prepare *now.* You can buy a few months' worth of food and water at Costco for less than $300. When the Zombie Outbreak occurs, you should be boarding up the house, laying low, and living off your supplies while the world outside collapses.

The last thing you should do is head for the Walmart. Aside from the whole "There's Zombies Outside" issue, you're exponentially increasing your odds of being shot or trampled while fighting over that last can of corn.

And that's just what's going to happen. Most people have more condiments in their refrigerator than they have food. As we have seen during real-life emergencies such as hurricanes, when people start to panic, grocery stores are sold out within hours, and supplies can be disrupted for weeks. The Zombie Apocalypse is not the time to go grocery shopping.

Then we get to the issue of carrying rifles and shotguns. Long arms are far and away the most effective weapons, but they are also among the least practical in a Zombie Outbreak. You can't carry a rifle around in pre-Zombie society. No matter how pimped your AR, it's simply not fashionably appropriate to wear one out of the house. Which means that you are unlikely to have one on hand during the initial day of the Outbreak, when you're at work or picking up the kids from school.

Perhaps you keep a rifle in your car. Once again, this is not as ideal as it sounds. Remember rush hour traffic? That's just people trying to get home on a normal day. Imagine if they were fleeing from Zombies in Downtown Anywhere, USA. After an Outbreak, roads will become parking lots, hysterical people will be running amok in the street, and it's just going to be a shit show.

It will be extremely difficult to navigate a crowd like that with a rifle, to say nothing of the unwanted attention that it will attract. Far from scaring off bad guys, people left and right will be trying to kill you for your gear so they can survive. And that's just the civilians.

The police and military will either confiscate your rifle Katrina style, or kill you outright because you look like an active shooter. *Not good.* In short, while rifles are better for fighting Zombies in the long run, brandishing them in the early stages of the Zombie Outbreak increases your odds of fighting armed humans — who, for the record, are far more dangerous than any Zombie.

So now we get to defending ourselves with handguns. But, once again, the media has sorely led us astray. While Rick and the gang seem to have no problem executing running, one-handed headshots on multiple Zombies without missing, that's just Hollywood bullshit.

In reality, statistics point out that the average police officer achieves a 1:3 hit ratio when in combat. That means that for every three bullets fired, only one round hits the assailant *anywhere* on his body. And that's a full-size, 6-foot tall criminal — not a 5-inch wide Zombie brain.

This is the reality that *The Zombie Shooting Guide* is designed to confront. Because of the impracticality of machetes and rifles, handguns are our best choice for defending ourselves during the beginning of the Zombie Outbreak. Yet if we simply replicate the static firing range practice used by most police agencies, we will only achieve a similar 1:3 hit ratio. And with that level of skill, we will quickly be killed due to our lack of headshot accuracy.

However, with proper training, we still have a chance for survival. In my research, I have come across data on law enforcement agencies that have bucked this trend of 33% hit mediocrity, and have achieved 80% to 90% hit rates.

I have taken their successful training methods and modified them for self-defense during a Zombie Outbreak. The result is a progressive training program that will take you from the very basics of marksmanship to making headshots on Fast Zombies.

Whether you are a total beginner or a seasoned shooter, there are exercises in *The ZSG* that will engage you at your current level, and then allow you to improve steadily until you have reached your goals.

In addition to being tailor-made for Zombie combat, this training does not cost any more than normal shooting techniques because much of the groundwork is done at home, using dryfire and inexpensive pistol simulation tools.

I cannot guarantee that you will survive the Zombie Apocalypse. But if you read *The Zombie Shooting Guide,* and apply the training techniques, you'll have a fighting chance.

WARNING

THE ZOMBIE SHOOTING GUIDE: SURVIVAL TRAINING FOR THE WORST-CASE SCENARIO IS FOR USE IN THE EVENT OF A ZOMBIE OUTBREAK ONLY. IT IS INTENDED ONLY FOR SELF-DEFENSE. UNLESS YOU ARE BEING ATTACKED AND YOUR LIFE IS IN IMMINENT DANGER, DO NOT USE ANY OF THESE TECHNIQUES.

BE SAFE. BE RESPONSIBLE. FOLLOW THE LAW.
AND ONLY USE YOUR POWERS FOR GOOD.

1

IT IS SAID THAT IF YOU KNOW YOUR ENEMIES AND KNOW YOURSELF, YOU WILL NOT BE IMPERILED IN A HUNDRED BATTLES; IF YOU DO NOT KNOW YOUR ENEMIES BUT DO KNOW YOURSELF, YOU WILL WIN ONE AND LOSE ONE; IF YOU DO NOT KNOW YOUR ENEMIES NOR YOURSELF, YOU WILL BE IMPERILED IN EVERY SINGLE BATTLE.

— SUN TZU, *THE ART OF WAR*

KNOW YOUR ENEMY

KNOWLEDGE OF THE enemy is essential to all military victory, while ignorance of the enemy is the chief cause of defeat. This ancient truism of the battlefield is key to confronting the multi-faceted threat paradigm that is the Zombie Apocalypse. To train effectively, you must know what you're up against.

THE TRADITIONAL ZOMBIE AKA WALKERS

When most of us think about Zombies, we think of the Romero-style lumbering corpses that relentlessly attack the living. From the 1968 film classic *Night of the Living Dead* to the wildly successful TV *The Walking Dead*, these are the Zombies that have dominated the popular imagination.

There have been many hypotheses as to what will cause the dead to rise and attack the living, including:

- Space radiation (*Night of the Living Dead*)
- The Solanum Virus (*The Zombie Survival Guide* and *World War Z* books)
- Aliens discovered in China (*Day by Day Armageddon*)
- The T-Virus (*Resident Evil*)

The truth is: We have no credible scientific theories on what would cause the dead to rise and feast on the living. And from a tactical standpoint, it really doesn't matter. Regardless of origin, all reanimated corpses have two defining characteristics: They are slow, and they are dead. These traits offer advantages and disadvantages.

The fact that Walkers attack at a leisurely pace is an obvious advantage. This allows survivors to outrun them, and it also makes it fairly easy to shoot them in the head. For this reason, an individual Zombie, or even a small pack, is not a huge threat as long as you are alert and properly armed.

However, the fact that these Zombies are dead is a huge drawback. They will never get tired, and can pursue you indefinitely. They won't starve to death. They can't bleed to death. And they cannot be killed with nerve gas, shrapnel, or wounds to major vital organs. This renders most military technology ineffective.

Since they are dead, these Zombies are hard to kill.

The only practical way to annihilate the Walking Dead is with precision gunfire. But not any shot will do. Although most human gunshot victims die from a loss of blood, Zombies don't require oxygenated blood to function, so blood loss is totally irrelevant to them. That mean even a shot through the heart is worthless.

Logically, then, the only way to stop the Undead dead in their tracks is to destroy the brain, causing all motor function to cease. Alas, that means making a headshot on a moving target that's about the size of a 3x5-inch note card. This would be a difficult shot at the shooting range. Imagine making it while under attack and in fear for your life.

Although Walkers are controlled by the brain, they also rely on the spine to transmit nerve signals to the limbs. So, if the spine were severed, the Zombie would be paralyzed from the waist down, causing him to collapse instantly. Although still capable of crawling and biting, its combat effectiveness would be greatly reduced. Unfortunately, the spine is only about 1-inch wide, so this is also an extremely difficult shot to make.

THE INFECTED AKA FAST ZOMBIES

The single biggest threat to man's continued dominance on the planet is the virus.
— JOSHUA LEDERBERG, NOBEL LAUREATE

The Infected are people who have been exposed to a virus that produces vast quantities of adrenaline, testosterone, and rage. Like the traditional Zombie, they lack fear, will never negotiate, and will relentlessly attack and infect all humans they come across.

There are two primary differences between The Infected and the Walking Dead: The Infected are not dead, and they don't walk. Instead, The Infected sprint at high speeds, making them infinitely more dangerous.

This scenario was portrayed in the 2002 film *28 Days Later,* where the "Rage Virus" turns most of England's population into Zombies. The video game *Left 4 Dead* espouses a similar scenario, where a "Green Flue" outbreak in Pennsylvania unleashes a Zombie Apocalypse.

Some Zombie purists have bemoaned the inclusion of Fast Zombies, claiming they are not "real Zombies" because they are not reanimated human corpses. I'm sure these guys will continue their semantic arguments until they are turned into corpses by The Infected.

WHILE THE PROSPECT OF THE DEAD RISING DEFIES SCIENCE AND LOGIC, A VIRUS THAT TURNS PEOPLE INTO BLOODTHIRSTY PSYCHOTICS IS WELL WITHIN THE REALM OF POSSIBILITY.

The virus could occur naturally, through some horrific rabies mutation leading to a Zombie Pandemic. Or, the Zombie Virus could be developed in a lab for use as a devastating biological weapon.

Virologists like Samita Andreansky, of the University of Miami's Miller School of Medicine, agree that this could happen:

"Mix rabies with a flu virus to get airborne transmission, a measles virus to get personality changes, the encephalitis virus to cook your brain with fever [to increase aggression further] and throw in the Ebola virus to cause you to bleed from your guts. **Combine all these things together, and you'll get something like a Zombie virus.**"

Nations are not above creating such a weapon. We have only to look at the hydrogen bomb, VX nerve gas, and weaponized smallpox to realize that governments are more than willing to build the tools of world destruction. The Zombie Virus would simply be another tool in their Apocalyptic toolbox.

Yet, given the advances in bioengineering and the democratization of laboratory technology, the Zombie Virus could also be created by a small group or determined individual. According to Brett Giroir, former head of the US Defense Advanced Research Projects Agency (DARPA):

"What took me three weeks in a sophisticated laboratory in a top-tier medical school 20 years ago, with millions of dollars in equipment, can essentially be done by a relatively unsophisticated technician. **A person at a graduate-school level has all the tools and technologies to implement a sophisticated program to create a bio weapon.**"

So, while some may protest that they're not "real Zombies," The Infected are a real potential threat, and you should prepare now to deal with them.

Because they are living humans infected with a virus that pumps them full of adrenaline and testosterone, it's like they're on killer steroids. Their muscles are on overdrive, so they're inhumanly strong, can sprint at high speeds, and fight with a berserk fury.

Numerous tests have shown that the average man can run 7 yards, or 21 feet, in 1.5 seconds. So, it's a safe assumption that The Infected will be at least as fast. This speed makes even a lone Infected more dangerous than a pack of lumbering Walkers.

In addition to speed and strength, the massive surge of adrenaline and other chemicals released by the virus makes The Infected immune to pain. Rather than giving up after being shot like a normal person, The Infected — much like their Undead cousins — will continue to attack relentlessly until they have been destroyed.

According to the FBI Firearms Training Unit:

"Even if the heart is instantly destroyed, there is sufficient oxygen in the brain to support full and voluntary action for 10-15 seconds."

That means that even with a perfect shot through the heart, The Infected can still sprint for up to 100 yards and attack you. Although they will die a few seconds later, it will be too late: You will be infected.

So, the only reliable way to stop The Infected is to disrupt the Central Nervous System — either by blasting the brain or severing the spine. Therefore, for combat purposes, The Infected are Zombies, just way faster and more dangerous.

The one upside, however, is that The Infected need food and water to survive, just like any other human being. That means that if you can find a secure location with enough supplies, you can wait a few months for them to starve to death.

However, if you're in a secure location with plenty of food and water, you will become the target of threats far more dangerous than Zombies.

OTHER THREATS

You know what's even scarier than Zombies? Desperate humans. And in the Zombie Apocalypse, there are going to be a whole lot of them. Much as we would wish that our shared struggle against a common foe would unite us as a species, the fact is there will be more close quarters killing than Kumbaya singing.

Our modern society is incredibly fragile. Even minor disasters, like an unusually heavy snowstorm in October, can leave millions without power. As we have seen from hurricanes Katrina and Sandy, state and federal governments are overwhelmed by regional emergencies. The result: massive blackouts, food and water shortages, and millions of people left to fend for themselves.

Now, imagine a nationwide, shit-hit-the-fan emergency — say, a dispersal of the Zombie Virus by North Korean commandos in 30 of America's largest cities. (Check out the short story, *30 Cities,* in the Epilogue.)

People are going to think, It's The End of the World, and they will act accordingly. There's going to be widespread panic, with rampant looting, arson, rape and murder — a Darwin-meets-Grand-Theft-Auto reality whose danger cannot be overstated.

BREAKDOWN OF INFRASTRUCTURE

In the first few days of the Outbreak, some will be celebrating their video game fantasy come to life. But soon the hard reality of a Zombie Apocalypse will set in. In the first 48 hours after Z Day, grocery stores, gas stations, and gun shops will have been picked clean. Power will be intermittent as employ-ees in the utilities sector stop showing up for work. Roads will be clogged, the phones down, and the Internet unreliable.

The average American has more condiments in their fridge than they have food. Due to poor PR and media programs such as *Doomsday Preppers,* being prepared for an emergency has been conflated with being a Survivalist nut job. Combined with the cognitive dissonance of the "It won't happen to me" mentality, only a small percentage of the population has even a week's worth of food and water on hand in case of an emergency.

The result is that within a week after Z Day, millions of Americans will begin to starve. The problem will only cascade, because modern grocery stores and super centers rely on a delicate network of "just in time deliveries" rather than large warehouses of supplies. Once they run out, they will be unable to order more food due to the inaccessibility of the roads, shortages of gasoline, and the breakdown of the electrical grid — all certainties in the aftermath of a Zombie Outbreak.

How cranky do you get when you haven't eaten for a few hours longer than normal? Now imagine three days without food. A week. How long until you did something crazy to survive? If you were starving, and you suspected someone had food, would you just sit around, waiting to die? Or would you do whatever it took to end the hunger?

If you're the kind of person who bought this book, chances are you already have at least a month's worth of food and water at your house. So the good news is, you won't be sitting around starving. The bad news is that now you're a massive target, because for every prepared household, there are going to be at least 10 starving ones. Meanwhile, 1 in 3 American households has a gun. . . .

Do you see where this is going?

POST-APOCALYPTIC OUTLAWS

As anyone who follows the news can tell you, America has no shortage of violent criminals. Unfortunately, they are likely to survive longer than most civilians in a Zombie Apocalypse, because their predatory nature makes them well suited to a breakdown of society.

To give an example of this, it's instructive to look at Argentina, which suffered an economic collapse from 1999 to 2002. After the collapse, people's savings were wiped out, social services plummeted, and the crime rate skyrocketed. There was a tremendous increase in predatory crimes such a robbery, rape, and murder, which continue to this day. By 2009, a survey by the the Argentinian newspaper *La Nación* concluded that, "nine out of ten people, or a direct family member, have been attacked by criminals in the last year."

Even more alarming, the crisis gave rise to a new form of commando criminality, where organized gangs would employ home invasion tactics against entire communities. According to Fernando "Ferfal" Aguirre, who lived through the economic collapse:

> "After the crisis in Argentina, it's not uncommon to hear about eight or more bad guys working together. Sometimes they just take over one house, use that as a command post, and spend the rest of the night robbing the rest of the houses on that block."

After Z Day, American criminals will likely start banding together to loot and pillage. We have already seen the violence of gangs that were simply motivated by money and turf. Now imagine what lengths they would go to if they were starving, and law enforcement had been wiped out by Zombies.

2
CHOOSING THE RIGHT WEAPON

AFTER GOD, WE SHOULD PLACE OUR HOPES OF SAFETY ON OUR WEAPONS, NOT IN OUR FORTIFICATIONS ALONE.

— EMPEROR MAURICE, *THE STRATEGIKON*, AD 600

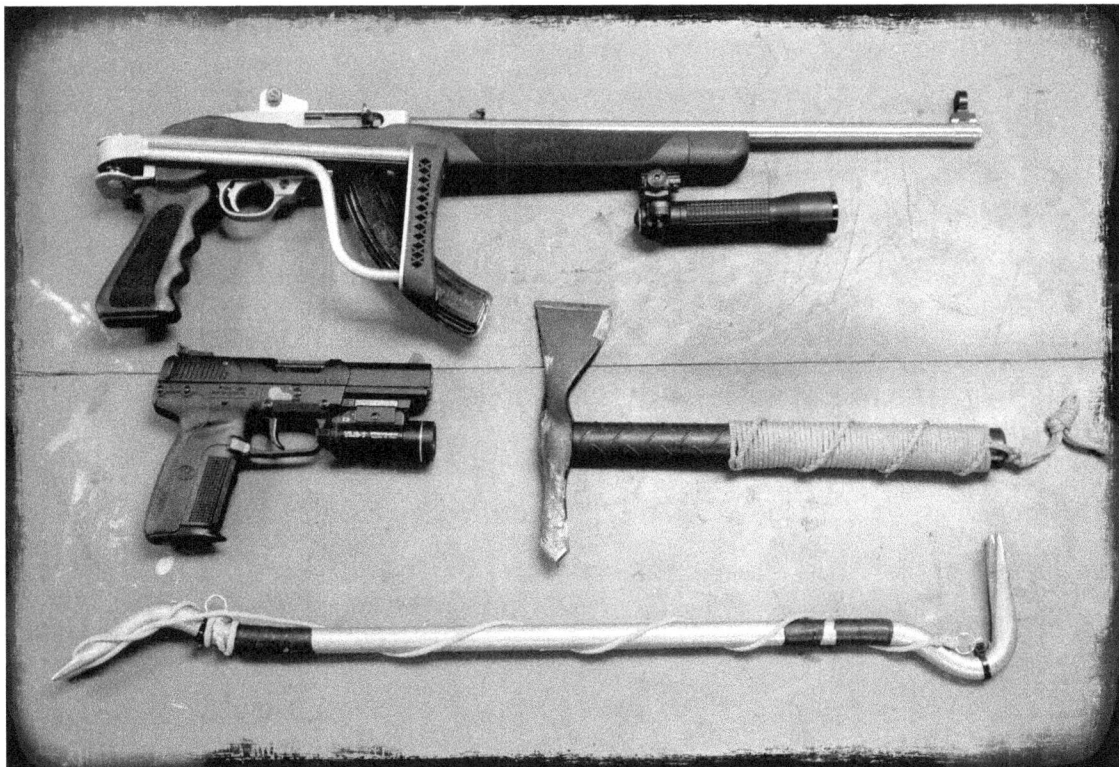

Anti-Zombie Weapons: Modified Ruger 10/22 with folding stock *(top)*; FN Five Seven Pistol with rail-mounted flashlight *(center, left)*; VTAC tactical tomahawk with paracord *(center right)*; 27" titanium crowbar with paracord carry sling *(bottom)*.

BY FAR THE most debated issue when it comes to Zombie survival is the "ideal" Zombie weapon. The truth is, there isn't one. Some are inherently better than others, however, and in order to make an informed decision about our armaments, it's essential to understand the strengths and weaknesses of all potential weapons.

GUNS VS. MELEE WEAPONS

It seems that many folks out there believe handheld weapons such as machetes and crowbars are the ideal anti-Zombie weapon, because they're cheap, quiet, and "never need reloading."

I've got two words that sum up the merit of melee weapons in a Zombie Outbreak: *ocular herpes.*

You see, if someone with herpes cums in your eye, you can get ocular herpes, which is a fancy term for eye herpes.

Think about that for a moment. Herpes. *In your eyes.* Now, consider this — ocular herpes is the leading cause of corneal scarring blindness in the United States.

The average amount of semen ejaculated by a male human is 2 to 5 ml. So this tells us that even small quantities of infected biological fluids are shockingly effective at spreading really lame diseases.

Where the hell am I going with this? Well, the point is this: The human body contains, on average, 5600 ml of blood. When a person becomes infected with the Zombie Virus, every single itty-bitty drop of his blood is now a highly infectious biological weapon that makes eye herpes seem like a trip to Six Flags on free cocaine day.

And when you go Gallagher on a Zombie's skull with a crowbar or sever its main carotid artery with a machete, you're going to be coated in more biological fluids than a German woman at a Bukkake festival. Think hundreds of milliliters at the minimum. If any of that blood comes in contact with your mucosal membranes — your eyes, your mouth, an exposed cut — you're infected. And if that Zombie had herpes, you probably have that as well.

MELEE WEAPONS ARE SUICIDAL WHEN COMBATING A HIGHLY INFECTIOUS ENEMY.

Even if you have WMD-grade protective clothing like a HAZMAT suit and gas mask, you would need a bioweapons-grade decontamination chamber in order to take off your blood-soaked gear without infecting yourself upon removal.

The moral to this story is: Use a gun. Or a crossbow. Or build an air cannon or high-power slingshot. *Anything,* as long as it's not a contact distance weapon. Otherwise you're just going to trade your life for the Zombie's. Although a gun can run out of ammunition, you will still live much longer than those who relied on a machete.

.22 RIMFIRE VS. LARGER CENTERFIRE CALIBERS

This is another fiercely debated topic in the world of Zombie Survival. Proponents argue that .22 caliber weapons are all that is needed, while naysayers decry the humble .22 as grossly underpowered.

Both arguments have their merits.

Advocates of the .22lr cite the low cost of the platform, as most rimfire weapons are approximately $200 to $300, and the ammunition itself is the cheapest on the market, with 500 rounds typically selling for less than $20. This low cost makes it easy to "buy cheap and stack deep," allowing even a Zombie hunter on a budget to prepare.

Also, due to the low-recoil of the .22lr, it can be easily handled by anyone, and follow-up shots are very rapid, a useful trait when engaging a Zombie horde. Further, the .22lr cartridge is very lightweight. Weighing in at 3.3 grams, a shooter can carry 4x more .22lr than they can 9mm or 5.56. This is a potentially lifesaving advantage should your home be overrun and you are forced to flee on foot, with only the gear you can carry on your back.

Finally, because the .22lr has the least muzzle blast of any caliber, it is the ideal cartridge to use with a suppressor (often incorrectly referred to as a silencer). While not "silent," a suppressed .22lr is the quietest firearm available, making it a superb tool when dealing with Zombies, who are attracted to noise.

In short: Given the overwhelming advantages offered by the .22lr, it's understandable why many consider it the ideal Zombie-fighting caliber.

However, opponents point out that while the .22lr has proven deadly over the years, there have been numerous cases of people surviving headshots from the .22lr — including failed suicides when the shot was taken at point blank range.

The human skull is one of the toughest materials on earth, and even larger rounds than the .22lr have been known to ricochet off it, depending on the angle of the shot. Therefore, many are uncomfortable relying on the .22lr for their primary anti-Zombie weapon due to its lack of brain destroying power.

**THE REAL ISSUE WITH .22LR AND ZOMBIES
IS NOT THE LACK OF POWER, BUT THE INHERENT
LACK OF RELIABILITY OF THE .22LR CARTRIDGE
AND THE WEAPONS THAT FIRE THEM.**

The .22 is the cheapest cartridge in the world, and is churned out by the billions. While this makes it superb for recreational shooting, the downside to this low cost is the poor quality control exhibited by most brands of .22lr ammunition.

The .22lr uses a rimfire ignition system, where a drop of impact-sensitive explosive is spun around the inner rim of the cartridge. However, sometimes the inner rim is not fully coated. So when the firing pin hits the cartridge, and it strikes an empty spot, there is a *click!* instead of a BANG! If that happens when a Zombie is right on top of you, you're (un)dead.

As an avid shooter of .22lr, I encounter dud rounds pretty much every time I go to the shooting range. By comparison, this has *never* happened to me with factory-produced centerfire ammunition, which utilizes a more reliable primer ignition system.

Also, due to the sheer volume of .22lr production, there is a much higher percentage of under-loaded and "squib" rounds, when the ammunition machine has accidently loaded the cartridge with too little smokeless powder. In a semi-automatic rifle or pistol, an under-loaded cartridge will not provide enough blowback for the weapon to cycle completely. This will cause a jam — something that is annoying at the shooting range, but potentially fatal in a Zombie attack.

Then there is the soft lead projectile of the .22lr, which is prone to becoming deformed and causing failures to feed. Unlike more expensive calibers, which utilize a full metal jacket that protects the projectile from damage, .22s utilize a soft lead bullet that is only slightly "gilded" with copper, making them much more susceptible to becoming deformed. When the weapon tries to load these misshapen bullets into the small 0.22" chamber, the gun jams. Once again, this happens to me fairly often at the shooting range, especially with bulk pack .22s.

Not only is the .22lr cartridge unreliable, but so are the weapons that fire them. Unlike defensive grade centerfire weapons, which are designed from the ground up to be used in life or death combat situations, .22s are designed to be sporting weapons and are not built to the same demanding standards.

If a Walther P99 jams, a person could die, and so the company builds them to exacting standards. By comparison, if a Walther P22 jams, the average shooter will just clear the jam and return to shooting cans, which is why the Walther P22 is made to much lower standards than the P99. Because of their recreational pedigree, rimfire weapons are not built to be as durable or as inherently reliable as their centerfire counterparts.

All weapons can jam, but the fact is that .22s jam way more than larger caliber weapons.

I *love* the .22lr — it's the caliber I shoot more than any other. But it also drives me crazy, because I experience at least one jam every time I go to the range. By comparison, I have rarely experienced a jam in the thousands of rounds I have shot through my centerfire defensive weapons.

In the event of a Zombie Outbreak, when there will be much less time for rigorous cleaning, I just can't trust the reliability of .22lr weapons with my life.

Now does that make the .22lr worthless? No! It's the most versatile caliber on Earth, and can be used to great effect in a Zombie Apocalypse. The key is to understand the cartridge's limitations — and to act accordingly.

Due to its unpredictability, it would be unwise to rely a .22lr when out in the open and under attack, because if the weapon were to jam you could be quickly overwhelmed and killed.

However, when firing from a position of relative safety, such as from the roof of a building or through gaps of your boarded-up windows, the .22lr is a great choice. It's powerful enough to get the job done, not terribly loud, and since the ammo is so cheap, hopefully you bought a whole lot of it before the Outbreak. When firing from a position where a jam would not be potentially fatal, it makes total sense to utilize the .22lr and conserve your centerfire ammunition for more dangerous missions.

In short, if you want my opinion on the .22lr vs. bigger-caliber weapons debate: Buy a larger caliber weapon, and then buy a .22lr conversion kit for it.

Conversion kits are available for the AR15 rifle and a half-dozen different centerfire pistols. They cost the same as a good .22lr weapon, but tend to be more reliable, easier to clean, and best of all, provide a much simpler and more reliable method of training. Rather than learning how to use two different weapon platforms, which could be confusing under stress, you can utilize one platform with both calibers.

WITH AN AR15 IN 5.56 AND GLOCK 9MM, PLUS .22LR CONVERSIONS FOR BOTH, YOU ARE IN A MUCH STRONGER POSITION THAN IF YOU HAD ONLY PURCHASED A .22LR WEAPON.

When on patrol or bugging out, the weapons would be loaded with the more reliable centerfire ammunition. But should you find yourself in a secure position, and under siege by a Zombie horde, you could convert to .22lr in under a minute, and take full advantage of what that wonderful caliber has to offer.

RIFLES VS. SHOTGUNS

One of the most common threads I see on the forums is whether a shotgun or rifle is better for Zombies. If you based your decision on *Dawn of the Dead,* it would seem that the shotgun is the ideal anti-Zombie weapon. After all, it barely needs to be aimed, and it blows their heads off!

However, it's important to differentiate myth from reality when it comes to the shotgun. There's a popular misconception that the 12 gauge has this huge spray that will provide a "wall of lead" and "knock down" multiple Zombies at once. All without aiming! You just point, shoot, and blow those Zombies away!

Folks, that's some more Hollywood bullshit right there.

A 12 gauge pump action shotgun with an open choke (for maximum spread) loaded with 9 pellet 00 buckshot has a spread of 1" per yard.

I repeat, for every yard the target is away, the shot only spreads 1". *That's it.*

To put that in perspective: At 7 yards — typically the biggest open area inside a home — the shot has only opened up a total of 7 inches, about the size of a Zombie's head. At closer ranges, such as around 10 feet — the width of the average bedroom — the pellets are so closely clustered together that it is practically one solid projectile.

So, at close range, where the majority of Zombie attacks are likely to occur, the shotgun's mythical wall of lead is just that — a myth. The groupings are tight, and the shotgun must be aimed carefully.

WITHIN 7 YARDS, THE SHOTGUN IS JUST A SLOW, HEAVY RIFLE THAT DOESN'T HOLD NEARLY AS MANY ROUNDS.

The shotgun's real benefit is out at 10 to 15 yards, against a moving attacker. Police have used them against criminals in this fashion for over a century, as the 10" to 15" spread of lead increases the chances of a torso hit on a running suspect. If you're fighting armed looters who are trying to rapidly flank your home's defenses, the shotgun's spread would be advantageous.

But as we've already discussed, torso shots are largely ineffective. Unless a lucky pellet strikes the Zombie's spine, he will continue to attack as if nothing has happened. Meanwhile, due to the spread of buckshot at ranges beyond 10 yards, it's possible that the pattern will have opened wide enough that the pellets will miss the head entirely.

However, the real nail in the coffin for the shotgun is the weight and bulk of the ammunition. For every 1lb of weight, you can carry 10 shotgun shells vs. 37 5.56 rifle bullets or 9mm pistol rounds. Furthermore, while rifle and pistol bullets are carried in neat, easy-to-load magazines, shotgun shells must be carried in awkward pouches and loaded individually. A centerfire rifle in an intermediate caliber can carry two to four times more ammunition than a 12 gauge, with less recoil, faster reloads, and vastly farther range.

In short, a shotgun is better than no gun, and is more practical than many types of bolt action hunting rifles. But, compared to a modern semi-automatic rifle, or even a good lever action rifle, there really is no competition — the rifle wins every time.

When it comes to Zombies, shotguns are best left to the movies.

RIFLES VS. HANDGUNS

The most effective Zombie-fighting weapon is a semi automatic rifle firing an intermediate power centerfire cartridge — ideally 5.7x28, 5.45x39, 5.56, 6.8 SPC, or 7.62x39.

These calibers are similar in weight to pistol cartridges, but more accurate and powerful. The rifles that fire them are rugged, reliable, and hold 30 to 50 rounds in standard magazines — with each round typically having four times the kinetic energy of a pistol round. Rifles can be used effectively by pretty much anyone — witness the child soldiers of Liberia — because they require relatively little training to use successfully.

By comparison, even trained professionals have difficulty using handguns effectively. Lacking a shoulder stock, and with a shorter sight radius, it requires much more finesse to shoot a pistol accurately. Furthermore, pistol calibers are much slower than rifles, and deliver far less kinetic energy down range. This creates a paradoxical situation, where handguns are the hardest firearms of all to shoot accurately, yet require the most precise shot placement to be effective.

So, if rifles are so much better than handguns, why are we not devoting our training toward them?

The answer is: Although a rifle is the most effective weapon, it is difficult to find a plausible scenario in which you would have one close at hand during the initial Zombie Outbreak.

To begin with, even a big ass handgun is significantly smaller than the most compact rifle.

Unless you have an NFA tax stamp for a short barreled rifle (which would be awesome) the smallest legal rifle in the US is 26 inches long, and typically weighs in excess of 6 lbs. A loaded AK47 with underfolder stock weighs 9 lbs.

26" long Ruger 10/22 rifle with folding stock next to discreet pistol bag.

Unzipped pistol bag fully loaded with supplies.

Pistol bag holds 450 rounds of 5.7x28mm ammunition, FN 5-7 pistol, 5 loaded pistol magazines, Fobus Holster, earplugs, pistol flashlight, 6 CR2013 batteries, FN 5-7 cleaning kit, and 3 magazine pouches.

**UNLESS YOU'RE ROLLING ULTRA MALL
NINJA STATUS WITH AN AK UNDERFOLDER IN
A TENNIS RACKET CASE AT ALL TIMES,
CHANCES ARE THAT YOU DON'T HAVE A RIFLE CLOSE
AT HAND WHEN YOU ARE OUTSIDE OF THE HOUSE.**

And given that the average workday is 8 hours long, and that the average American only has 12 paid vacation days, most of your time is spent at work, away from your rifle.

Conversely, 39 of the 50 states have Shall Issue Concealed Carry Weapons (CCW) permits. When combined with a comfortable holster, a CCW permit allows you to carry a handgun all day, every day (with a few exceptions). This will be a tremendous practical advantage in the initial Zombie Outbreak, because it is likely to catch everyone off-guard and you will most likely be at work when they arrive. While you won't have your rifle, having a pistol on your side sure beats fighting Zombies with a stapler.

However, the real crux of the issue is that even if you have access to a one, it's probably still not a good idea to be openly carrying a rifle around. While a rifle increases your ability to shoot Zombies, it also increases the likelihood of getting shot.

During the initial stages of the Outbreak, when law enforcement and National Guardsmen are out in force, they will not be happy to see a person with a semi-automatic rifle. They will either attempt to confiscate your weapon, as happened in New Orleans after Katrina, or shoot you outright because you look like an active shooter.

To top it off, a rifle singles you out for unwelcome attention by the other side of the law — namely, desperate people who would kill you for your pimp ass rifle and the goodies in your tactical BUGOUT bag.

This is not desirable. Human beings are much smarter and deadlier than Zombies, and having people deliberately targeting *you* in particular is major bad news. Even the "sheeple," as we are fond of calling them, will be pretty wolf-like after going three days without food.

To quote military contractor James Grey of *Death Valley Magazine:*

"During an Urban Survival situation, I give someone about 15 minutes of walking down the street with a big-ass backpack and an AR on their chest before they get shot and robbed."

In short: Although a rifle would increase your ability to fight off Zombies, openly carrying one makes you a bullet magnet.

So in a Zombie Outbreak, rifles should be kept in your vehicle, in your home, and in your secondary BUGOUT location. But when you're trying to get to any of these locations on foot, the safest option is to move swiftly with a concealed pistol in order to draw as little attention to yourself as possible.

3
THE VERSATILITY
OF PISTOL TRAINING

ALTHOUGH *THE ZSG* is focused on pistols, it's important to understand that this training has crossover benefits for rifle shooting. Within 200 yards, shooting a pistol operates on the same basic principles as shooting a rifle: The sights are lined up correctly, and the trigger is prepped and pressed until the shot breaks.

However, a handgun is much more difficult to shoot because it has a heavier trigger, a shorter sight radius, and lacks a shoulder stock. Therefore, to shoot a handgun accurately, you need much better muscle coordination.

From a training standpoint, this is actually a great benefit. Once the pistol has been mastered, it is extremely easy to pick up a rifle and shoot it well, as the mechanics are the same, just easier.

I came to this epiphany a few years ago when I was invited to a rifle shoot outside Las Vegas. Until then, I had focused on shooting pistols almost exclusively, and was comfortable firing my FN 5-7 out to 200 yards. Although I had not shot an AR15 before, or any other rifle from a standing position, compared to shooting my pistol, it was ludicrously easy to drop man-sized targets out to 200 yards off hand. I didn't miss once in 30 rounds.

My long range pistol shooting had provided all the basics I needed to shoot that rifle to good effect. With just a few minutes to familiarize myself with the controls, I would have been able to fall back on my pistol training and use that rifle with confidence in a Zombie Outbreak.

By comparison, having observed rifle-dominant friends and strangers at the range, the reverse is not true at all. Because everything is easier with a rifle than with a pistol, people get spoiled, and there's little crossover training benefit even though the same mechanics are at work.

A GOOD PISTOL SHOT CAN BE A GOOD RIFLE SHOT WITH MINIMAL TRAINING, BUT EVEN A GREAT RIFLE SHOT CAN BE LOUSY WITH A HANDGUN UNLESS HE HAS TRAINED EXTENSIVELY WITH A PISTOL.

It's the same with working out. Hard exercises, such as pull-ups, make less challenging exercises, such as lat pulldowns, easier to do. While lat pulldowns target the same muscles as pull-ups, they are significantly easier to perform. The result is that if you spend most of your time doing lat pulldowns at the gym, pull-ups will still be very challenging. Conversely, if you spend your time doing pull-ups, lat pulldowns will be a snap.

What this means: If you devote the majority of your training to handguns, but are lucky enough to have a rifle, you'll be better than OK, because the same shooting mechanics apply, only everything is much easier.

4
GUN MYTHS

WITH THE EXCEPTION OF HITS TO THE BRAIN OR UPPER SPINAL CORD, THE CONCEPT OF THE RELIABLE AND REPRODUCIBLE IMMEDIATE INCAPACITATION OF THE HUMAN TARGET BY GUNSHOT WOUNDS TO THE TORSO IS A MYTH.

— SPECIAL AGENT UREY W. PATRICK, FBI FIREARMS TRAINING UNIT

THE ONLY RELIABLE way to stop a Zombie immediately is with a shot to the head or spine. This may sound obvious to any Z fan, but it's important to understand why. It's not simply because that's what the Zombie mythos has told us to do — Hollywood is not reality, nor is it the basis of our training. The reason we will be targeting the Central Nervous System is because of the realities of combat anatomy and the limitations of firearms.

But in order to understand those limitations, we need to dispel some of the firearms myths we have been conditioned to believe.

MYTH #1: GUNS KNOCK PEOPLE DOWN

In movies, we see a bad guy get shot with a pistol, and he's knocked off his feet. And, if he's hit with a shotgun blast, he might go flying back.

Guys, that violates the Laws of Physics.

THE ZOMBIE SHOOTING GUIDE

According to Newton's 3rd Law of Motion, for every action, there is an equal and opposite reaction. In terms of shooting, a gun launches a bullet out the barrel at high velocity (action) and the weapon recoils back with the same amount of force (reaction). This is why guns "kick," and the more powerful the gun, the more "kick" it has.

So now that we've accepted Newton's 3rd Law, let's look at this whole "knockdown power" concept. If the impact of the bullet had enough force to knock a man down (action) then the kick of the firearm would be so severe that the shooter would also be knocked down (reaction).

This does not happen. Even the most powerful handgun in the world, the .500 S&W Magnum, does not knock a shooter on his ass when he fires it. It just makes his arms move upward. Likewise, even the mighty shotgun just thumps the shoulder a bit when it fires.

**IF THE SHOOTER CAN ABSORB THE RECOIL OF
THE WEAPON WITHOUT FALLING DOWN,
THEN IT IS PHYSICALLY IMPOSSIBLE FOR
THE BULLET TO KNOCK DOWN THE ATTACKER.**

Knockdown power is a myth.

To illustrate this, let's quantify the relative impact strengths of 9mm and .45ACP pistols. According to FBI tests:

"A ten pound weight equals the impact of a 9mm bullet when dropped from a height of 0.72 inches . . . and equals the impact of a .45 when dropped from 1.37 inches."

So, the big bad .45 has as much "knock down power" as a girl's fitness weight dropped from the height of a plastic army man. To put it more succinctly, a pistol bullet strikes with approximately as much energy as a fast-pitched baseball.

Therefore, we cannot rely on powerful firearms to knock Zombies down so that we can run away. The only way to protect ourselves is to stop their attack permanently.

MYTH #2: HANDGUNS ARE VERY DEADLY

In films and TV shows, people get shot with a handgun, and they fall down dead. *Bang! You're dead!* Although we've seen this countless times on the screen, in reality that's the opposite of the truth.

According to statistics compiled by the National Center for Biotechnology Information, a branch of the National Institutes of Health, 80% of people who get shot with handguns survive.

I repeat, for every 100 people shot with a handgun, only 20 of them die. I'm not saying that it doesn't totally suck to be shot, nor am I overlooking the thousands killed by gunfire every year. But, when it comes to defending yourself, it's absolutely essential to understand this:

**IF YOU ARE SHOT, YOU ARE NOT DEAD.
YOU'RE NOT DEAD UNTIL YOU'RE DEAD!**

And statistically, you're likely to survive as long as you (a) kill the guy who shot you before he finishes you off and (b) get prompt medical attention. The lesson, to quote Sir Winston Churchill: "Never, never, never give up."

The flip side of this lesson is: Just because you shot the attacker doesn't mean that he's going to give up. Undead Zombies obviously need a headshot, but what's less obvious is that The Infected are also very hard to stop.

There have been many cases of killers continuing to attack after suffering multiple gunshots. For example, in the infamous 1986 Miami Shootout, *uber* badass Michael Platt killed two FBI agents and wounded five more — and he did this with a collapsed lung and a 9mm bullet lodged an inch from his heart, not to mention 11 other gunshot wounds.

Now, for those of you who subscribe to Colonel Jeff Cooper's oft-quoted wisdom, "The 9mm is for killing Europeans, for truly dangerous people you need a .45," here's another example:

In 2009, a 37-year-old Gangster Disciple robbed a bank outside of Chicago. When he was pulled over, he exited his vehicle and opened fire on Police Sgt. Timothy Gramin. A 56-second gun battle ensued, and Gramin shot the suspect 14 times with his .45ACP Glock 21 — including hits to the heart, right lung, left lung, liver, diaphragm, and right kidney. Despite these "fatal" gunshot wounds, the assailant continued to attack as if nothing had happened. The fight only ended when Gramin shot the suspect three times in the head. No drugs were found in the assailant's system. He was operating only on adrénaline and the will to kill.

These case studies are instructive when examining the threat posed by Fast Zombies. The Infected are fueled by adrenaline and the urge to kill. Therefore it is a safe assumption that they will also be able to continue to attack even after suffering multiple gunshots in much the same way as the above attackers.

That is why the only way to reliably stop a Zombie attack is with a shot to the head or spine.

5
LESSONS FROM LAW ENFORCEMENT

YOU DON'T HURT 'EM IF YOU DON'T HIT THEM.

— LT. GENERAL LEWIS "CHESTY" PULLER

I STUDIED MILITARY history in college, and one of the most crucial lessons I took away from it was: If it didn't work then, it won't work now.

For example, wearing red into the battlefield was a disaster during the American Revolutionary War, when guerrilla fighters dressed in muted colors easily picked off the conspicuously attired British Redcoats.

This history lesson was ignored at the outset of WWI, when the French were deployed along the Western Front wearing bright red pants. Even though the other Nations had switched to drab uniforms that were harder to see, the French Minister of War, Eugene Etienne, insisted, *"The pantaloon rouge c'est le France!"*

Translation: "The red pants are France!"

The easy-to-spot French soldiers were mowed down by the thousands because their leaders had not learned from history.

IN CONDUCTING RESEARCH FOR *THE ZSG*, MY GOAL WAS TO AVOID THIS *"PANTALOON ROUGE* PHENOMENON" — THAT IS, GETTING KILLED BY DOING SOMETHING HISTORY HAS ALREADY PROVEN WRONG.

I believe that by analyzing as much historical data as possible, and figuring out what doesn't work, we can stop doing stupid shit, and focus on figuring out a logical and effective solution to the problem at hand.

The problem that I was trying to solve was: "What kind of training is the most effective for shooting Zombies in the head?" Since there haven't been any confirmed Zombie attacks, I began my research by analyzing combat shootings to discover which training techniques worked, and which didn't.

SHOOTING DATA

There are three primary groups of shooters from which data could be gained: The US military, law enforcement, and armed civilians who have used firearms in self-defense.

The US military is the deadliest fighting force the world has ever seen, but it fights its enemies from a position of overwhelming superiority with groups of men armed with automatic weapons engaging an enemy 50 to 500 yards away. Data from these lopsided engagements have little to offer the civilian Zombie shooter, who will likely be fighting alone, armed with a handgun, against multiple attackers at close quarters.

On the other end of the spectrum is the civilian who has defended himself with a firearm. At first glance it would appear that this is the ideal source of shooting data to apply to Zombie self-defense. However, it is not.

Unlike the military or law enforcement, which have standardized armament and training regimens, American civilians are armed with anything from .22 derringers to custom 1911s, with training ranging from dumb luck to competitive shooting. Therefore, due to the wide variety of weapons and training, this data is too inconsistent to provide useful insight into which training techniques would be effective.

Fortunately, law enforcement provides an excellent source of shooting data from which we can glean effective training techniques.

Police officers typically work alone or in pairs, and are armed with semi-automatic handguns loaded with modern hollow point ammunition — precisely the weapons and conditions likely for a civilian defending himself during a Zombie Outbreak.

Another similarity is that police shootings occur at close range — almost always within 10 yards — and are frequently against aggressive, highly motivated attackers. While not a Zombie *per se,* some cop killers, such as Michael Platt from the 1986 Miami Shootout, have exhibited Zombie-like symptoms, where they have continued to fight after multiple gunshot wounds, and were only stopped by a shot to the Central Nervous System.

Lastly, what makes law enforcement data so useful is the fact that police training is relatively standardized across the nation. When combined with the hundreds of police shootings that occur each year in the United States, law enforcement shooting data provides a rich trove of information for analysis.

THE 1:3 HIT RATIO

When I analyzed the available police shooting data, I was surprised by the results. Not only were head and spine shots rare, but the vast majority of shots fired were complete misses!

**WHILE THIS IS A BIT OF A GENERALIZATION,
THE MAJORITY OF MAJOR POLICE DEPARTMENTS
NATIONWIDE AVERAGE A 1 IN 3 HIT RATIO. THAT
MEANS FOR EVERY 3 SHOTS FIRED, ONLY 1 ROUND
HITS THE SUSPECT ANYWHERE ON HIS BODY.**

Some departments performed even worse than the 1:3 ratio. From 1990-2001, The Miami police fired around 1,300 rounds in combat — and missed 1,100 times — achieving a 15.4% hit ratio.

Meanwhile, some departments, such as the California Highway Patrol and Salt Lake City PD, did significantly better, achieving an 80% hit ratio or above. The causes of this discrepancy will be discussed later, as it is highly relevant to our training.

However, the take away is this: If a civilian Zombie shooter were trained in a similar fashion as the average police officer, he would probably average a 1:3 hit ratio or worse. Which, due to the incredible resilience of Zombies to gunfire, would simply be unacceptable.

In order to survive a Zombie Outbreak, we will have to be significantly better trained than the Police.

6

UNDERSTANDING THE 1:3 HIT RATIO

IN ORDER TO solve a problem, it's essential to understand the underlying cause. Based on my research, the experts seem to agree that the two primary causes of the 1:3 hit ratio are: (1) a lack of rigorous and realistic firearms training and (2) the effects of Survival Stress on human physiology.

INADEQUATE TRAINING

As civilian shooters preparing for the Zombie Outbreak, we have the luxury of picking our training regimen, and taking it as far as we want. And, let's face it, most of us enjoy shooting.

Police departments do not have those same advantages. Many of the recruits, especially those from urban areas, are not recreational shooters and gun nerds. Police departments need to teach people who are not "into guns" how to shoot, in addition to dozens of other skills needed for police work. Furthermore, police departments operate on a tight budget, which have been decimated by budget cuts brought about by the Great Recession.

The result is that many departments have pretty mediocre firearms training programs. Recruits only fire a limited number of rounds, and typically only at stationary paper targets. Alarmingly, "nearly 6 in 10 departments reported that they do not require that officers hit the target with all their shots in order to pass."

Once officers have "qualified" according to this low standard, supplementary shooting experience is often minimal, with only 28% of surveyed departments emphasizing additional training beyond the basics learned in the police academy. Instead of teaching new and improved skills, most departments focus on having officers "re-qualify" using the same mediocre "rote courses-of-fire" that do little beyond preparing the officers to shoot a paper target. Furthermore, most departments only have requalification shoots four times a year, with some agencies, like the NYPD, only reevaluating their officers twice a year.

However, the real issue is not the lack of shooting experience. For example, the LAPD shoots 12 times a year, yet their effectiveness is basically identical to the NYPD. The issue is a lack of realistic training.

Only 43.3% of surveyed departments train their officers to engage multiple attackers. Shockingly, only 18.6% of departments had their officers engage moving targets — despite the fact that the majority of shootings occur against moving adversaries. By relying exclusively on stationary paper targets, the majority of police officers across the country are only being trained to put holes in the next piece of paper they encounter.

Even if an officer is superb at stationary marksmanship, he has not been taught the skills he is likely to use in a real shooting — which will almost always involve a moving target, frequently at night, under extreme stress.

Not surprisingly, officers who have not been trained to shoot moving targets at the range have difficulty hitting moving targets on the street — especially when those targets are shooting back.

SURVIVAL STRESS

There is solid evidence to support that the problem of multiple shots with few hits is partly the result of a fear-induced stress response.
— Lt. Col. Dave Grossman, *Killology Research Group*

The other cause of the 1:3 hit ratio, and this cannot be overstated, is the effect of Survival Stress on human physiological performance.

It's relatively easy to make free throws with a basketball when shooting hoops with your friends. However, have you ever tried to make one in the middle of the big game, with everyone watching? Pretty hard, right? Well that's nothing compared to the difficulty of trying to shoot accurately when someone is trying to kill you.

The cause of this reduction in performance is Survival Stress.

WHEN A PERSON'S LIFE IS IN DANGER, THE BRAIN ACTIVATES THE "FIGHT OR FLIGHT" RESPONSE, AND DOZENS OF HORMONES ARE PUMPED INTO THE BLOOD, MANY OF WHICH HAVE SIMILAR EFFECTS TO HALLUCINOGENIC DRUGS.

During the stress of the Fight or Flight response, the heart rate skyrockets, eyes dilate, and muscles constrict, priming the body to run fast or fight hard.

Back in the caveman days, this was totally awesome, as this survival response allowed man to outrun a Woolly Mammoth or shatter a rival's skull with a wooden club. Regrettably, our bodies have not evolved with our weaponry, and the same biological response that was so helpful for most of history is now a tremendous hindrance to our combat performance with a firearm.

When a modern man with a modern firearm is hit with the fight or flight response, much of his modern training goes out the window. The firm yet balanced grip and smooth trigger press are replaced by a convulsive death grip and trigger jerk. The front sight, lauded as being essential to accuracy, becomes blurry as the pupils dilate. Rather than standing still and firing deliberate shots with both hands, many shooters will instinctively move away from their attacker while firing as fast as they can with one hand. This is especially prevalent in close quarters encounters, where Survival Dtress is so acute.

According to a study of police gunfight survivors conducted by criminologist David Klinger, 94% of officers experienced at least one sensory distortion due to the effects of stress hormones.

TRAINING FOR STRESS

After analyzing the 1:3 hit ratio and its underlying cause, I began to look into what some of the higher performing police agencies were doing differently that allowed them to make hits in the 80% range or higher.

THE LARGEST SINGLE PREDICTOR FOR AN AGENCY'S HIGH PERFORMANCE CAME FROM THE USE OF FORCE ON FORCE (FOF) SCENARIO TRAINING TO INOCULATE THEIR OFFICERS TO THE STRESS OF COMBAT.

In FoF training, officers are armed with airsoft or Simunition training pistols, and are placed in realistic scenarios that closely mimic conditions on the street. In most scenarios, officers may have to shoot the "bad guy," who is also armed with a training pistol.

During these exercises, both the officer and the suspect are shooting at each other at close range, which results in a skyrocketing state of stress similar to actual combat conditions. Meanwhile, both the officer and the suspect are moving, making marksmanship much more difficult than if the officer was-shooting at a stationary paper target.

The benefits of Force on Force training will be covered extensively in later chapters, but briefly, this type of training achieves two very important objectives. First, it allows trainees to observe how their previous firearms training holds up when the target is moving and shooting back. Second, because the scenarios are realistic, and training guns hurt, Force on Force triggers many of the same chemical reactions created by the fight or flight response.

The stress response is the crucial characteristic that makes FoF training so effective. By repeatedly exposing officers to high levels of fear and stress, they become progressively "inoculated" to its effects.

Much like a person who is allergic to bees can become immunized by being injected repeatedly with bee venom, repeated exposure to the stress of Force on Force training can immunize officers to the negative effects of the fight or flight response. Instead of becoming panicked during a gunfight, their stress-inoculated brains remain functional, and they are able to fall back on their training and employ their weapons successfully.

Because stress is the chief limiting factor in defensive shooting, officers who have had these "inoculations" shoot consistently better in real-world shootings than those who have not experienced such realistic levels of training. The result is that these departments shoot in the 80% range, while departments that neglect this vital training perform at a much lower level.

APPLYING SHOOTING DATA TO ZOMBIES

When I applied the *pantaloon rouge* phenomenon to the available shooting data, it was apparent that the static firing range practice employed by most police agencies would get us killed in the advent of a Zombie Outbreak. With 15-50% hit rates, against Fast Zombies, we'd be lucky to live long enough to run out of ammo — and we can kiss the dream long-term survival goodbye.

Now that we know what not to do, the question is, what should we do to prepare for the Zombie Outbreak?

The answer from the shooting data is pretty clear: We need to train ourselves to make head shots on moving targets, and then we need to practice those skills under realistic levels of Survival Stress through Force on Force training. Only then will have the physical and mental preparation needed to keep our head — while shooting the Zombies in theirs.

7
TRAINING EQUIPMENT

YOU WILL NEED the following tools to train effectively to defend yourself in a Zombie Outbreak.

- Semi-Automatic Handgun
- 22 Conversion Kit
- Centerfire Ammunition
- Laser Training Cartridge
- Shoot-N-C Targets

- Airsoft Training Pistol
- Stun Gun
- Balloons
- Face Mask
- Safety Goggles

SEMI-AUTOMATIC CENTERFIRE HANDGUN

Any gun is better than no gun in a Zombie Apocalypse, but a modern, high capacity semi-automatic handgun is the most practical weapon for Zombie shooting. It offers good firepower in a compact, easy-to-carry package that can be used with one hand while on the move.

Because there will be countless Zombies in your area, you should select a handgun that holds as many bullets as possible. Since Zombies can only be reliably stopped by disrupting the Central Nervous System, shot capacity is more important than bullet size. Stick to handguns with double stack magazines that hold 10 or more rounds, as they are more effective when dealing with multiple Zombies. When under attack, every bullet counts.

When selecting a handgun, you first need to decide on the caliber. I personally recommend the 9mm for your first pistol, as 9mm ammunition is about half the cost of .45 ACP. Cheaper ammo means that you will be able to practice more, which will make you a better shot. And being a better shot is far more important than the marginal increase in effectiveness offered by more powerful cartridges.

Once you have settled on a caliber, it's time to select the right pistol. There are dozens of great handguns out there, but for Zombie shooting they need to meet two mandatory criteria for training with this guide:

- The gun must have a .22 conversion kit, or a 1:1 .22 analog
- The gun must have an Airsoft analog for Force on Force training

Here are the only pistols that currently meet these requirements:

- Glock (all models)
- CZ 75
- Beretta 92 (conversion kits available but rare)
- Sig 226
- Smith and Wesson M&P (only .22 analog, no conversion kit)
- 1911

I personally recommend the Glock 19, as it is small enough to carry in all weather conditions, and holds 15+1 rounds of 9mm. The G19 is the world's most popular 9mm handgun, so many shooters share my opinion.

However, any of the listed pistols will serve you well. What matters most is that they fit your hand, and that you can shoot them well. So, go to your local shooting range and rent them all, and see which one suits you the best.

I recommend renting at least three pistols and lining them up at the shooting bench. Set up a target with three *Shoot-N-C* targets. Begin by dry firing each pistol 20 times at the bullseye to get a feel for the trigger. Then load each magazine with 10 rounds, and fire each pistol 10 times, one right after the other in a side-by-side competition.

Observe your results, and eliminate the least accurate pistol. Then have a showdown between the remaining two. The gun you shoot the best is the one you should use.

.22 CONVERSION KIT

The most important firearms training tool you can have is a .22 conversion kit for your weapon. In order to master the high levels of marksmanship and point shooting needed to make headshots on moving targets, thousands of rounds of ammunition will need to be expended.

At 2012 prices, 1,000 9mm practice rounds cost about $200, or $.20 a shot; 1,000 40 S&W around $300, or $.30 a shot; 1,000 .45 ACP costs around $350–$400, about $.40 a shot. By comparison, a 525-round box of Federal Bulk pack .22lr can be purchased at WalMart for around $20, less than $.04 a shot.

During the initial stages of marksmanship and point shooting, when you will be missing frequently, it's a waste of money to spend $.20 to $.40 per miss when you can run the exact same drill with a .22lr conversion kit at a fraction of the cost. Additionally, when working on one-shot drills, such as drawing a pistol from concealment and making a fast, first round hit, training with .22lr is just as effective as with a .45 since successful performance is a function of speed and accuracy rather than recoil control. Centerfire ammo should be conserved for Rapid Fire Drills and Zombie defense.

The most effective .22 training pistol is a .22 conversion kit for your defensive handgun. The .22 conversion kit consists of a replacement slide and magazine. This allows you to switch from centerfire to .22lr for low cost training, while still maintaining the feel of your defensive handgun. If this were a car, it's the equivalent of switching your powerful V8 engine to a fuel efficient 4-cylinder at the push of a button in order to save money while driving around town.

Advantage Arms .22 Conversion Kit for the Glock 21: replacement slide, magazine, cleaning supplies, and carrying case.

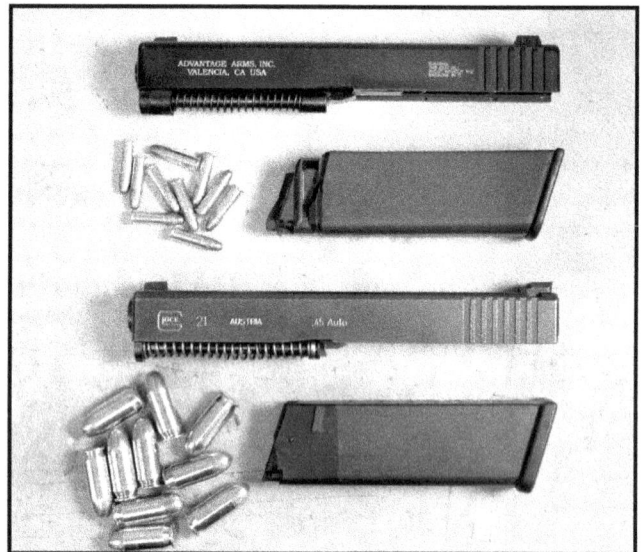

The .22 conversion slide and magazine (top) compared to the original .45.

By switching the slide and magazine, the Glock can fire either .22lr or .45 ACP, depending on the needs of the shooter.

The conversion process takes less than a minute, and requires no tools.

1. Begin with a Glock .45.

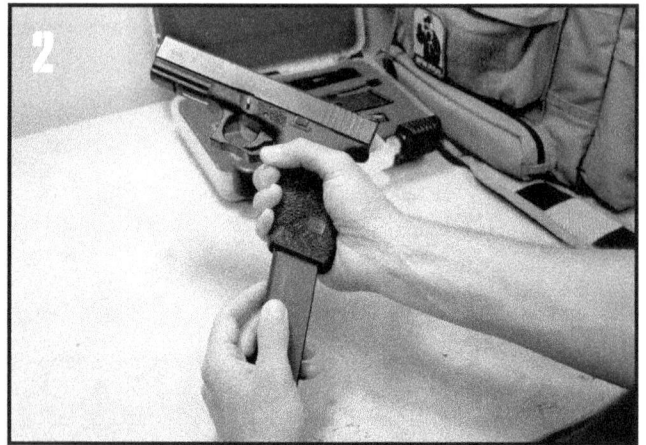

2. With finger off the trigger (Safety Rule 3), eject the magazine.

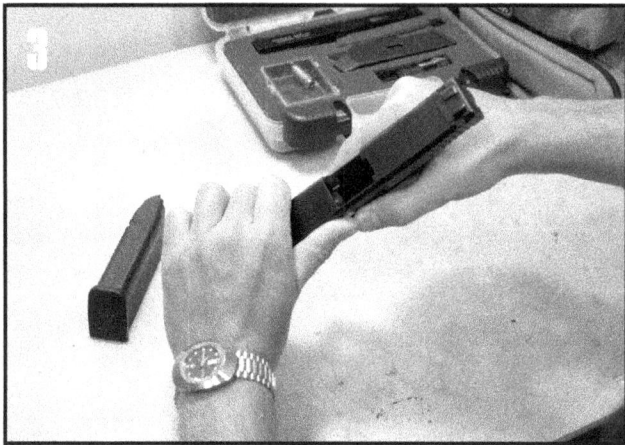

3. After removing the magazine, rack the slide back, and then lock it open with the slide stop.

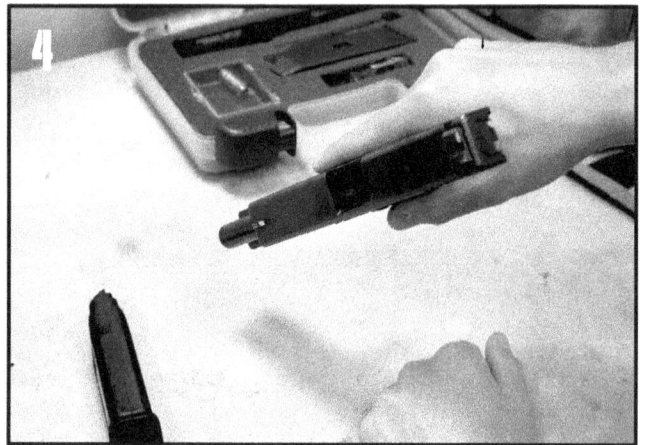

4. Inspect the chamber to confirm that the pistol is unloaded.

5. To disassemble the Glock: Press the slide forward slightly while depressing the takedown lever.

6. Remove the slide.

7. The Glock is now field stripped.

8. Remove the .22 conversion slide.

9. Attach the slide to the Glock frame.

10. The Glock .22 conversion kit is a bit weird. You have to press the barrel in with your palm until you hear a *click!* Otherwise, the kit will not work. Don't forget: Keep your finger off the trigger!

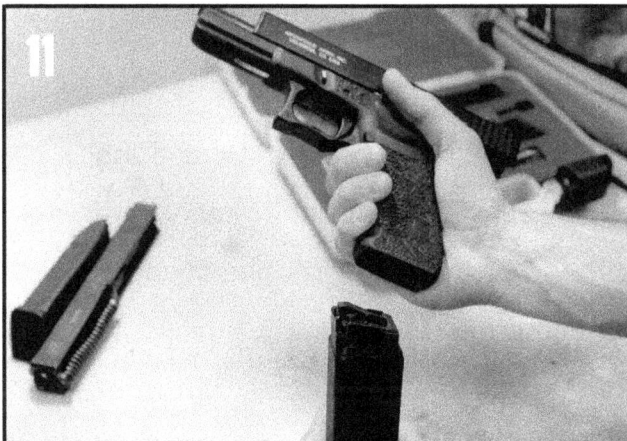

11. The new .22 conversion magazine is inserted into the pistol.

12. The .22 conversion is now complete, in under a minute.

Glock with .22 conversion kit compared to .22 Colt Woodsman.

What's so terrific about a .22 conversion kit is that you are still practicing with your gun — the trigger, sights, controls, grip angle, and point of impact are all the same. The only differences are the lower cost and less recoil, making it easier and more affordable to master the fundamentals of any drill.

When a Glock .22 conversion kit is compared to a traditional .22 target pistol, the training benefit becomes obvious. The conversion kit feels and operates exactly like the Glock .45. By comparison, the traditional .22 target pistol has different sights, a different grip angle, a different magazine release, and a different trigger. When it comes to building muscle memory during training, these differences are critical.

Most conversion kits cost around $300 to $400, but due to the tremendous cost savings of practicing with .22lr, they pay for themselves within the first 1000 to 2000 rounds. This cost savings cannot be overstated. Without a .22lr conversion kit it would be prohibitively expensive to train at the levels needed for Zombie shooting.

Another advantage of the .22 conversion kit is that it allows you to continue shooting when centerfire ammunition becomes scarce. Whenever gun control is front-page news, the gun-owning collective gets scared, and they hit the stores like locusts. During the great panic of the 2008 election, it was almost impossible to find any .45 ACP on the shelves. But because I had my .22 conversion kit, I was able to keep training without having to dip into my emergency centerfire ammo reserves.

CENTERFIRE AMMUNITION

Due to the high cost of ammunition, as well as its limited availability in times of political uncertainty, *The Zombie Shooting Guide* has made every attempt to maximize the use of other training tools to reduce your consumption of centerfire ammunition.

That being said, you simply cannot become a proficient shooter without expending large amounts of centerfire ammunition. You will use dryfire, laser dryfire, airsoft, and .22 conversion kits to learn the fundamentals of each drill. But to consider the drill mastered you must perform it successfully with the full recoil of centerfire ammunition. This is especially true with the Rapid Fire Drills in later chapters.

In order to save money, as well as increase your preparedness for a Zombie Outbreak, you should get your ammunition in bulk 1,000 round cases.

When you shoot 500 rounds, get another case, and save the rest for emergencies. For a Zombie Outbreak, you want *at least* 100 loaded magazines worth of ammunition on hand; for a 15 shot Glock 19 you should have at least 1,500 rounds in reserve.

That being said, if it's a choice between training and hoarding ammo, it's always better to train. When the Fast Zombies come, a highly trained shooter with a 100 rounds will have a better chance of survival than a lousy shot with basement full of lead.

So don't be a useless ammo hoarder.

Be an effective one.

LASER TRAINING CARTRIDGE

In recent years a product has come onto the market that is useful for practicing marksmanship and point shooting at home. Known as a Laser Training Cartridge (LTC), it's essentially a miniature laser pointer the size of a bullet, and works in 9mm, 40 S&W, and 45 ACP pistols.

The Laser Training Cartridge compared to a .45 ACP cartridge.

When the pistol's firing pin strikes the little black button *(far left)*, the laser dot will appear for a fraction of a second on the spot where the bullet would have struck.

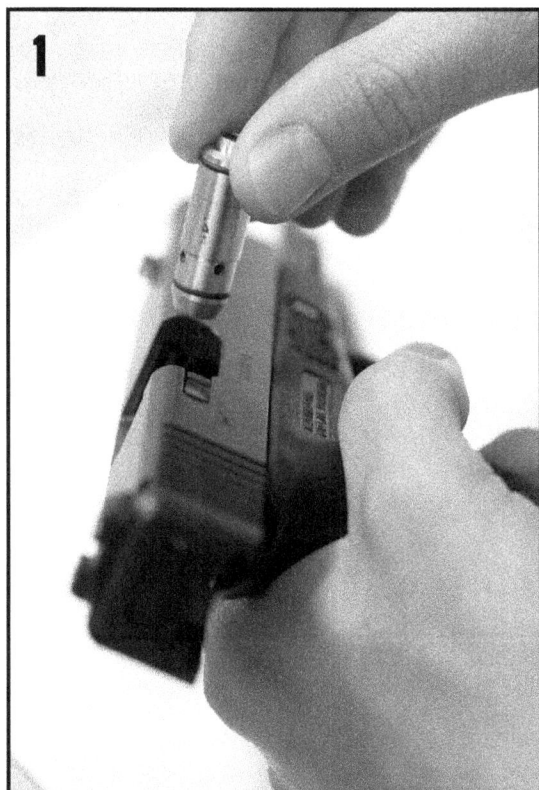

1. Begin with an unloaded pistol and the Laser Training Cartridge (LTC).

2. Insert the LTC into the pistol's chamber.

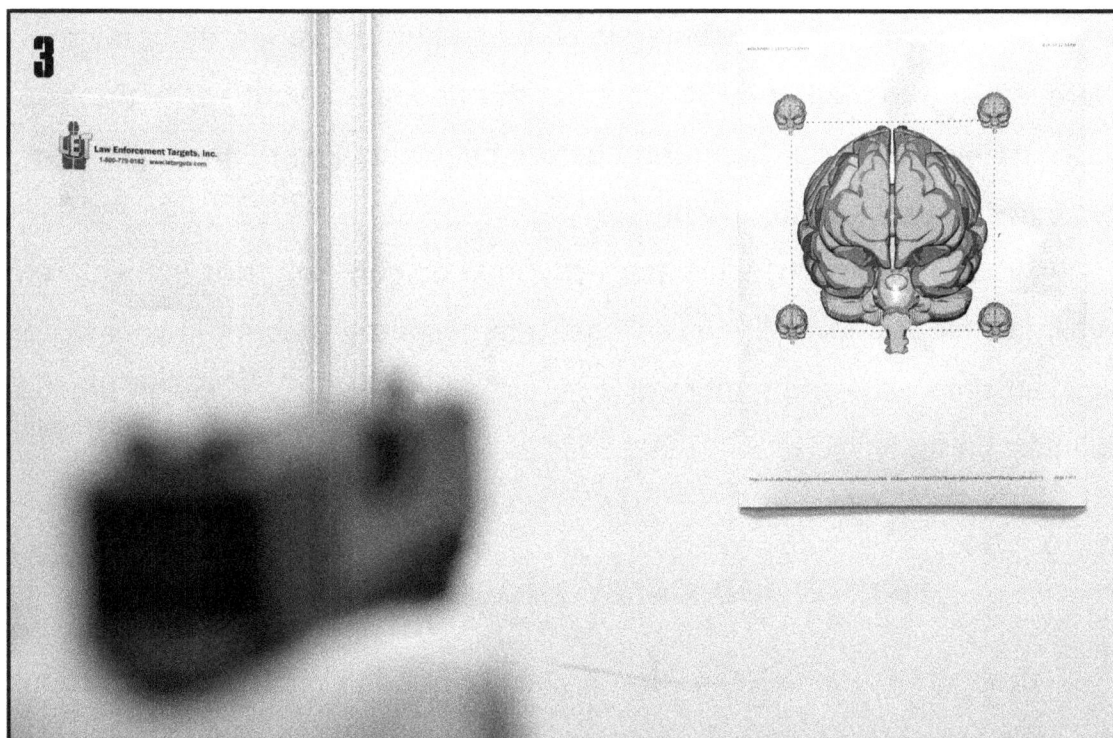

3. When the pistol is "fired," a laser dot will momentarily appear on the target where the bullet would have struck.

For about $80, the Laser Training Cartridge is a fun and effective way to practice your marksmanship at home. It becomes truly invaluable when you start practicing Point Shooting. Because Point Shooting does not use sights, conventional dryfire training is ineffective. But because the laser provides a visual index of where the bullet would have struck, you can learn the fundamentals of Point Shooting at home.

However, it's important to mention that the LTC does not work perfectly with all guns. It may be dead on with one pistol, and totally off with another.

**IT IS ABSOLUTELY ESSENTIAL THAT YOU
ONLY PRACTICE WITH THE LTC WHEN IT IS
100% TRUE TO YOUR SIGHTS.**

This happened to me. I had just gotten a new set of sights, and didn't realize that the laser was actually shooting 3" high and to the right. . . . Well, a month of constant laser training later, when I hit the range, all of my shots were low and to the left by 3". Don't let this happen to you! Verify that your Laser Training Cartridge is accurate before beginning Point Shooting training or you will create a terrible habit!

If the LTC does not work perfectly in your gun, return it immediately. While it's nice to have, if you can't get a laser trainer to work in your pistol, you can simply substitute more dryfire, airsoft, and .22lr conversion practice to make up for it.

BIRCHWOOD CASEY SHOOT-N-C TARGETS

Although the Zombie Qualification Target included in the back of this book provides a useful metric for gauging your shooting skills, when first learning to shoot at the range, I highly recommend the use of Shoot-N-C (SNC) targets.

What makes these targets so useful is that they produce a neon yellow burst of color when they are shot.

The bright yellow splash of a SNC target provides immediate visible feedback when shooting, making it much easier to verify your shooting accuracy, and adjust your aim accordingly. Beyond 7 yards, or when shooting in dark indoor ranges, it is nearly impossible to see where shots have landed if you're shooting a plain paper target. But with a SNC, you can confirm hits out to 25 yards, which is a lot more fun than guessing whether you hit the target.

SNC targets have an adhesive backing that allows them to be attached to any target of your choice, and come in a variety of sizes. For beginners, or those shooting at ranges beyond 7 yards, I suggest the 6-inch bullseye targets, which are available in packs of 60 for about $20 on Amazon.

For more advanced shooters, I'm very partial to the 2-inch bullseyes, which are both cheaper and more challenging. 108 targets can be purchased for $9 on Amazon, and they work perfectly when combined with the printable "dot torture target" from pistol-training.com.

AIRSOFT REPLICA OF YOUR DEFENSIVE PISTOL

I've heard of one officer who would take primed cartridge cases and press the case mouths into blocks of soap, forming a hard soap "bullet." He would load these into his service Wesley. In the garden he would have his servants surround him, armed with a variety of sticks and bludgeons, then at random rush him. Our hero would then respond with well-placed shots to his human targets, giving him practice in reactive accuracy.
— DENNIS MARTIN, *C.Q.B. Services*

Although the old school, soap bullet method was state of the art in 1914, in this century we conduct our Force on Force training with airsoft guns. Specifically, you will need a gas blow back (GBB) version of your defensive firearm — not just some cheap toy from Walmart.

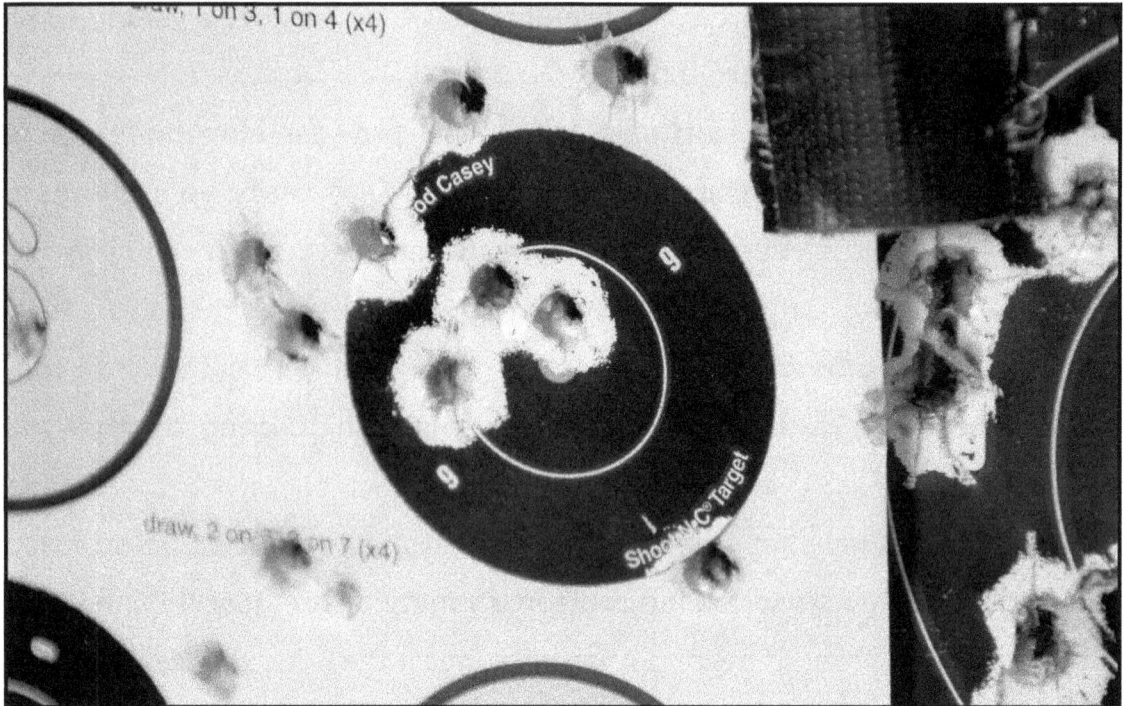

Shoot-N-C in Action: The black sticker is a 2-inch SNC attached to a "Dot Torture" target. As you can see, the bright burst of color upon impact makes the bullet holes much more visible.

Real Glock *(top)* compared to the KWA airsoft training pistol.

A gas blowback airsoft pistol *(bottom)* operates identically to its real steel counterpart — except it shoots 6mm plastic BBs instead of .45 caliber hollow points.

A GBB Airsoft clone will have the same size, sights, grip angle, and controls as your defensive handgun, making it a valuable tool for building muscle memory in training. It also allows you to use the same holster and magazine pouches, so you can practice your draw and magazine changes. Within 7 yards, it will also share the same point of impact as your handgun, so no changes in marksmanship habits are required.

In addition to being fairly realistic, airsoft is also one of the least expensive training tools available. A gas blow back airsoft gun costs around $150. 3,000 black airsoft BBs costs around $15. A can of Green Gas propellant is $8, while an adapter that allows you to fill your pistol from a propane tank costs $14. In comparison to a .22 conversion kit ($300+), centerfire ammunition ($200+ per case,) or training with Simunitions (hundreds of $ per day) airsoft is dirt cheap.

Airsoft Supplies: KWA Glock 17 airsoft pistol, 3,000 black airsoft BBs, Green Gas propellant, safety glasses, and Tokyo Marui magazine loader. Everything you need, for less than $200.

To give you a sense of just how incredibly inexpensive airsoft training is, think about this: For the cost of a single shot from my .22 conversion kit, I can shoot 10 rounds of airosft. Still not impressed?

FOR THE PRICE OF FIRING A SINGLE ROUND OF .45 ACP OUT OF MY GLOCK 21, I CAN FIRE 100 6MM BBS OUT OF MY KWA GLOCK TRAINING PISTOL.

**Airsoft Price Comparison: 1 round of .22lr = 10 shots of airsoft *(top)*.
1 round of .45ACP = 100 shots.**

Lastly, when compared to the cost of a single Simunition cartridge, which costs $0.85 per shot, I can fire 200 rounds—enough to run 10-20 Force on Force drills.

What makes airsoft so effective as a training tool is not just its similarity in aesthetics to a "real gun," but the fact that airsoft guns sting when they shoot you — from small bruises at a distance, to nasty bleeding welts at close range. Because of this discomfort, airsoft training induces a good amount of stress, an essential ingredient for realistic Force on Force training.

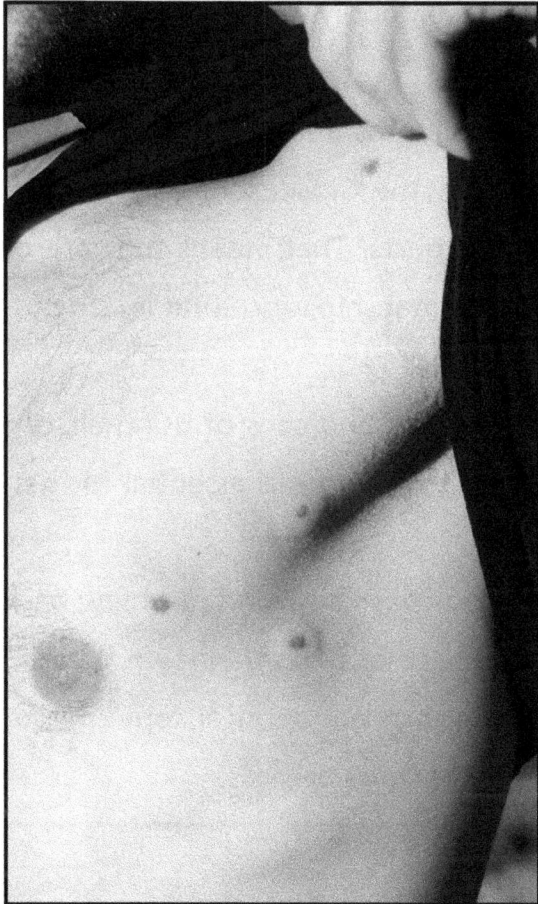

Painful welts like these makes Force on Force realistically stressful.

Another benefit of airsoft is that the small plastic BBs leave very little mess behind. This allows you to train pretty much anywhere — in a park, near parked vehicles, even inside your house. Unless you have the most understanding spouse ever, chances are that you will not be shooting paintballs in your living room.

Although airsoft has many advantages, it does have some drawbacks. One is its limited range. Due to the lightweight nature of airsoft BBs, the maximum realistic training range is 10 yards. However, because the vast majority of attacks will occur within 7 yards, this is not a huge deal.

Another issue is the low velocity and bright white color of airsoft BBs. Because they can be seen in mid-flight, the shooter can adjust his aim much as if he were firing tracers. Since this is obviously not going to be possible with a real firearm, this "tracer effect" can lead to unrealistic outcomes.

Luckily, this issue is easily solved by using **black airsoft BBs,** which cannot be easily seen in flight, especially when shooting in subdued lighting. For this reason, it is essential that all Force on Force be done with black airsoft BBs.

Another problem is that airsoft guns have very little recoil — about the same as a Glock equipped with a .22 conversion kit, but nowhere near the recoil of a real centerfire firearm. This lack of recoil makes it easy to fire rapidly with good accuracy — something that is not nearly as simple with a centerfire handgun. Be aware of this in training, because if you find yourself defaulting to Rapid Fire under stress, you will need to make doubly sure to practice Rapid Fire with centerfire ammunition at the range.

By far the biggest issue with airsoft training as an analog for real firearms is the trigger pull. Airsoft guns, especially the Glock clones, have much lighter triggers than their "real steel" counterparts. That means they are of very little use for practicing conventional marksmanship, since that is largely a matter of trigger control.

While not perfect, when we analyze the pros and cons of using airsoft, it's clearly a useful and cost-effective training tool, and it is essential for getting the most out of this guide.

If you can, it is recommended that you purchase a second gas blow back pistol for your training partner to use. If your partner owns their own firearm, get an airsoft version of their gun. Otherwise, buy an identical copy of your existing airsoft gun, to serve as a backup should yours break.

To let everyone know that you are training with fake guns, it is essential to have your airsoft pistol clearly marked. The little orange tip on the barrel is not enough. You must also coat the slide and grip frame with bright blue painter's tape. This will allow anyone within 25 yards to clearly see that your gun is not real, and that you are not a threat.

Airsoft pistols coated with bright blue painter's tape. This tape is sold at any hardware store, and can be removed without leaving sticky residue behind.

SAFETY NOTE:

AIRSOFT PISTOLS ARE SO REALISTIC THAT THEY CAN EASILY BE MISTAKEN FOR REAL FIREARMS. ALTHOUGH THIS IS COOL FOR PEOPLE WHO PLAY AIRSOFT, THIS IS NOT COOL AT ALL WHEN YOU ARE TRAINING IN YOUR BACKYARD OR A PUBLIC PARK. IF PEOPLE THINK YOU ARE WAVING REAL GUNS AROUND, THE POLICE WILL BE CALLED, AND YOU MIGHT END UP GETTING SHOT IN THE FACE DUE TO THE CONFUSION. MAKE SURE YOUR AIRSOFT PISTOLS ARE COVERED IN BLUE TAPE TO IDENTIFY THEM AS TRAINING TOOLS.

STUN GUN

Airsoft is an ideal, off-the-shelf solution for mimicking a gunfight. Unfortunately, there is no off the shelf training analog for simulating a Zombie bite. Believe me, I looked around. This was an issue, because without something scary about the "Zombie," this type of Force on Force training would be useless.

So, to make our Zombies terrifying enough to induce a Survival Stress response, they will be equipped with a handheld stun gun.

I was inspired to use stun guns by self-defense instructor George "Mercop" Matheis, who uses stun guns to train his students in knife defense. I always thought that would make for some really badass training, so I bought a $9 "Terminator" stun gun on Amazon, and decided to give it a try.

Although not as horrible a fate as getting mauled by a Zombie, the threat posed by a training partner running at you with a stun gun is more

If you can't tell: Getting tazed sucks!

Stun Gun in Action.

than enough to induce a Survival Stress response. So, until a more effective Zombie bite simulator is devised, our partners will be armed with stun guns. Even the cheap ones are painful, so there is no need to get anything too crazy.

BALLOONS

In most Force on Force training, people attempt to shoot someone who is trying to shoot them, and the fight is over when the opponent is hit. In typical airsoft rules, that means if they're hit anywhere on the body. But in a Zombie scenario, only a hit to the head or spine will stop the fight.

To simulate the spine your training partner will be equipped with a long balloon, used for making balloon animals, which will be taped to the center of his chest.

When the area of the spine is hit, the balloon will pop, and the drill should stop. Conversely, if you don't hear the pop, that means that you have missed the spine, and need to transition to a headshot.

Now, in reality, the spine is only one-inch in diameter, and is on the back, protected by the torso. So, this balloon spine simulation is not perfect. However, I still feel that it's a worthwhile addition to training, because it provides an immediate indicator if your shots are at least on centerline. Much like the stun gun, it's not perfect, but it works.

FACE MASK

Because the FoF training drills in *The ZSG* are designed to teach you how to shoot a Zombie in the head, you and your partner must wear protective face masks that cover your entire head and throat, as well as safety goggles to protect your eyes. This is very important, as both of you will be getting shot by airsoft guns at close range, and if the BBs strike any exposed skin, you're going to bleed.

We found this out the hard way the very first time we ran the Fast Zombie Drill. My training partner was wearing a protective Balaclava and goggles, but I failed to notice that the bridge of his nose was not covered. Well, in a mixture of excellent shooting and bad luck, that's exactly where I shot him!

Zombie Training Outfit: Face mask, protective goggles, balloon spine, protective gloves and stun gun.

Skull Balaclava: This is our photographer Sam Goldenberg's favorite photo.

He started bleeding immediately, swore that he would never train with me again, and had a nasty blood welt on his face for over a week. Learn from this, and **make sure to double check that all of the sensitive skin of your face and neck is covered.**

In choosing a face mask, it's really up to you and your partner to decide just how much pain you're each willing to endure.

The bare minimum protection is a Balaclava, which is just a fancy word for a ski mask.

The advantage of the Balaclava is that it transfers enough pain that your partner will almost always stop as soon as he is shot in the head. This is useful when it's just you and him, with no third party to referee and decide whether a headshot has occurred. With these masks, there is no ambiguity about your accuracy — you will be able to count the welts on your partner's face to confirm your hits.

The downside to this, of course, is that these masks do almost nothing to minimize the pain of being shot in the face — they prevent the skin from being broken, but little else. If you're only going to run the drill once or twice a day, a Balaclava is an acceptable mask. However, very few people will want to continue training after being shot at close range wearing one of these. At 7 yards, a shot to the face stings. At 7 feet away — which is where the majority of headshots will occur — *it sucks.* I find it more painful than being zapped by the stun gun.

In general, I like the Balaclava for FoF drills like The Showdown, when shots will be taken at 5 to 7 yards and headshots are unlikely. I also like it as the protective mask for the shooter in the Zombie drills, as the mask helps protect the skin in case he's accidently hit in the face with the stun gun.

However, for protecting the partner playing the Zombie in the Fast Zombie Drill, a single Balaclava is really just too painful. I suggest wearing 2 or 3 Balaclavas on top of each other.

On the opposite end of the spectrum is a professional paintball mask. Designed to stop .68 caliber paintballs, these masks provide exceptional protection to the face, with no feelings of pain. For this reason, the majority of Force on Force instructors have their students wear these types of masks.

The problem with this much protection is that your partner will frequently be unaware he has been shot, since the airsoft rounds will simply bounce off without transferring any impact whatsoever.

Unless your partner hears the sounds of the BBs striking his mask, he is likely to continue onward and taze you mercilessly, which is frustrating to say the least. This is especially likely if your partner is keyed up with adrenaline, which

"Gates of Hell" Latex Zombie mask, designed by Chuck Jarman of Bump in the Night Effects.

not only makes him more aggressive, but also suppresses hearing. If you have a third person to referee the drills and observe the hits, then paintball masks can work well.

The option I have had the most success with is a rubber Zombie mask.

What's cool about this mask is that it genuinely looks like a Zombie is attacking you, which greatly adds to the fun of the drills. Plus, the thick Latex absorbs the majority of the impact from the airsoft BBs, making getting shot in the head relatively pain free.

And, unlike the rigid paintball mask, the rubber Zombie mask buckles and vibrates under impact, providing both a tactile and auditory confirmation that a headshot as occurred. As long as your partner isn't totally lost in the throes of an adrenaline rush, he'll know when he's been hit.

The downside to this mask is that it is extremely hot and claustrophobic to wear, especially with a set of goggles underneath. However, given the level of fun and protection this mask offers, it is still my #1 recommendation for Zombie FoF training.

PROTECTIVE EYEWEAR

Chicks dig scars, but there's nothing sexy about losing an eye. Since the majority of our Force on Force training will involve shooting and being shot in the face with an airsoft gun, it should be pretty obvious why you need to wear protective eyewear. Always wear ballistic eye protection when training.

DO NOT WEAR SUNGLASSES!!

They will not stop an airsoft round and you will shoot your eye out!

I personally had an airsoft BB shoot right through the left lens of a pair of Hugo Boss sunglasses I was wearing from 49 feet away. If I had not been closing that eye to aim, I would be blind in my left eye.

I recommend high-impact plastic shooting glasses, which can be purchased online for around $10, just to be extra safe.

Even if they say "high impact" on the label, it's always wise to confirm this. When you get your new goggles, place them on the ground and shoot each lens 3 times from 5 feet away with your airsoft gun. If they pass this test, then they're tough enough.

8

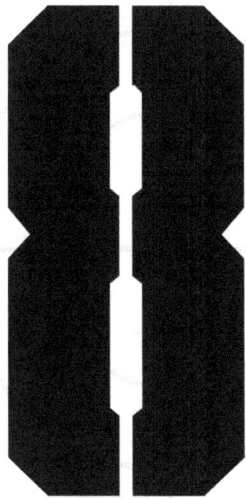

FIREARMS SAFETY

THE MOST IMPORTANT shooting skill you need to know is firearms safety. You must always follow these rules. Your life — and those of others — depend on it. With only four rules, there's no excuse to forget.

THE FOUR RULES OF FIREARMS SAFETY

1. TREAT ALL FIREARMS AS IF THEY ARE LOADED.
2. NEVER POINT THE MUZZLE AT ANYTHING YOU ARE NOT WILLING TO DESTROY.
3. KEEP YOUR FINGER OFF THE TRIGGER UNTIL YOU ARE POINTING AT THE TARGET AND READY TO SHOOT.
4. BE AWARE OF YOUR TARGET, AND WHAT IS BEYOND IT.

First, before we talk about Firearms Safety, we need to familiarize ourselves with the parts of a pistol.

FRONT SIGHT SLIDE SLIDE STOP REAR SIGHT

BARREL

ADVANTAGE ARMS, INC.
VALENCIA, CA USA

BACKSTRAP

FRAME

TRIGGER GUARD TRIGGER MAGAZINE RELEASE MAGAZINE

RULE 1: TREAT ALL FIREARMS AS IF THEY WERE LOADED

Violating the 1st Rule of firearms safety is the primary cause of accidental firearms deaths. For some reason, many people see a gun, pick it up, and assume it's unloaded. *Bam!* They were wrong.

Dead wrong.

HOW TO CHECK IF PISTOL IS LOADED:

1. Begin by following the basic safety rules:
Because the gun could be loaded, when you pick it up, keep your finger off the trigger (Rule 3), and keep the muzzle pointed in a safe direction (Rule 2).

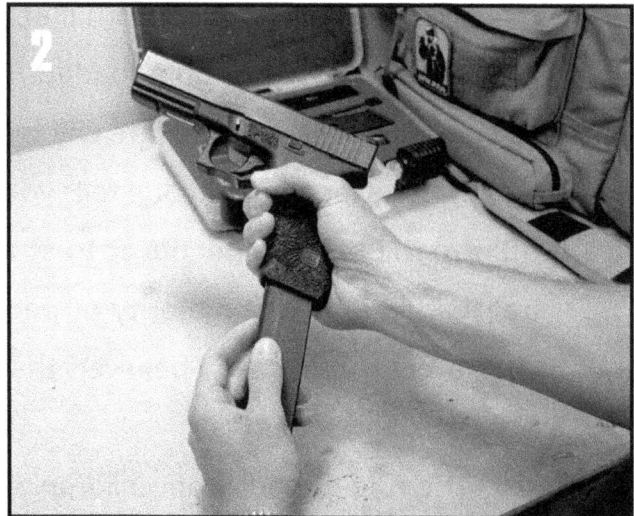

2. Eject the Magazine: Press the mag release, which is a small button on the left-hand side of the pistol's grip frame, typically located at the base of the trigger guard. The button will release the magazine, which you should then remove and place aside.

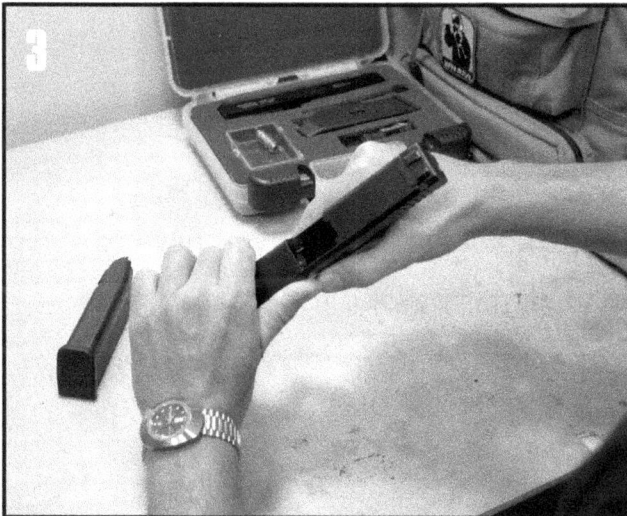

3. Clear the Chamber: Pull the slide backwards and lock it open using the slide stop. This should eject the cartridge from the chamber on most pistols. If the pistol does not have a slide stop, simply hold the slide to the rear.

4. Inspect the Chamber: With the slide locked back, visually inspect the chamber. Is there a bullet inside? If you cannot see it clearly, or if lighting conditions are poor, insert your finger into the chamber to physically verify that the gun is unloaded.

Understand this: Guns are designed to shoot attackers. They accomplish this by firing bullets. Without bullets, they are useless for self-defense. That's why people keep their guns loaded. Therefore, it is only logical to assume that the guns you encounter in life will be loaded. *Never* forget this.

No matter what anyone tells you, no matter how much you trust them in other parts of your life, **never trust anyone when they tell you that a gun is not loaded.** The vast majority of people who have accidently killed someone with a firearm honestly believed that the gun was unloaded — until it went off and killed someone.

This rule extends from children to world-class shooters like Bill Jordan, who accidently killed a fellow police officer because he didn't remember that he had reloaded his .357. If a legend like Jordan can make a mistake, so can you.

YOU MUST ALWAYS PERSONALLY DOUBLE-CHECK TO MAKE SURE THAT THE GUN IS UNLOADED.

Never become complacent.

So, in order to handle a firearm safely, the first thing that you have to do is personally verify that the gun is unloaded. It is beyond the scope of this book to describe how to check every type of firearm. If in doubt, you can look online for the owner's manual.

ONLY AFTER YOU HAVE EJECTED THE MAGAZINE *AND* CHECKED THE CHAMBER IS THE PISTOL UNLOADED.

Always double-check the chamber. Many "professionals" have shot themselves, or others, because they forgot to check the chamber.

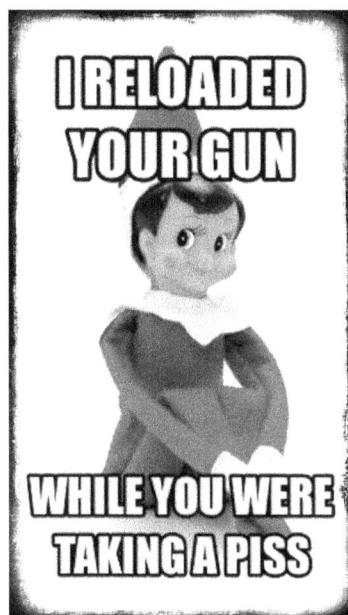

Another part of this rule is that the pistol is only unloaded as long as it's in your hand. **As soon as you set the gun down, even for a moment, you should assume that it has been loaded again.** When you pick it back up, you must double-check to make sure that the gun is still unloaded. There have been many tragedies caused by someone forgetting that they have reloaded their "unloaded" gun.

I like to call this the **"evil elf principle,"** and it is the foundation of my personal firearms safety habits. Whenever I set my unloaded gun down for even a moment, I assume some sick fucking elf has snuck back and reloaded it while I wasn't looking. So I double-check to make sure that it is still unloaded before I resume my dryfire practice. It sounds silly, but the ingrained habit ensures that I never pull the trigger on any firearm without personally verifying its status.

If you're going to be around firearms, Rule 1 needs to become ingrained into your subconscious. I realized this one night when I had a dream that someone handed me a pimped out bullpup 10/22.

Even in my dream, I checked the chamber.

RULE 2: NEVER POINT THE MUZZLE AT ANYTHING YOU'RE NOT WILLING TO DESTROY

Guns are only dangerous in front of the muzzle. Therefore, this safety rule is very easy to follow:

IF YOU DON'T WANT TO PUT A HOLE IN SOMETHING, DON'T POINT THE MUZZLE OF A GUN AT IT!

THE ZOMBIE SHOOTING GUIDE

Always keep the muzzle of any firearm pointed in as safe a direction as possible.

Now, there is no truly "safe" direction — a bullet fired up into the air can travel over a mile and strike some unlucky guy like a miniature asteroid, and a bullet fired into the ground can ricochet with fatal results. But, that being said, if the gun in your hand were to go off, it's much better that it be aimed at the ground or in the air than at your friend's kneecap.

Therefore: Always be aware of where your muzzle is pointing so that you don't carelessly point your gun at yourself or anyone else. This is known as sweeping someone with the muzzle, and it's a potentially fatal breach of social etiquette.

RULE 3: KEEP YOUR FINGER OFF THE TRIGGER UNTIL YOUR GUN IS POINTED AT THE TARGET

Rule 3 is known as "The Golden Rule" because it is the cause of every negligent discharge in modern history. Modern firearms are designed to withstand hard drops to the floor and other abuse without accidently firing.

**GUNS DON'T "GO OFF ACCIDENTALLY."
THE ONLY WAY A MODERN GUN CAN FIRE IS IF
SOMEONE PULLS THE TRIGGER.**

Therefore, if you want to prevent an accident from happening, keep your finger off the trigger until your gun is pointed at the target and you are ready to shoot.

The best way to accomplish this is to keep your finger at the "full limit of extension," off the trigger and above the trigger guard.

Your finger should be in this position until your gun is pointed at the target and you are ready to fire.

Trigger finger discipline is one of the marks of a true professional. When you see someone in a photo with their finger on the trigger, you know that they're an untrained newb. By that same token, if someone has their finger at the full limit of extension, you know that they have at least a basic familiarity with firearms.

For a fun game, watch movies and TV shows, and note how few actors have proper trigger finger discipline. Although you may never become famous, at least you can say that you have better safety habits than they do.

RULE 4: BE AWARE OF YOUR TARGET, AND WHAT IS BEYOND IT

It's very hard to stop a bullet. Made of lead, and traveling faster than the speed of sound, a bullet can travel hundreds of yards after piercing its original target. Therefore, it is essential that you not only be aware of your target, but also what is beyond it.

First, you need to be aware of your target. What material is the target made of? Will it stop a bullet? For example, if you are shooting at a can on top of a fence, the can will not stop the bullet. Instead, it will pierce right through and continue flying for hundreds of yards.

So if you're shooting cans on a fence, you need to know what is beyond the target, for a very long distance away. If your neighbor's house is 100 yards behind the can you're shooting, this is clearly not a safe place for target practice.

FOR RECREATIONAL SHOOTING, YOU WILL NEED AT LEAST A MILE OF CLEAR GROUND BEYOND THE TARGET, OR A FIRM BACKSTOP SUCH AS A HILL. TO BE SAFE, STICK TO LICENSED SHOOTING RANGES.

9

FAST IS FINE, BUT ACCURACY IS EVERYTHING.

— WYATT EARP, FRONTIER LAWMAN & GUNSLINGER

MARKSMANSHIP: FROM BASICS TO BULLSEYES

MARKSMANSHIP IS THE careful use of the sights to achieve maximum accuracy. The front and rear sights are aligned on the target, the trigger is properly pressed, and the bullet goes where it's supposed to go. Using a well-made pistol, you can use your marksmanship skills to put a bullet through another bullet hole at 7 yards, or hit a standing Zombie out to 200 yards. The trick, of course, is practice.

GRIP

Described by WW2 legend Grant Taylor as "fitting the metal hand of war," a proper grip on the pistol is the beginning of all shooting. There's a very specific way to hold the pistol in order to ensure optimum accuracy and recoil control, and this is where your training will begin.

First, double-check to confirm that your pistol is unloaded.

1. With your finger off the trigger, pick up your pistol. You want the upper web of your dominant hand to reach the top of the backstrap of the gun, with your middle finger pressed up beneath the trigger guard. Basically, grip the pistol as high as possible.

   The purpose of this high grip is to place your hand close to the height of the barrel, which will minimize the leverage exerted by recoil. This will limit muzzle rise and reduce recovery speed between shots, essential for accurately engaging multiple Zombies.

2. Wrap your support hand around your shooting hand, with your thumb pointed forward toward the target. Your wrist is angled properly if your hand is pointed downward at a 30-degree angle.

3. Your proper grip looks like this: Both hands should overlap, with your thumbs pointing toward the target and your finger off the trigger.

4. The most important part of your support side hand is the placement of the thumb. Place the thumb on the side of the pistol frame, below the slide. Where exactly on the frame depends on the size of your hand and the design of the pistol. What matters is that it's in a natural and comfortable position, with a secure purchase on the frame. I prefer my thumb pointing forward toward the target, as this provides a biomechanical indicator of where my pistol is pointed, and puts the most amount of skin on the frame.

**THE THUMB GRIP IS ESSENTIAL BECAUSE
IT PROVIDES FRICTION VERY CLOSE TO THE BORE
LINE. THIS HELPS MINIMIZE RECOIL AND IMPROVE
SHOT-TO-SHOT CONSISTENCY.**

I have a tendency to shoot a bit to the left, so I also find that this thumb position helps keep my shots centered on the target. Even if you are already an accomplished marksman, I encourage you to try this simple trick for yourself, as every person I have shown this to has experienced improvements in their shooting.

The result should be a two-handed, thumb-over-thumb grip that covers the pistol equally on both sides with your hands. This provides maximum skin contact on all sides of the pistol, ensuring optimal recoil control. When combined with a good trigger press, you can shoot very accurately with this grip.

In terms of grip pressure, your support hand should be exerting more "squeeze" than your dominant hand, and the thumb of your support hand should be pressing into the side of the pistol frame. Think 60/40 support hand to dominant hand pressure. By having the support hand exert the lion's share of pressure, the dominant hand is better able to achieve its primary goal, which is pressing the trigger correctly.

STANCE

There are several different shooting stances, and in an actual Zombie attack, stance will be irrelevant, since you will be shooting while moving. However, when starting out, a stable, consistent stance is important for learning to shoot accurately, since it reduces unpredictable variables and allows you to focus your attention on your grip, sight alignment, and trigger press.

The stance we will be using is called the Isosceles, which is the most popular stance with completive shooters, law enforcement officers, and military personnel. It is a biomechanically solid stance that absorbs recoil and allows for accurate shooting. However, the most important characteristic of this stance is that the body automatically assumes it under stress. According to Bruce K. Siddle, author of *Sharpening the Warrior's Edge:*

> "[Our natural] response, when suddenly attacked especially in close quarters, is to face our opponent squarely with our hands and arms extended out in front of us. This is a natural stance assumed by all animals who defend themselves on two legs. Add a handgun and you have an Isosceles stance."

More complex stances such as the Weaver place the body in an unnatural firing position. Although it works very well at the shooting range, the Weaver has been shown to break down in the presence of heightened stress, which causes the body to revert to a more natural stance. In Westmoreland's 1989 study, he tested a group of primarily Weaver-trained shooters to see how they reacted under stress. When attacked spontaneously, 92% instinctively reverted to the Isosceles stance.

Because the Isosceles is based on our natural "action stance," we will be able to assume this stance when facing a Zombie attack.

Let's begin with the footwork. Face the target head on, with one foot slightly back. Most people will

When all is said and done, your Isosceles stance should look something like this.

How to Get into the Isosceles Stance From the Draw:

1. Establish a secure grip on your pistol.

2. Draw the pistol straight up out of the holster.

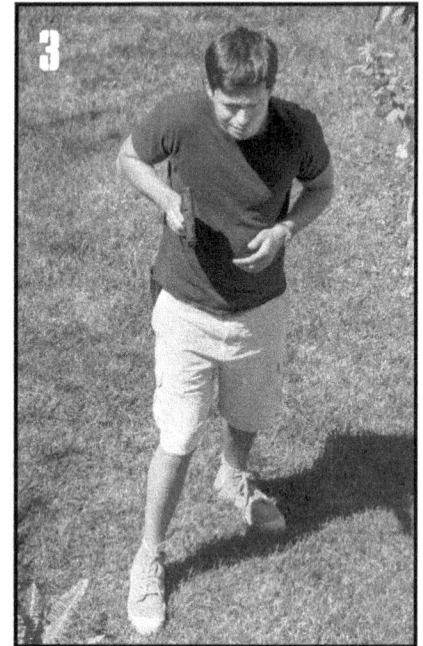

3. Rotate the pistol forward 90 degrees, so that the barrel is parallel with the ground and pointed toward the target. Your support hand should be coming up so you can get into a two-handed grip.

4. With your pistol in a two-handed grip, drive the pistol forward toward where your eye is focused.

5. Continue driving the pistol forward while focusing on a small part of the target. This strict target focus is key to rapid accuracy.

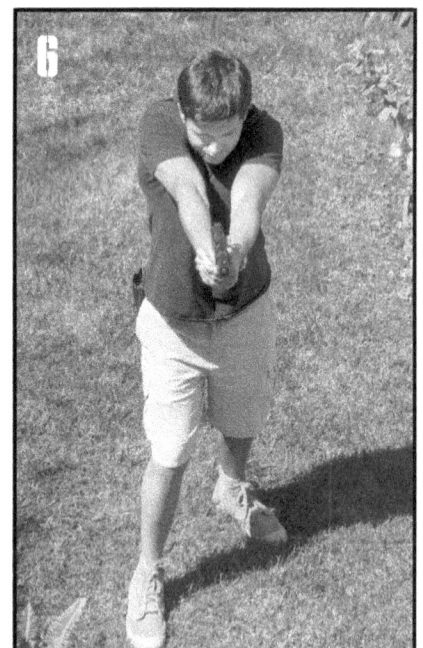

6. When your arms are fully extended, your pistol will be at eye level. With a proper draw, the gun will automatically be on target, with the sights properly aligned.

be more comfortable with their dominant foot held slightly back. Your toes of your rear foot should be in line with the center of your front foot. Bend your knees, but do not crouch.

Extend both arms in front of you to their full limit of extension, but not locked at the elbows. Lean forward, with your "nose over your toes," similar to the way that you would lean into a heavy wind. This forward lean will help absorb recoil, and make you harder to knock over.

Now, everyone's built differently, so feel free to mess around with the footwork until you feel comfortable. As long as your upper chest is square to the target, and both of your arms are fully extended in a triangle-shaped turret, you're golden.

Correct Sight Alignment: The front sight sits evenly spaced in between the rear sight notch, and the tip of the sight blade is equal with the top of the rear sight. Note that the front sight is crystal clear, while the rear sight is slightly out of focus and the target is blurry. This is how your eyes should be focused when going for maximum accuracy.

SIGHT PICTURE

At 7 yards and under, the sight picture is really not that important — even with the sights seriously misaligned you will be able to keep your shots in the head as long as your trigger control is good.

However, because "perfect practice makes perfect," it's foolish not to use a good sight picture when doing slow precision fire. And proper sight alignment is essential for engaging Zombies at longer range.

Different weapons will have different sights, but the general rule is that you want the sights aligned and

THE ZOMBIE SHOOTING GUIDE

flat. So, the front sight is in the notch of the rear sight, with the top of the front sight corresponding with the top of the rear sight.

While it's easier to learn to use the sights by closing one eye to aim, it's essential that you learn how to shoot with both eyes open for close-quarters combat shooting:

> "Both eyes have to be open for engagement when tracking a moving target. This does not matter if the assailant or the officer is moving. . . . As two eyed individuals, many of the body's functions are dependent on the efficiency of both eyes being open and working together. These functions include balance, depth perception, bodily movement, tracking and eye-hand-body coordination."

Additionally, when in fear for your life, your body simply will not allow you to close one eye, because with one eye closed, you deprive the brain of 60% of the visual infomation needed for fighting. For that reason, you want to practice shooting with both eyes open.

TRIGGER CONTROL

The difference between a good marksman and someone
who can't hit the proverbial "bull in the ass with a brass fiddle"
almost always boils down to a matter of trigger control.
— Andy Stanford, *Surgical Speed Shooting*

The key to good marksmanship is not a good gun, a steady hand, or a sharp set of eyes. Although those are all nice to have, **the most essential ingredient to precision shooting is good trigger control.** It is more important than grip, stance, and sight picture combined.

Basically, the trigger is a tiny lever. Archimedes said that with a big enough lever he could move the world. By that same token, your trigger has more than enough leverage to move your weapon out of alignment if

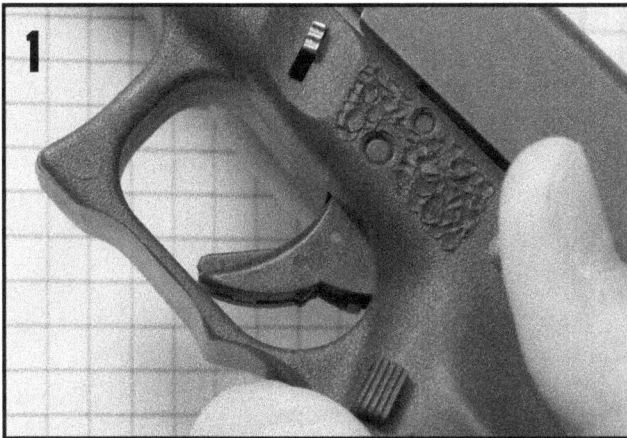

1. Standard Glock Trigger.

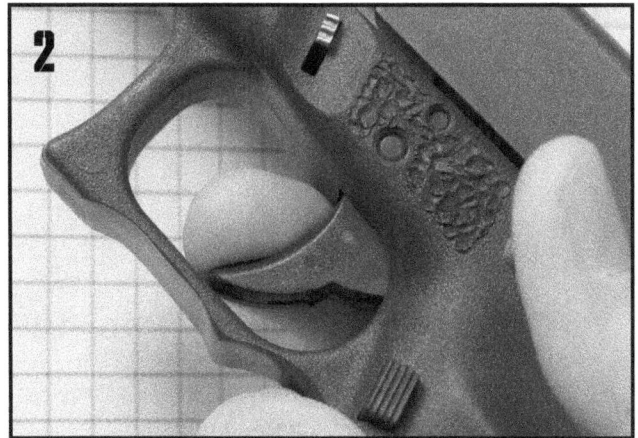

2. The empty space behind the trigger is mostly "slack."

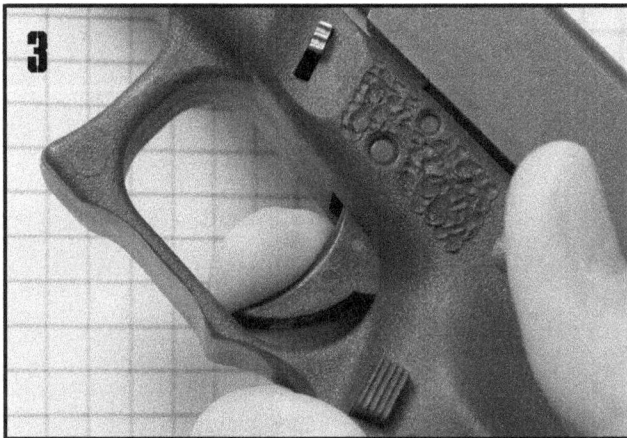

3. When you feel your finger encounter firm resistance, you are at the "set." Note how far the trigger has moved: this was all useless slack.

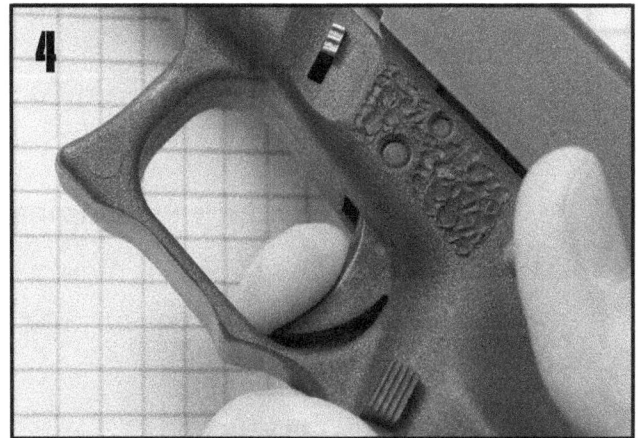

4. Glock trigger fully depressed. Note how little the trigger has moved from being at the "set" to firing. By minimizing trigger travel, you maximize accuracy. That is why you should always take out the slack before firing.

it is pulled incorrectly. In order to shoot well, it is essential that you learn to press the trigger properly.

DRYFIRE: GETTING TO KNOW YOUR TRIGGER

Because 90% of accuracy is good trigger control, you need to master the proper trigger technique. What's great about this skill is that the majority of your practice can be done for free, at home, through what is known as dry-fire practice.

TO BEGIN, EJECT THE MAGAZINE OF YOUR FIREARM, AND THEN CHECK THE CHAMBER TO MAKE SURE IT'S UNLOADED.

Then check again. Once you have verified the gun is unloaded, point it at something you are willing to destroy (Kevlar vest, pile of phone books) and press the trigger.

Now that you have confirmed that your pistol is unloaded, dryfire can commence.

Most triggers on semi-automatic pistols have two stages—the initial "slack," where the trigger is moving but there is no real resistance, and then the "set," where you exert pressure on the trigger until the sear "breaks."

Stages of Trigger Press

1. To pull the trigger correctly, the first step is to take out the slack, which makes up the majority of the overall trigger travel. Pull lightly until you encounter firm resistance. Then stop.
2. When resistance is felt, the trigger is at the "set."
3. Slowly, apply light but deliberate pressure until the trigger fires. Pulling it too abruptly will result in a trigger jerk, causing the shot to hit low.
4. If the trigger is pressed properly, the gun will barely move at all.

One way to test your trigger control is to place a dime on the tip of your front sight. If the dime doesn't move, you're doing it right. If the dime moves, or falls off, more practice is needed.

DRYFIRE DRILLS

Fifteen minutes a day of dry practice . . . will make an immense differ-ence in the ability to deliver highly accurate fire during a life-threatening encounter. Fifteen minutes a week could easily make the difference in terms of weapon presentation, sight alignment, and trigger control.
— KENNETH R. MURRAY, *TRAINING AT THE SPEED OF LIFE*

Trigger control is not something that is learned right away. It takes prac-tice, and due to its critical importance to marksmanship, it is a skill that should be practiced for the rest of your life.

Dryfire practice can be as informal as watching *Dawn of the Dead* and pulling the trigger every time a Zombie pops up on screen. But you will achieve better results through a formal, conscientious routine that is regularly followed.

Here's a routine that you can use:

1. At the farthest distance you can find in your house, tape a Zombie Qualification Target to the wall at head height. There are a few in the back of the book that you can cut out and use. The brain is to scale.

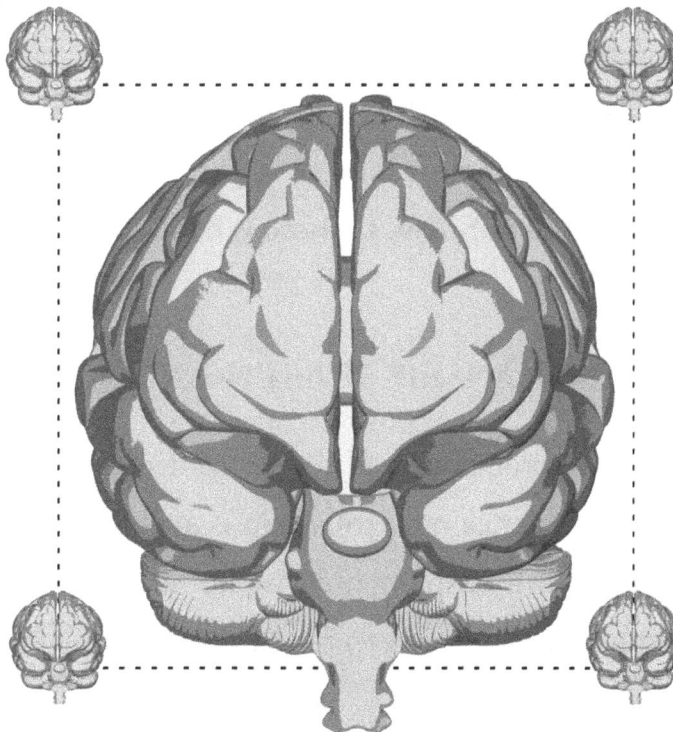

2. Check and re-check that your pistol is unloaded.

3. In your shooting stance, with a two-handed hold on your pistol, aim for the Small Brain in the upper left-hand corner of the target.

4. Slowly dryfire àt the brain, imagining that the gun is loaded, and that you are at the range trying to make the shot.

5. Fire 10 slow "shots" into the brain.

6. Lower your arms for 60 seconds to let them rest.

7. Switch to the Small Brain on the upper right-hand of the target, and repeat the drill.

8. Shoot all four Small Brains following this routine, then do the dime test.

The more seriously you take the drill, the better your results.

HERE ARE SOME DRYFIRE TRAINING GOALS:

1. Pass the dime test with two-handed grip using primary hand.

2. Pass the dime test with two-handed grip using off hand.

3. Pass the dime test with primary hand only.

4. Pass the dime test with off hand.

Complete at least Level 1 before proceeding to live fire at the shooting range, and make sure to complete all four levels as soon as you can. It's simple, free, and can be done at home, so there is no excuse.

MARKSMANSHIP TRAINING AT HOME

Marksmanship is a combination of trigger control and sight picture. Obviously, the best way to practice marksmanship is at the range, but it will save ammunition to master the fundamentals at home beforehand. Also, these drills will let you stay sharp in between range sessions.

You can perform basic marksmanship training at home using your Laser Training Cartridge and/or your airsoft gun. If using your LTC, you can simply "shoot" at your dryfire target. If firing your airsoft gun, I recommend that you attach the target to an empty cardboard box to trap the BBs.

1. Set up a Zombie Qualification Target from the back of this book.
2. Step back 7 yards from the target, or as far as you can.

   1 yard ≈ 1 long stride.

3. Assume a two-handed stance, align your sights, and aim for the Big Brain in the center of the target.
4. Remembering your proper trigger control, take out the slack, and then press the trigger until the shot breaks.
5. Click! Thump! Depending on whether you were using your LTC or your airsoft gun, there should be either a laser dot or a small hole in the brain.
6. When you can keep all of your shots in the Big Brain using two hands firing with your primary, start shooting using two hands, but firing with your off hand.
7. Once that is mastered, switch to firing with just your primary hand, and after that, fire with just your off hand.
8. When you can keep all of your shots in the Big Brain with either hand, run your next drills aiming at the small brains, repeating the same cycle.

THE 5 TARGET DRILL

Once you feel that you have made sufficient progress in your home marksmanship training, it's time to hit the range.

Using your Shoot-N-C's, set up a target with 5 bullseyes.

1. With your pistol unloaded, start the range session by dry firing 10 times at the bullseye, just to re-familiarize yourself with the trigger.

2. Now load 10 rounds of centerfire ammo into your magazine. Fire into the center target, using the good trigger control and proper sight picture you have been practicing. This center target represents your control target, serving as a record of your current level of skill at the beginning of the day. This will allow you to gauge how much you have improved by the end of your range session.

3. Now it is time to switch over to your .22 conversion kit. Double check that your gun is unloaded, then follow the conversion procedure of your particular kit.

4. Using your .22 conversion kit, fire 10 rounds into each of the remaining targets, maintaining proper trigger control and sight picture.

5. Assess if you are shooting with sufficient accuracy with the .22 for the given level of skill you are trying to build. For example, if I'm practicing to shoot left-handed, and all of my .22 shots are grouped closely together in the bullseye, then I am shooting accurately enough to move back to centerfire. However, if I'm not yet achieving good groups, then I should continue to practice with the .22.

6. Either set up a new target, add more Shoot-N-Cs, or cover the holes with the supplied little black dots.

7. Continue with the .22 conversion kit until you have mastered your skill for the day.

5 Target Drill, Round 1: Sam's initial 10 rounds of 45 ACP to the center target showed inadequate accuracy. The three missed shots below the bullseye were caused by jerking the trigger due to poor trigger control. He switched over to the .22 conversion kit and shot the remaining 4 targets. As his familiarity with the trigger increased, his accuracy improved. By his last target (bottom left), 7 out of 10 shots were perfect. Good, but not good enough.

CENTERFIRE TRAINING DRILL

Once you have perfected a given skill with your .22lr conversion, swap out the slide and convert back to centerfire. The recoil will be different, and it may take a few rounds to get used to but because the sights, trigger, and grip angle are identical, the learning curve should be minimal.

5 Target Drill, Round 2: Now that Sam is familiar with the trigger, he keeps all 10 rounds of .45 in the black, with 9 touching in a nice grouping. However, he's still not satisfied with that level of accuracy, so he switches to the .22 conversion kit and shoots the remaining 4 targets. His last target (bottom right) is perfect, with all 10 shots in the bullseye. With 15 minutes of practice, Sam has just shot the best grouping of his life.

1. Set up a new 5 bullseye target and switch back to centerfire.

2. Shoot the center target 10 times as your control target, taking it slow. You will likely notice an improvement in accuracy.

3. Assess. **If you were doing great with the .22, but poorly with your centerfire, that means that you are anticipating the recoil, causing you to flinch.** If that is not the case, skip ahead to step 5.

4. If you're flinching / having issues with the recoil, dump your next magazine into the center of the target rapid fire as fast as possible, forcing yourself to keep both eyes open. Congratulations! You're still alive, the recoil and noise didn't kill you. Personally, I found that doing this a few times helped me get over my fear of recoil, and I highly recommend you do the same if you're having issues with flinching.

Remember, once you've fired, the bullet has already left the barrel and is heading toward the target before you feel the recoil, so there is no need to try and compensate for it. Just use a firm grip and go with the flow, and focus on using the great trigger control you have been working on. If you do your part, the recoil will take care of itself.

5. Shoot your remaining four targets. If you just had a 50-round box of ammo, shoot 10 rounds into each of the two bottom targets, and then shoot 5 rounds into each of the top ones.

6. Compare your control target to your final five targets, and gauge your progress.

MARKSMANSHIP GOALS

There are all kinds of marksmanship standards being espoused today. For the purpose of *The Zombie Shooting Guide,* marksmanship is based on the Zombie Qualification Target available in the back of the book. This provides a free and versatile metric for evaluating your skill. Remember, because of the unique challenge posed by the Zombie menace, your marksmanship is held to a higher standard.

For slow-fire, precision shooting, you should strive to attain the following levels:

Basic Z: All shots hit the Big Brain at a distance of 7 yards when using two hands with both eyes open.

Intermediate Z: All shots hit the Big Brain at 7 yards one handed (left and right) with both eyes open. All shots hit the Small Brains two-handed using sights 7 yards.

Advanced Z: All shots hit the Big Brain at 25 yards using two hands with both eyes open. All shots hit the Small Brains one handed (left and right) using sights 7 yards. All shots hit the 8.5x11-inch paper at 50 yards using sights.

Expert Z: All Shots hit the Big Brain at 50 yards. All shots hit the 8.5 x 11-inch paper at 100 yards.

Before progressing to the next chapter on Point Shooting, it is highly recommended that you master at least Basic Z level of precision marksmanship. If you can already accomplish this, move up a level.

Regardless of your current level of skill, you should use the full array of training tools available to you before switching to centerfire ammunition. This will allow you to master the mechanics of the drill without the cost and recoil of full caliber ammunition.

EXAMPLE TRAINING DRILL PROGRESSION

If you were attempting to master precision shooting with your left hand, a typical regimen would go as follows:

AT HOME

1. Dryfire with your left hand, extensively (10 to 100 times a day until you pass the dime test).

    Cost = $0

2. Laser dryfire at home with your left hand. Set up a Z Qualification Target in the farthest part of your house and work on hitting the Big Brain, and then the Small Brains with the laser. Continue until you hit them 100% of the time.

    Cost = $0 (excluding the onetime cost of the LTC).

AT THE SHOOTING RANGE

1. Begin with 10 shots of centerfire ammunition with your left hand, on the Z Qualification Target you used at home, at the same distance (ideally around 7 yards). This is your control target, to see where your shooting level lies within the given drill.

Cost = $2 to $4, depending on caliber.

2. Switch to .22lr conversion, and shoot till you have mastered, or at least improved on, the drill. The number of rounds could be as few as 50 or as many as 500, but 100 to 300 is a comfortable amount.

Cost = $5 to $15, depending on # of rounds.

3. When the drill is mastered in .22lr, switch to centerfire and shoot 40 rounds.

Cost = $6 to $16, depending on caliber.

4. If you still cannot complete the drill, call it a day and try again later, or keep shooting if you can afford it.

Total ammo cost per range session: $15 to $35, depending on the caliber of your pistol.

10

PHYSICAL FIGHTS AND ARMED ENGAGEMENTS OCCUR IN LESS THAN IDEAL CONDITIONS. LIGHTING IS POOR, INFORMATION IS IMPERFECT, THREATS ARE DYNAMIC, SITUATIONS ARE DETERIORATING QUICKLY, BLOOD CHEMISTRY IS RAPIDLY CHANGING, AND HUMAN PHYSIOLOGY IS PRIMING ITSELF FOR THE FIGHT OF ITS LIFE. MARKSMANSHIP SKILLS AND PSYCHICAL TECHNIQUES SUDDENLY BECOME SERIOUSLY IMPAIRED, IF AVAILABLE AT ALL.

— KENNETH R. MURRAY, *TRAINING AT THE SPEED OF LIFE*

POINT SHOOTING: THE EMERGENCY MARKSMANSHIP SKILL

IN THE INITIAL chaos of the Outbreak, your focus will more likely be on the 6-foot tall Zombie that is trying to eat your face, and not on the $\frac{1}{8}$–inch tall sights on the tip of your pistol. Therefore, to increase your chances of survival, you should have a backup shooting method that will allow you to deliver accurate fire at close quarters, under stress, without using the sights. That backup firing method is called Point Shooting.

Research indicates that when a person is suddenly confronted by an attacker at close range, he will tend to point his gun at the threat, not look at his sights, and just start spraying. This, unsurprisingly, leads to terrible results, with the 1:3 hit ratio being typical, and with innocent bystanders sometimes hit as well.

It's important to understand: This is not Point Shooting. This is pointing AND shooting. Pointing AND shooting is an unpracticed, panic response that relies on luck and sheer volume of fire to work. By comparison, Point Shooting is a honed skill that allows for the accurate delivery of shots without the use of sights.

Although the names sound similar, the results are utterly different. One describes a trained and accurate response, the other an utter breakdown in training.

WHY PRACTICE POINT SHOOTING

Point Shooting is a necessary skill for surviving a Zombie attack.

Here's why: Hundreds of after-action reports compiled over decades of shootings have stated that the majority of shooters, when surprised by a life-or-death attack, did not look at their weapons' sights.

Although you may have already achieved a high level of marksmanship, it is always wise to profit from the experience of others. If countless shooters have reported not using their sights when under attack, it's foolhardy to assume that you will be the exception, especially during the terror of your first Zombie attack. Hopefully you will be able to use your sights, but it's very important to have a backup shooting method should you need it.

One reason you may not be able to use the sights is the effect of Survival Stress on the human eye. According to Bruce K. Siddle, author of *Sharpening the Warrior's Edge*:

> "The lens [of the eye] is normally held in a flattened, distance viewing state by tension of the radial ligaments. Parasympathetic excitement contracts the ciliary muscle, which releases this tension allowing the lens to become more convex. This causes the eye to focus on close objects. During sympathetic response, the eye cannot focus; thus one will see the front sight out of focus, which will result in a heightened state of stress. . . . **Therefore, trying to use the front sights during survival stress is counterproductive to the normal function of the eye.**"

What this means is: Should the attack be terrifying enough to induce the Survival Stress response, your eyes may be physically incapable of focusing on the front sight.

In the madness of your first Zombie attack, it seems highly likely that your Survival Stress response will be activated. If so, it is essential that you are able to make a headshot without looking at the sights. And in order to do that, you will need to practice Point Shooting.

POINT SHOOTING TECHNIQUE

The basic Point Shooting technique has three main ingredients: target focus, driving the pistol, and pistol-eye coordination. You look intently toward a small target — say, a Zombie's mouth — and then you drive the pistol forward, as if you were trying to punch the target with the tip of your barrel. With lots of practice, you will develop the pistol-eye coordination necessary to instinctively "feel" that you are on target. This will allow you to shoot accurately without relying on the sights.

TARGET FOCUS

When Point Shooting, the most important thing is to focus intently on a small part of the target. This focus point serves as your sights, because "the bullets go where the eyes go." This is similar to the "aim small, miss small" philosophy of aimed fire.

For example, if you aimed your pistol at a big blank sheet of paper, your shots would most likely be spread out around the paper. However, if you aligned your sights on a small dot in the center of the paper, your shots would be in a nice grouping.

The same thing is true with Point Shooting. If you just look at the entire target, your shots are going to be all over the place. But by focusing on a specific part of the target as your bullseye, you will have a precise goal for your pistol-eye coordination.

When it comes to Point Shooting for Zombie combat, you don't want to just look at the Zombie and start shooting. Rather, stare intently at his face and use it as your target. Then drive your pistol toward it, and fire.

In short, "Focus tight. Hit right."

DRIVING THE PISTOL

Once you have a precise target focus, the next step is to "drive the pistol" toward that target. This provides the biomechanical feedback necessary for building effective pistol-eye coordination.

Fundamentally, the Point Shooting Draw is identical to the regular draw used in aimed fire. The beauty of this is two-fold. First, it prevents the need for learning a new "Point Shooting Draw," which would be confusing under stress. Instead, you are performing the exact same draw that is already familiar to you. The only difference is that instead of firing when you see the sights are on target, you will be firing when you "feel" that your weapon is on target.

The second benefit is that target focus is a very natural, evolutionary response to stress. When humans are under attack, they instinctively focus their attention on the threat. During the Outbreak, we will be focusing our attention on the Zombie's horrifying face as it attacks us. So, by combining this natural target focus with our familiar draw, Point Shooting will happen of its own accord.

However, though Point Shooting is an instinctive technique in principle, it is essential that you build up your pistol-eye coordination.

Target Focus: Although the pistol is raised to eye level, I am focusing on a small part of the target, and not the weapon's sights.

1. With your eyes locked on the target, draw the pistol straight out of the holster.

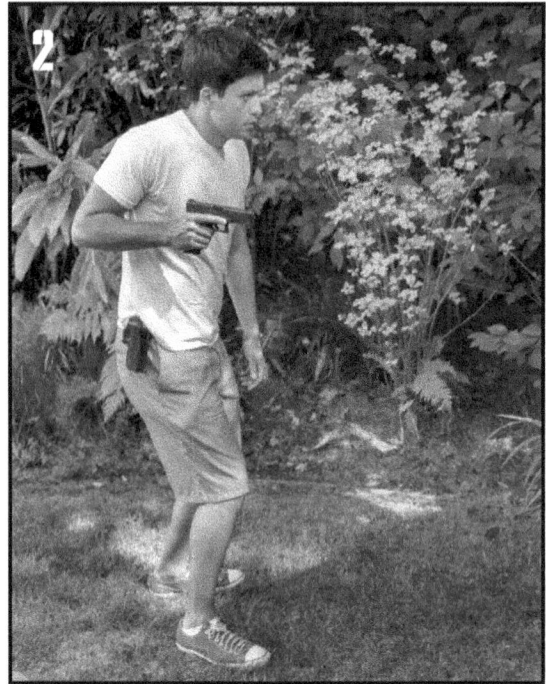

2. When your pistol reaches your ribs, rotate it forward, muzzle toward the threat. At this point, try and keep the pistol flat, with the barrel parallel to the ground. This biomechanical trick will help keep your shots straight and on target.

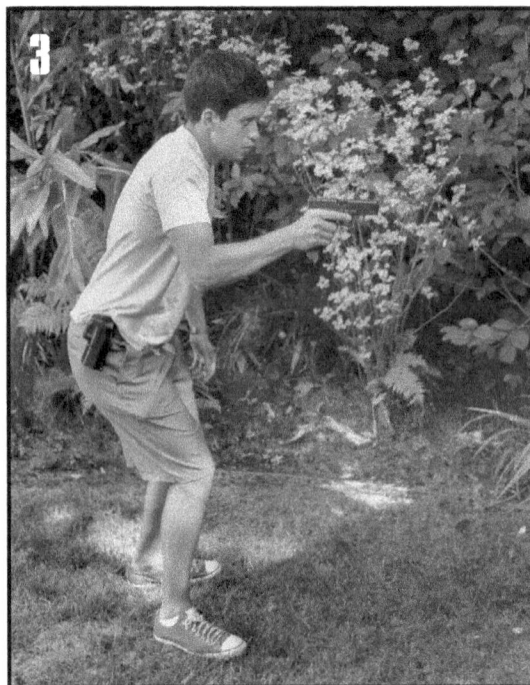

3. Drive the pistol toward where your eyes are focusing, as if you were trying to stab the target with the barrel. Try and keep the pistol flat and parallel to the ground. Maintain strict target focus as you continue to drive the pistol forward.

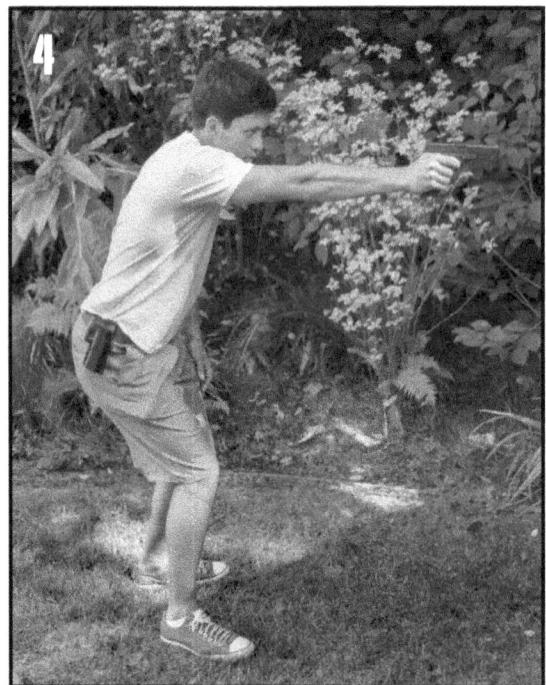

4. When the gun reaches eye level and you "feel" that the gun is on target: Fire.

PISTOL-EYE COORDINATION

Hand-eye coordination is a fundamental human skill. In its simplest form, it allows us to look at something, such as a bird in flight, and intuitively point our finger right at it. As hand-eye coordination improves, it allows us to throw a ball accurately into a red plastic cup, or a dart into the bullseye.

Taken to the limits of human potential, hand-eye coordination is responsible for some remarkable feats. When a batter hits a 90mph fastball out of the park, a running quarterback throws the perfect touchdown pass, or a hockey player scores a goal from halfway across the rink while skating, these are all examples of peak performance in hand-eye coordination.

Compared to the hand-eye coordination required for most sports, our Point Shooting challenges are actually pretty modest. Although handguns are less accurate than rifles, they are worlds more accurate than a football or hockey puck. So if a quarterback can make a 30-yard pass with a lump of pigskin, it shouldn't be too difficult to master a 3-yard headshot with a precision machine. Remember, every other sport in the world relies on hand-eye coordination for accuracy. Shooting should be no different.

But, like other sports, developing your pistol-eye coordination takes lots of practice. Fortunately for our wallets, the majority of our Point Shooting training can be performed at home for free.

USING LASER DRYFIRE TO PRACTICE PISTOL-EYE COORDINATION

Although the Laser Training Cartridge (LTC) is a fun and useful tool in general, it is invaluable when it comes to learning Point Shooting. The reason is simple: Point Shooting is the firing of a pistol without using the sights, but dry firing relies on the sights for target verification. So, without sights, the LTC is necessary to show where your shot has landed.

Of course, for this training to be accurate, it is essential that the LTC be accurately aligned in your pistol. Although a cool bit of technology, the LTC is not perfect, and it does not align precisely with the sights in some guns. This can be a disaster, because if the laser is inaccurate, you will be programming an incorrect targeting system into your brain.

Before training, verify that your LTC is 100% on target. Otherwise, you are better off skipping the LTC and going directly to your airsoft trainer and .22 conversion kit.

POINT SHOOTING TRAINING AT HOME

1. Tape a Zombie Qualification Target to the wall, 5-foot 10-inches off the ground to mimic the height of the average male Zombie.
2. With your LTC in the chamber, and your gun in the holster, stand 3 yards away from the target.
3. Focus your eyes on the center of the Big Brain, draw, and slowly drive the pistol toward the target.
4. When the gun reaches your eye level, and you "feel" it on target: Fire.
5. Repeat this drill again and again, maintaining that slow drive and precise target focus. When you can make 25 slow headshots in a row, start doing it faster.
6. When you can make a Point Shooting headshot at 3 yards as fast as you can, step back to 4 yards and repeat.
7. Continue practicing until you can make a fast Point Shooting head-shot out to 7 yards.
8. When you have mastered it at 7 yards, start back at 3 yards, using only your dominant hand.
9. Master out to 7 yards, going as fast as you can.

10. Start again at 3 yards, using only your other hand.

11. Master out to 7 yards.

12. Perform all of the above drills again, now using your airsoft trainer.

LIVE FIRE POINT SHOOTING

Once you have mastered Point Shooting to at least 3 yards using your laser and airsoft trainers, it's time to start practicing using live fire at the range.

1. Begin with a Zombie Qualification Target set up at a distance of 3 yards, using your .22 conversion kit in a holster. Start slow, focusing on the Big Brain.

2. When you can perform 25 Point Shooting headshots in a row with your .22 conversion kit at 3 yards, switch back to full power centerfire ammo. Repeat the same drill, going slow.

3. When you can perform 25 perfect slow fire PS headshots with your full power centerfire ammo, switch back to your .22 conversion kit. The target will remain at 3 yards, but now your goal is to improve your speed. Starting slow, gradually increase in speed until you are making PS headshots at full speed.

4. After 25 perfect headshots at full speed using your .22 conversion kit, convert back to centerfire. Repeat the above drill, until you can shoot at full speed with your centerfire.

5. When you can fire 25 Point Shooting headshots with centerfire ammo at full speed at 3 yards, step back to 4 yards and start over again with .22 conversion kit.

6. Continue this progressive training until you can perform a full speed Point Shooting headshot with centerfire ammunition at 7 yards.

11
MOVE YOUR ASS

ONE OF THE most important elements of shooting for self-defense is movement. Yet it is also the least practiced skill since a traditional firing range, with its delineated fields of fire and strict safety rules, is not conducive to action shooting. You're forced to stand in one place, and shoot at a stationary target. Imagine if some guy at your local range suddenly started sprinting sideways while firing one-handed as fast as possible. That would probably not go over so well.

Yet shooting while moving is exactly what we need to start practicing.

If we treat the Zombie Outbreak like another Sunday afternoon at the shooting range, we're not going to survive for very long. A Fast Zombie can clear 7 yards in 1.5 seconds. A looter with decent shooting skills can shoot you twice in the chest in the same amount of time. Given the speed with which we can be killed, it's essential that we make ourselves a harder target.

A moving target is hard to hit, and a moving target that is shooting back is even harder.

**REMEMBER: NOT BEING HIT IS JUST AS IMPORTANT,
IF NOT EVEN MORE IMPORTANT, THAN MAKING HITS.**

This is especially true in a Zombie / SHTF (Shit-Hit-the-Fan) scenario, when there will be a breakdown in emergency medical care. With ambulances and phone service, 80% of handgun wounds are survivable. Without medical attention, in a disease-ridden wasteland, not so much. And of course, there is no cure for the Zombie Virus.

So the name of the game is: Don't get hit, and don't get bit.

And to do that, you're going to need to *move your ass.*

OODA, ACCURACY, AND SURVIVAL

In the 1950s, a US Air Force Colonel named John Boyd came up with a concept known as the OODA loop that would fundamentally change the study of human conflict. Boyd's OODA loop stands for "Observe, Orient, Decide, Act," and it is essential to all decision making. It's especially pertinent to combat and self-defense.

Here's how it works: First, you **observe** something. The next stage is **orient,** when your brain compares the observation to past experience. Based on this information, you **decide** the appropriate action to take. Then you **act.**

We are running through the OODA loop constantly, whether it is suddenly slamming on the brakes in response to seeing the red taillights of a car ahead of us, or flirting with a girl because she smiles at us.

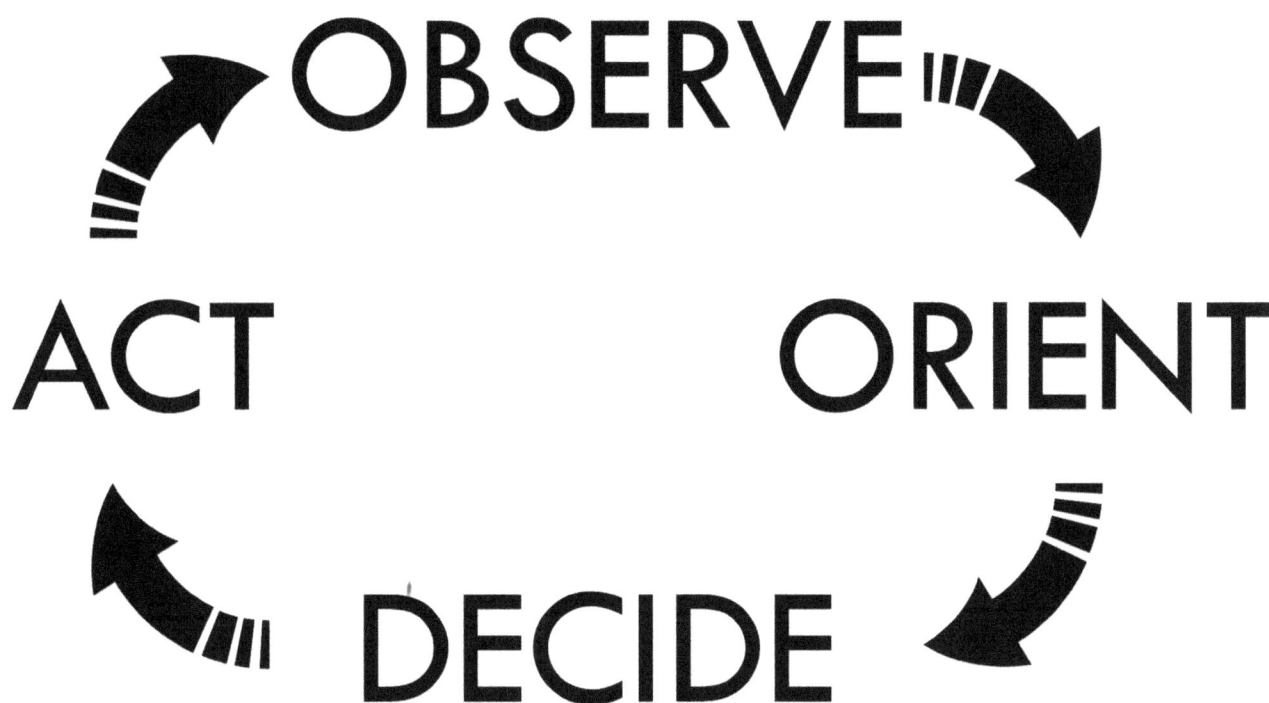

OBSERVE

ORIENT

ACT

DECIDE

OODA loop

The OODA loop will be especially important for surviving a Zombie attack. For example, you observe a grotesque horror of a man, blood dripping from his mouth and screaming incoherently. Then he starts running toward you.

It's OODA time.

Your optic nerve sends this observation to the brain, which orients the information based on past experiences — in this case, you remember the Zombie movies you have seen with similar attackers. Your brain decides that based on the threat's rapid approach, your only chance is to shoot him. You act by drawing your pistol and making a headshot.

THE SPEED IN WHICH YOU RUN THROUGH THE OODA LOOP IS OFTEN THE KEY TO YOUR SURVIVAL.

In the above scenario, you would have survived because you observed the threat, and oriented what you saw based on your previous knowledge of Zombies. This allowed you to rapidly make a decision to draw your gun, and you acted in time to save yourself.

Since Zombies are fundamentally human, it's safe to assume that they also operate using the OODA loop. The Zombie observes you. His optic nerve (or sense of smell or hearing, whatever he has left) sends that information to his brain. He remembers the previous humans he has attacked. Those humans were tasty, so he decides to kill you. He turns toward you, raises his arms, lets out a terrible groan, and heads your way.

Now, here's where *Move Your Ass* comes in: If you just stood in place shooting, the Zombie's brain is still set to attack. However, if you *move your ass* by sprinting sideways while shooting, the Zombie's brain must momentarily reset to the beginning of the OODA loop.

He observes you moving away. Now he must figure out your relative distance and direction in relation to himself. He must decide to change direction, and then his entire body must act to change direction and continue his attack.

The speed of Zombie brain processing is still unknown, but the uninfected human brain runs through the OODA loop in roughly 0.25 of a second. But—and this is crucial — the human body can also sprint and shoot very quickly. If a human can run 21 feet in 1.5 seconds, that's 14-feet-per-second. Which means that if you reset the attacker's OODA loop back for just 0.25, you can move 3.5 feet away.

So even if it takes the Zombie only 0.25 of a second to run through the OODA loop, if you *move your ass,* you have gained at least one extra stride away from him. And, if you have your pistol already in hand, you have managed to fire at least one shot. The more shots you can put into him, and the more distance you can put between you, the better your chances of survival.

When it comes to surviving a gunfight, the benefits of movement are more obvious. A clay pigeon sitting 5 yards away is a relatively easy target to

shoot. However, a clay pigeon only 5 feet away is difficult to shoot if it is flying through the air.

Here's another example. Look at the width of my chest.

I'm 6-feet tall and weigh 175 lbs, and my upper chest can be covered by the width of a sheet of paper. Even one large sidestep will put me three chest-widths away from my attacker's original point of aim. As his OODA loop attempts to catch up to my actions, he no longer has the initiative. *Now he's reacting to my initiative.* And that gives me time to access my pistol and bring it into the fight.

The lesson is clear: When a Zombie is charging toward you, or someone is shooting at you, *move your ass!*

WHERE TO MOVE

The ZSG is all about progressive training, so learning how to *move your ass* begins at an easy level, and then increases in difficulty and intensity as you gain confidence with the technique.

The first step is understanding where to move.

Unless you have no other choice, you do *not* want to move straight back. There are several reasons for this. First, the human body moves forward and sideways much faster than it can move backward.

Second, you do not have eyes in the back of your head. So when moving backward, it is easy to trip over some random piece of debris, or stumble into a Zombie who is coming up from behind.

The third point — and this is essential to surviving an attack by post-Apocalyptic outlaws — is that moving straight back is ineffective if you want to avoid getting shot. A pistol bullet can travel hundreds of yards. So, no matter how far back you move, as long as you're still in the path of the bullet, you're going to get shot.

IT'S ESSENTIAL TO *MOVE YOUR ASS* TO GET OUT OF THE LINE OF FIRE.

Remember the picture of how wide my chest is — even moving one step to the side is enough to get me out of the path of the bullet. This principle is known as "getting off the X."

Here I *move my ass* to the 9 o'clock position as the Zombie charges.

So, for the purpose of dodging Zombies and bullets, your training will focus on moving sideways and at a diagonal. If you are at the center of a clock, and your attacker is shooting at you from the 12 o'clock position, you want to focus on moving to your 3 or 9 o'clock. Or, go to your 1 or 11 o'clock.

As long as you're not standing still, or moving straight back toward the 6 o'clock, you can move in pretty much any direction. Timing and terrain will largely dictate where you move. The most important thing is *moving your ass* as soon as you perceive a threat. This will involve programming your brain to recognize threatening movements.

THREAT STIMULUS

A threat stimulus is a physical action that indicates an attack is about to occur. For our purposes, if a Zombie locks eyes on you and begins moving in your direction, *move your ass!* Likewise, if you encounter a looter and he is reaching for his waistband or swiftly moving his arm up in your direction, these are universal signs that he has a weapon, and you need to *move your ass!*

Zombie Threat Stimulus: The first indicator that a Zombie is going to charge is in the legs.

If you see a Zombie start to lift his leg, you need to *move your ass* and start shooting.

1. Weapon Threat Stimulus: Pay attention to the hands or you'll be looking down the barrel of a gun!

2. If a stranger suddenly reaches for his waistband, it's not so he can scratch his crotch: He's going for a weapon.

THREAT STIMULUS DRILL

Now that you understand threat indicators, it's time to begin training yourself to *move your ass* as soon as you see one. Do it at least 20 times.

1. You and your partner stand 15 feet apart, with your partner concealing an **unloaded airsoft gun.**
2. At a time of his choosing, he should suddenly draw his airsoft gun or sprint toward you as fast as he can.
3. As soon as you perceive either threat stimulus — *move your ass* by exploding in any direction — preferably sideways to the 3 or 9 o'clock, or diagonally forward to the 11 or 1 o'clock.
4. Continue running the drill, mixing up your moves each time.

MOVE YOUR ASS DRILL

To make things more interesting, we're going to add some very minimal Force on Force training. The purpose is to increase your stress and the need for speed.

1. You and your partner must each **wear goggles and face masks.**
2. Your partner will load one round into his airsoft gun, and tuck the pistol in his waistband. You will be unarmed.
3. Place a white paper plate or other large visible marker directly behind the spot where you're standing. This will represent the "X."
4. Standing 15 feet away from each other, your partner suddenly draws his pistol at a time of his choosing. He is to fire straight ahead, in the direction of the paper plate. If you *move your ass* fast enough, the round will miss. If you're too slow getting off the X, you will get shot.

Note: The goal is for him to shoot straight over the plate, not to track your movement and shoot at you.

5. Repeat this drill until it seems childishly easy.

DRAWING WHILE MOVING DRILL

The next step is drawing your pistol while moving. In this exercise, we will use airsoft guns and introduce a stun gun. Your airsoft pistol should be in your concealed holster if you have a Concealed Carry Weapon (CCW) permit, or in your open carry Zombie shooting holster if you do not. Remember: Train like you fight. If you carry your weapon concealed, you need to practice drawing from concealment.

1. Stand 21 feet away **wearing goggles and face masks.**
2. Your partner should load one round into his airsoft gun to play the role of the looter. In his pocket should be the stun gun to simulate a Zombie attack. Your airsoft gun is unloaded. Have a paper plate or other visible marker behind you designating the "X."
3. At a time of your partner's choosing, he is either to draw his airsoft gun and fire straight down the X, or sprint toward the paper plate with the stun gun. Either way, his goal is to attack the X, not to track your movements and attack you.
4. As soon as you perceive the threat stimulus, you are to *move your ass* off the line of attack, to either the 3, 9, 1, or 11 o'clock position. If you are fast enough, you will not be shot or tazed. If you are too slow, you'll know!
5. While moving, draw your unloaded airsoft pistol and "shoot" your partner. Even though it's unloaded, try and make a headshot.
6. Repeat this drill until it feels natural and smooth.

12
THE BACKYARD MOVING TARGET

WHETHER YOU ARE engaging Walkers, Fast Zombies, or armed looters, they will all be moving much faster than a stationary paper target. Therefore, in order for your training to be realistic, it is essential that you practice shooting moving targets.

Unfortunately, most shooting ranges are not equipped with moving target facilities, and only have fixed targets. Some ranges do offer moving targets, but they are unrealistically linear, usually moving either horizontally on the X-axis, or straight toward you on the Y-axis. This is much better than a stationary target, but since no real attacker moves strictly sideways or forward, it's still not ideal.

The best training is with a robotic moving target system, which is basically a giant radio-controlled car with a human-sized target on top. The Marines are testing systems like the Australian R-TMS, while similar systems such as the TRACS and Motoshot are available on the civilian market. These robots are controlled by remote, and can move rapidly over uneven terrain, with 360-degree movement. In short, they're totally awesome.

Bad news is, they cost upwards of $2,000.

Luckily I've come up with a DIY moving target that offers much of the same benefit as a robot, but it only costs about $2 and can be used in your backyard.

THE BACKYARD MOVING TARGET

The Backyard Moving Target (BMT) is designed as an inexpensive and convenient way to practice your accuracy against an unpredictable moving target. It is not as realistic as using live fire against moving targets, of course. But using airsoft against the BMT is still 1,000x better than performing no moving target drills at all.

BMT practice will help prepare you for the upcoming chapters on Force on Force training, when the targets will not only be moving, but will be trying to hurt you. So this is a useful intermediary between the static range and dynamic Force on Force training. Unless you enjoy getting mauled by your training partner, it is highly recommended that you do not skip this section before moving onto FoF.

The BMT is constructed out of several cardboard boxes and some tape, and can be built in about 10 minutes.

Here's how the BMT works: When an airsoft round strikes the target, it will pierce through the first layer of cardboard, allowing you to verify your accuracy. However, if you used sturdy cardboard boxes, the BBs should not pierce through the double-thick cardboard shield behind it. Still, for safety reasons, **the person holding the BMT must always wear protective goggles** in case a round fully penetrates the box.

1. You will need 3 flat, sturdy, medium-sized cardboard boxes. Also, some duct tape, 4 binder clips, a marker, and a sharp knife.

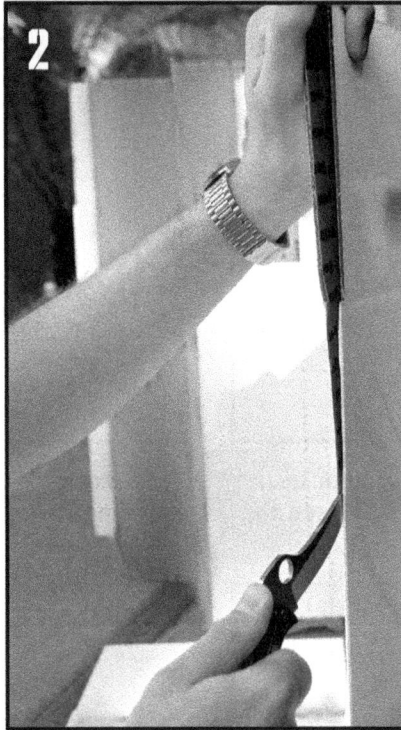

2. Begin by cutting one box in half by slicing along the seams.

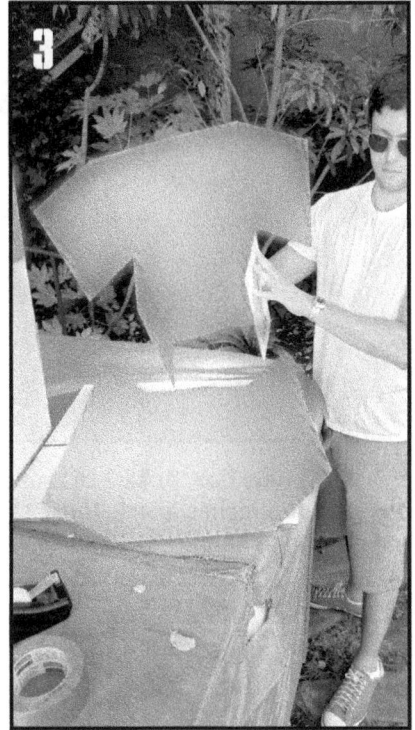

3. Reorient the box halves so that the box is as long as a Zombie's torso.

4. Fold the two halves together to form a new box. You now have the Zombie box torso.

5. Attach the halves together with binder clips.

6. Using a new box, poke 2 slits on each side of the box, about 6 inches apart. These slits will be used for the duct tape handles.

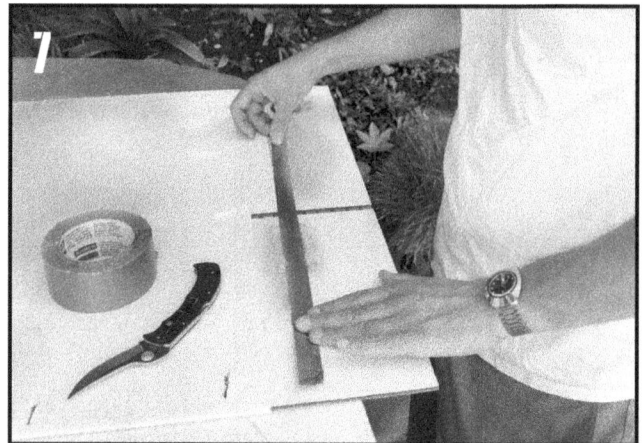

7. Tear off a 12-inch strip of duct tape, and fold it in half lengthwise so that the adhesive is covered.

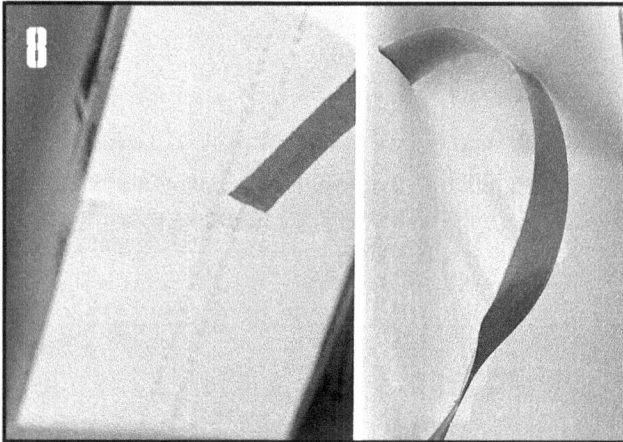

8. Insert this strip of duct tape into the slit that you had cut with your knife. Leave enough space on one side for a comfortable handle.

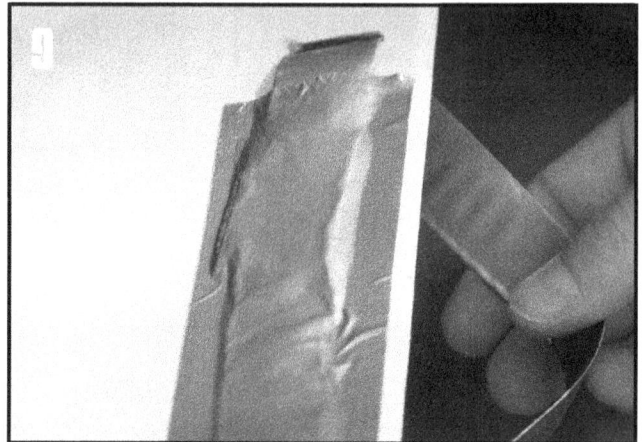

9. Tape the loose ends of the handle together, and then tape the handle directly to the cardboard. Test to make sure it feels solid, and if needed, affix more tape.

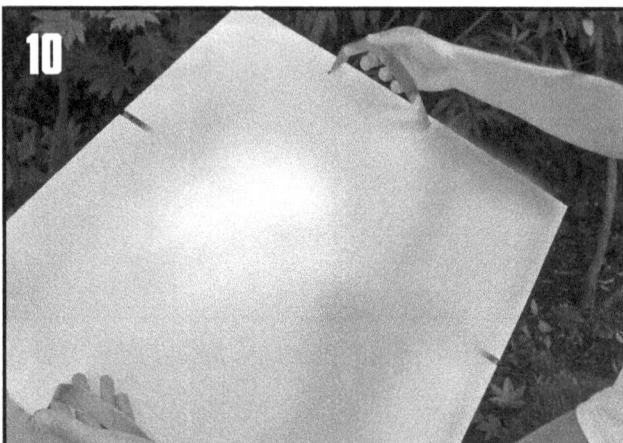

10. Place the box with the duct tape handles on top of the unused box, to form a double layer.

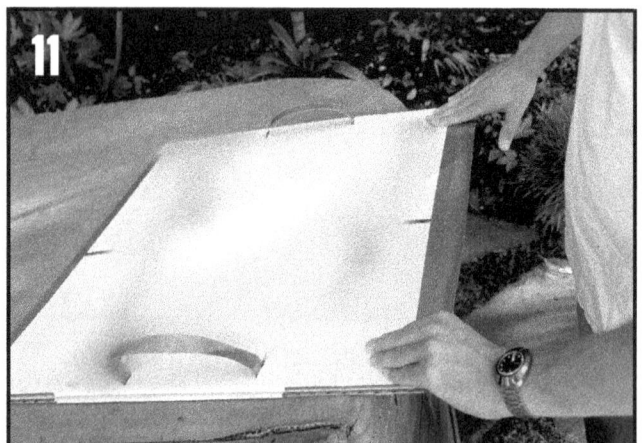

11. Tape the two boxes together to create a double-layered box shield.

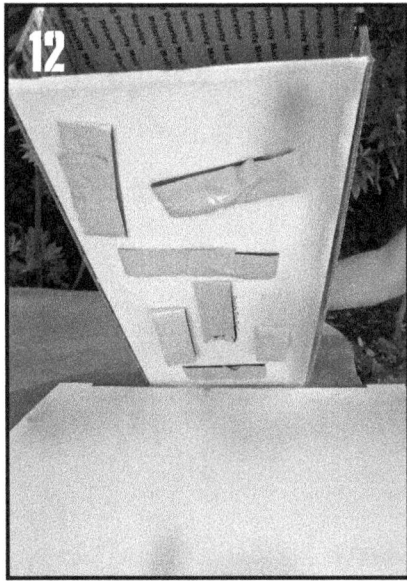

12. Tape the box torso to the box shield.

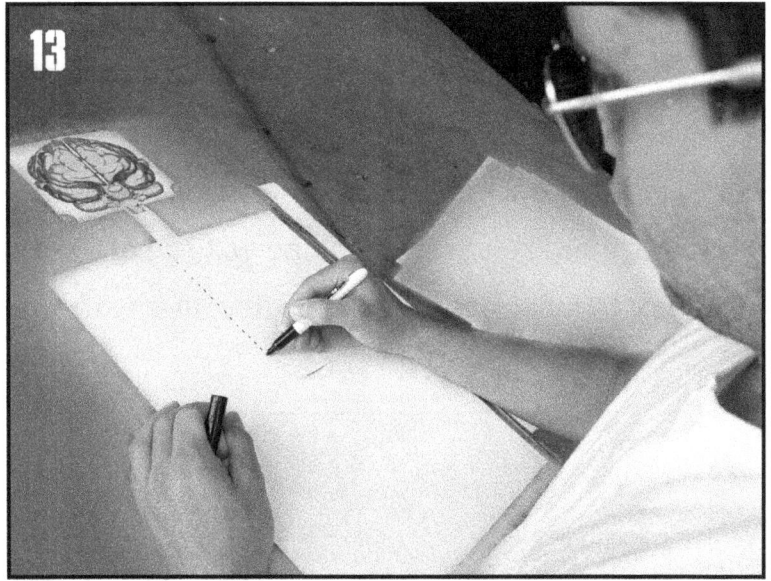

13. Cut out the Big Brain from the Zombie Qualification Target, and tape it to the top of the box. Six inches below the brain, affix two pieces of printer paper widthwise. Draw a one-inch wide strip down the middle of the two pieces of paper. This will represent the Zombie spine.

14. The Backyard Moving Target (BMT) is now complete.

Now you may be wondering, how is this thing going to move? Am I going to tape it to a sturdy RC car? Attach it to an elaborate pulley system? Nope! That's all too complex and would cost too much. No, what puts the "moving" into the Backyard Moving Target is that the BMT will be held by your training partner like a shield, and he will run around in unpredictable ways while you try to make accurate hits with your airsoft trainer.

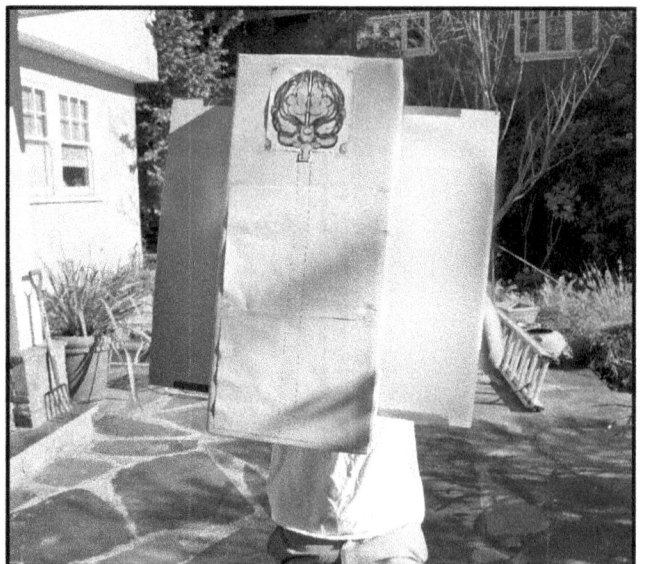

Using the Backyard Moving Target: Training partner holds BMT like a shield, and runs forward while you try to make a spine hit or headshot.

As the saying goes: If it's stupid, but it works, then it isn't stupid. And though crude and ugly, the BMT does provide the challenge of engaging a dynamic moving target, an essential skill in preparing for the upcoming Force on Force drills.

BACKYARD MOVING TARGET DRILLS

Like all training in *The ZSG,* BMT drills should begin slow, and steadily increase in difficulty as you progress.

Bring two different colored markers or pens when you train. One color is for you, the other for your partner. After each drill, mark off your hits with your designated pen, so that you and your partner can compare your accuracy.

WALKER DRILL

Level 1W: Stand 3 yards away from your partner, with your loaded airsoft pistol held at the low ready with 2 hands. At a time of his choosing, he will walk forward or sideways slowly while holding the BMT in front of him. When you perceive him moving, raise your pistol and go for a headshot. The goal is to make a headshot as soon as possible.

Level 2W: When you can make 10 headshots in a row at 3 yards, step back to 5 yards and repeat.

Level 3W: When you can make 10 headshots in a row at 5 yards, step back to 7 yards and repeat the drill.

BRISK DRILL

Once you have mastered the Walker Drill out to 7 yards, it's time to repeat the same drills, but this time your partner will be moving briskly, at a speed-walk pace. Begin at 3 yards, and work your way up to 7 yards as described above.

RUNNER DRILL

Once you have mastered the Brisk Drill out to 7 yards, it's time to move onto targets representing the high speed, Infected Zombie.

Level 1R: Because Fast Zombies will usually be heading right for you, your first Runner Drill begins with your partner standing 10 yards away holding the BMT. Your pistol is held at the low ready.

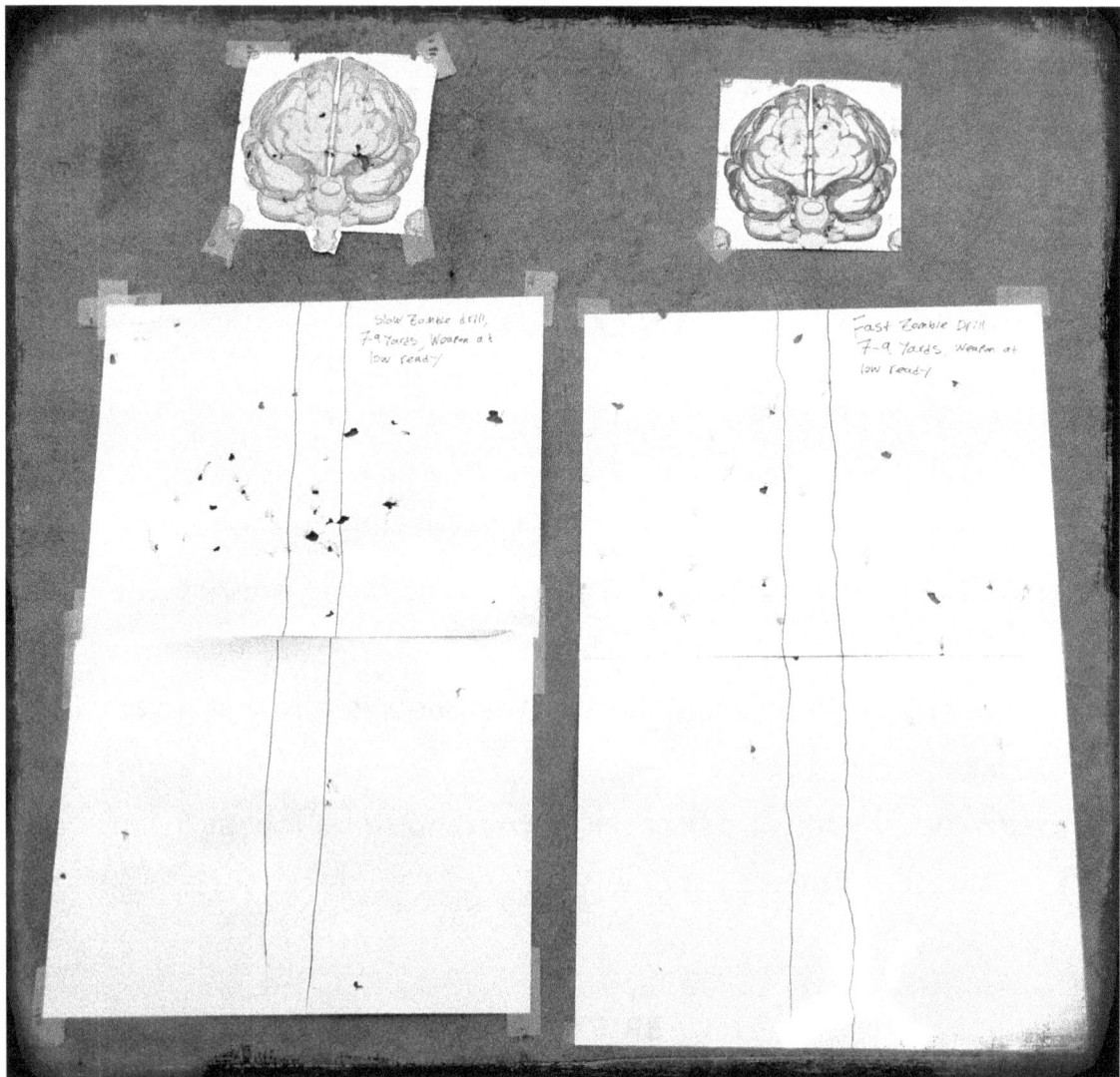

Accuracy Comparison: The Walker Drill *(left)* has a higher number of shots clustered in the spine and chest. It also has more brain shots. Meanwhile, we see a corresponding lack of accuracy in the target from the Runner Drill *(right)*. Clearly, it is harder to hit a Fast Zombie.

At a time of his choosing, he will suddenly charge explosively toward you like a rage-filled Zombie thirsting for blood. Raise your pistol and go for a three-to-four round burst to the chest, and then a headshot before he gets to you. Your partner should continue running forward, so remember to *move your ass,* or he will knock you over!

Level 2R: When you can make 10 headshots in a row with your partner starting at 10 yards, decrease the distance to 7 yards.

Level 3R: When you can make 10 headshots in a row at 7 yards, decrease the distance to 5 yards.

Level 4R. Once you have mastered the forward rush, it's time to move on to dealing with unpredictable movement patterns. Standing at 7 yards and holding the BMT, your partner will suddenly explode in a direction of his choosing — forward, sideways, or diagonally forward.

For this drill, it is useful to create a boundary area. Set up two parallel lines, 15 yards across, using paper plates. You must make a head or spine shot before your partner crosses the boundary line on either side. Otherwise he has "gotten behind cover" and the drill starts again from the top.

ONE-HANDED DRILL

In the Zombie Apocalypse, you might be forced to shoot one-handed. Maybe you're holding a family member's hand as you run to safety. Maybe you're holding a bag of supplies. Maybe a post-Apocalyptic warlord has chopped off your hand with a Katana. Shit happens, and it's best to be prepared. Therefore, it's essential that you be comfortable engaging moving targets with either hand.

Using only your dominant hand to shoot, practice the Walker, Brisk and Runner drills. When you have mastered all three, start again using only your other hand.

HOLSTER DRILL

Once you are comfortable shooting with one hand, it's time to step up the realism and engage moving targets from the holster. Although in the movies the main characters walk around with weapons in hand, it seems far more likely that your pistol will be in a holster — especially on Day 1 of the Outbreak. If you can't engage a moving target from the draw, you may not live to see Day 2.

Start from the top with the Walker Drill, except that instead of having your pistol in the low ready, it should be in a holster. Concealment garments can do some strange things to your draw, so it's good to find that out now, before the Zombies arrive.

13
MOVING & SHOOTING

TO HALT UNDER FIRE IS FOLLY. TO HALT UNDER FIRE
AND NOT FIRE BACK IS SUICIDE.

— GENERAL GEORGE S. PATTON

BY NOW YOU know how hard it is to hit a moving target. This is both good and bad. A running Zombie is hard to kill. But, when you're the one who's running, you're hard to kill. As we've already discussed, moving resets your attacker's OODA loop, allowing you to create distance between you and the Zombie's teeth or a looter's bullets.

THE SOONER YOU *MOVE YOUR ASS*, THE MORE LIKELY YOU ARE TO SURVIVE.

In this section, you are going to be integrating the *move your ass* concept with drawing and shooting from concealment. You will begin with fixed targets, and as you progress, the targets will move faster and faster. Finally, you will be shooting running targets while running yourself — a skill that could save your life in a world overrun by Fast Zombies and Outlaws.

I call these the Move Your Ass and Shoot (MYAAS) Drills. You will be armed with a loaded airsoft training pistol, and your partner will be holding the Backyard Moving Target (BMT). **For each of these drills, you and your partner must wear protective goggles.**

TURN AND SHOOT DRILL

The Turn and Shoot Drill is the most basic of the MYAAS exercises. It is designed to teach you how to move, draw, and shoot while moving in response to an outlaw reaching for his weapon. In this drill, your partner will be holding the BMT while facing sideways. When he turns towards you, this represents the threat stimulus of an attacker going for his gun.

Level 1: Your partner stands 3 yards away, holding the BMT. He is facing sideways. Stand with your loaded airsoft trainer held in the low ready.

At a time of your partner's choosing, he will suddenly turn toward you with the BMT. The second you perceive this movement, *move your ass,* either sideways or diagonally forward. While moving, raise your pistol and engage the target. The goal is to move as quickly as you can while still making spine and head shots.

Level 2: When you're consistently making accurate hits while moving at 3 yards, repeat at 5 yards.

Level 3: It's time to start working with your pistol in the holster. The drill begins with your partner at 3 yards, only now your pistol is concealed and your hands are empty. When your partner suddenly turns toward you, *move your ass.* While moving, draw your pistol, and shoot. The goal is a headshot, although a burst to the spine is also acceptable.

Level 4: Repeat, but at 5 yards.

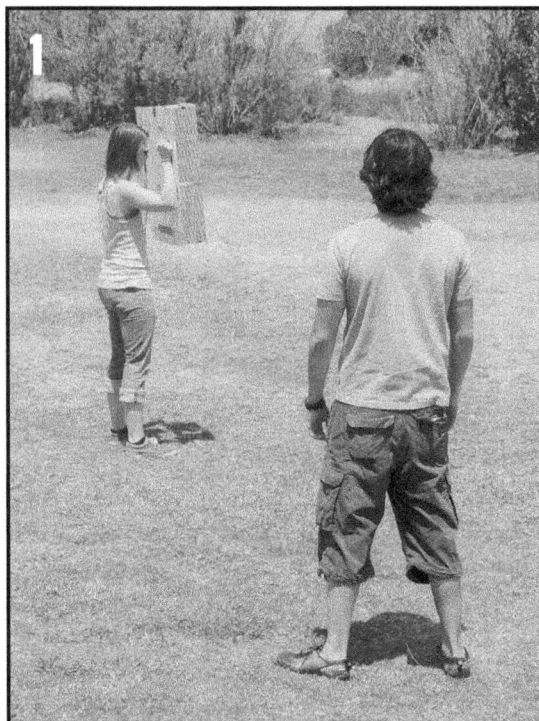

1. The Turn and Shoot Drill begins with my partner Kelsey turned sideways and holding the BMT. When she turns toward me, that is the signal that the attacker is reaching for their weapon.

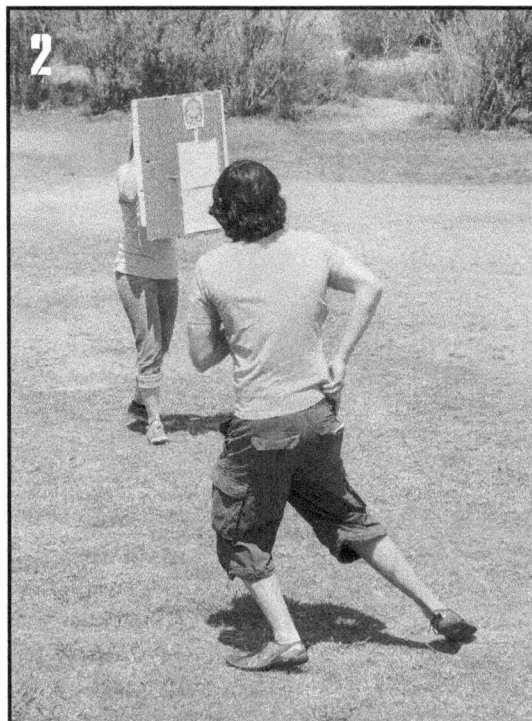

2. I observe her beginning to turn, so I *move my ass* by exploding left while simultaneously reaching for my airsoft pistol.

3. My gun is coming up as I continue to move toward my 9 o'clock.

4. I continue moving while driving my pistol toward the target.

5. I'm three steps off the X, firing with a two-handed grip, This entire sequence has only lasted a few seconds.

MYAAS ZOMBIE DRILL

Now your partner will be playing the role of a Zombie. He will hold the BMT, and either walk or run straight toward you like a Zombie on the attack. You will need to move, draw, and make a spine or headshot before he touches you.

Level 1: Begin 5 yards apart, facing each other. Your partner will hold the BMT, while you stand with your airsoft pistol in a concealed holster. At a time of his choosing, he will start walking toward you like a Slow Zombie. *Move your ass* off the line of attack, draw, and make a headshot.

Level 2: Repeat, with your partner 3 yards away. *Move your ass.* If he touches you before you can make the shot, consider yourself bitten.

Level 3: Your partner will now begin 7 yards away, and he will speed-walk toward you like a very hungry Walker. You need to get off the X, draw, and make a spine or headshot. If he touches you, you're infected.

Level 4: Now the drill becomes really challenging. Your partner will begin at 7 yards away. Stand facing him with your pistol in the holster. At a time of his choosing, he will suddenly charge like a bloodthirsty Fast Zombie. He is to continue running toward you until you draw and make a spine or headshot. If he touches you, you're infected, so you'll need to move quickly.

Level 5: Repeat, beginning at 5 yards.

1. I observe the Zombie's feet moving, which is a threat stimulus that tells me I need to *move my ass.*

2. I start to *move my ass* to the 9 o'clock while drawing my pistol.

3. I'm now one step off the line of attack, and my handgun is out.

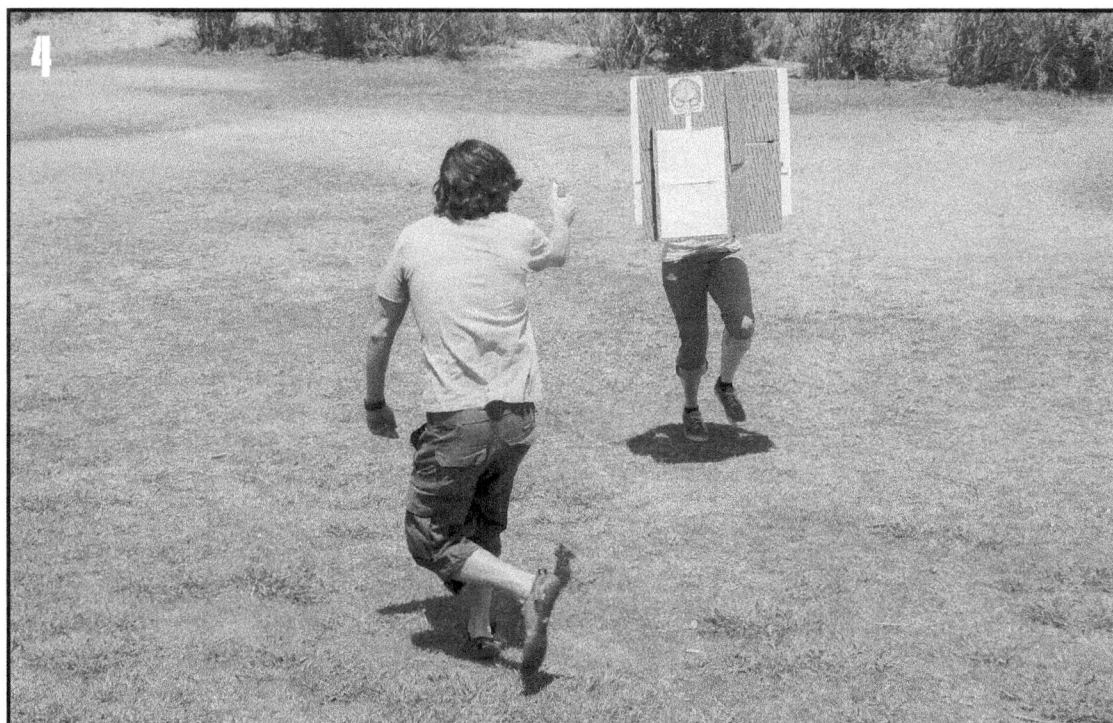

4. I drive my pistol toward the Zombie while continuing to move.

5. Safely off the line of attack, I start shooting the Zombie in the chest.

6. I continue to *move my ass* while shooting the Zombie as fast as I can pull the trigger.

MULTI-THREAT DRILL

In the first two MYAAS drills, you were training for either Zombies or outlaws. Now, you're going to be training for both, with your partner moving in unpredictable ways. You won't know who's coming at you until he starts moving.

If the target is charging you straight on, he's a Zombie, so *move your ass* and make the headshot. But, if your partner moves sideways or diagonally forward, he's an armed looter trying to flank your position and shoot you. Whichever direction he moves in, you need to *move your ass* in the opposite direction. So if he goes to your right, move left, etc.

The critical distinction between an armed looter and a Zombie is the danger level. Although Zombies are harder to kill, it's also harder for a Zombie to kill you — the creature has to make physical contact with you. However, a post-Apocalyptic outlaw with a gun can kill you from much farther away.

Therefore, when dealing with outlaws, avoiding getting shot is just as important as making the shot. So, if it's a choice between moving fast while making a 3-shot burst to the chest vs. slowing down to make a headshot but risk getting killed, the choice should be obvious.

It's impossible to be 100% accurate, but once you have achieved a 75% hit rate, you're ready to move up to the challenges of Force on Force training.

14

MENTAL PRACTICE BENEFITS PERFORMANCE BECAUSE IT ALLOWS THE PARTICIPANT TO COGNITIVELY PREPARE FOR AND PLAN PERFORMANCE. THE SEQUENTIAL ASPECTS OF THE TASK CAN BE REHEARSED, TASK GOALS CAN BE CLARIFIED, POTENTIAL PROBLEMS IN PERFORMANCE CAN BE IDENTIFIED, AND EFFECTIVE PROCEDURES FOR TASK EXECUTION CAN BE PLANNED.

— BRUCE K. SIDDLE, *SHARPENING THE WARRIOR'S EDGE*

MENTAL PRACTICE

EVEN WHEN YOU can't train with a partner, you can still enhance your OODA loop response time through the use of Mental Practice.

Mental Practice is a thought exercise where you role play various scenarios in your mind, then plan out how you would respond if that situation were to occur in real life. By programming a mental response into your brain ahead of time, you will greatly increase the speed of your response in a real emergency. Remember the OODA loop? The more past experiences the brain has to rely on, the faster you can go from observing to acting.

These experiences do not need to have occurred in real life — even imaginary scenarios can be effective if they are realistic in detail.

For example, if you are in your office, you can mentally role play how to respond to a fire. You would envision the location of the fire exits in your building, and then imagine yourself responding to the fire alarm by quickly moving toward those exits and fleeing the building. If a real fire were then to occur, your brain would quickly retrieve the memories from your mental preparation, and you would be able to respond quickly to the threat stimulus (the fire alarm) by defaulting to your pre-programmed mental response (heading for the exits and fleeing the building).

So, rather than wasting valuable time trying to come up with a plan during the chaos of an emergency, you would simply execute the plan you have already come up with through Mental Practice. This allows you to act immediately instead of freezing up.

We can apply this same technique to any type of survival situation — even the Zombie Outbreak.

MENTAL ROLE PLAY:
RESPONDING TO A ZOMBIE ATTACK

In a relaxed situation, when you are not distracted, close your eyes.

1. Imagine your day-to-day life. Everything appears normal, calm. Just another day at the office.
2. Visualize yourself at your desk, fiddling with a TPS report from HR.
3. Suddenly, you hear the sickening sound of screams from down the hall.
4. You bolt up out of your chair, and step out to see what's happening.
5. A shocking scene confronts you: A coworker, soaked in blood, has the boss's secretary pinned to the ground. He's ripping off her face with his teeth.
6. Just then, you hear a growl behind you. You turn, and there is another blood-soaked man at the opposite end of the hall. His eyes are bloodshot, the same color as the handprints on his formerly white shirt.
7. He sprints toward you, his tie flapping as he accelerates.

8. As soon as you see his feet begin to move, you *move your ass* to your 3 o'clock, to get out of his line of attack and into your office.

9. As you move, you clear your concealment garment with your left hand, and access your pistol with your right.

10. You come up into a two-handed grip, and extend the pistol to eye level.

11. The Zombie appears in your doorway, less than 10 feet away.

12. You superimpose the pistol over his face, and pull the trigger twice.

13. The bloody brains on the white wall are startling, but you don't lose your head.

14. You realize it's the Zombie Apocalypse, and that you need to execute your pre-planned escape route.

15. You sprint down the hall, away from the stricken secretary, toward the fire exit.

16. Heading down the stairs, you load a fresh magazine, because you can hear the screams outside.

Now this is just a hypothetical Zombie situation, and you will need to adjust it to your own life. But, as you can tell, this is a powerful method of visualization, and when done correctly, with enough imagination and intensity, these mental role-playing exercises can release small amounts of adrenaline. More important, they provide a free and effective way for you to program your OODA loop, without even having to get out of your chair.

Think of it as emergency daydreaming.

In the next chapters, we will begin Force on Force training. Before you perform any of those drills, spend some time doing Mental Practice. Think through each step of the exercise, and plan out how you need to respond. This will greatly improve your performance.

AUTHOR'S NOTE

I began writing this book about a month before I had done any of the Zombie Force on Force exercises. But every single day, I imagined how the drills would unfold in real life. I visualized how my partner would move toward me, the crackle of the stun gun, how I would draw my pistol, and where I would aim.

On our very first drill, my partner Rex ran at me at full speed with the stun gun. If I didn't pop his balloon spine or make a headshot, I was going to get tazed.

The second the drill began, all my previous Mental Practice clicked into place. I wasn't scared. I wasn't confused. I didn't need to think. I simply executed the pre-programmed plan I had run in my mind so many times before.

On that very first drill, I popped his balloon spine, shot him in the throat, and put my last round right between his eyes.

That's the power of mental practice.

1. The Zombie, played by my buddy Rex, sprints toward me with the stun gun from 7 yards away. You can't see me yet, but as he gets closer, I begin drawing my pistol.

2. He's 5 yards away and my gun is now out. Notice how he still has his balloon spine.

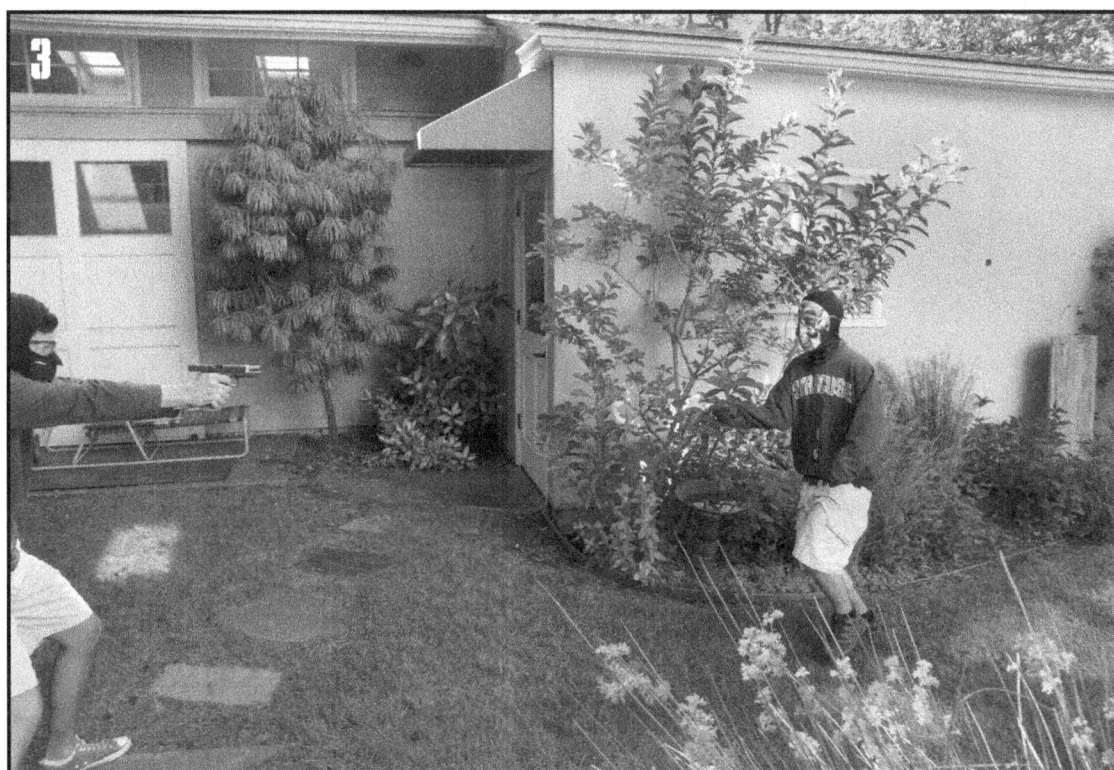

3. I pop his balloon spine with my second shot.

4. He doesn't understand the drill, and continues coming toward me with the stun gun. I transition to a headshot.

5. He turns away sharply: I've just shot him in the face from point-blank range.

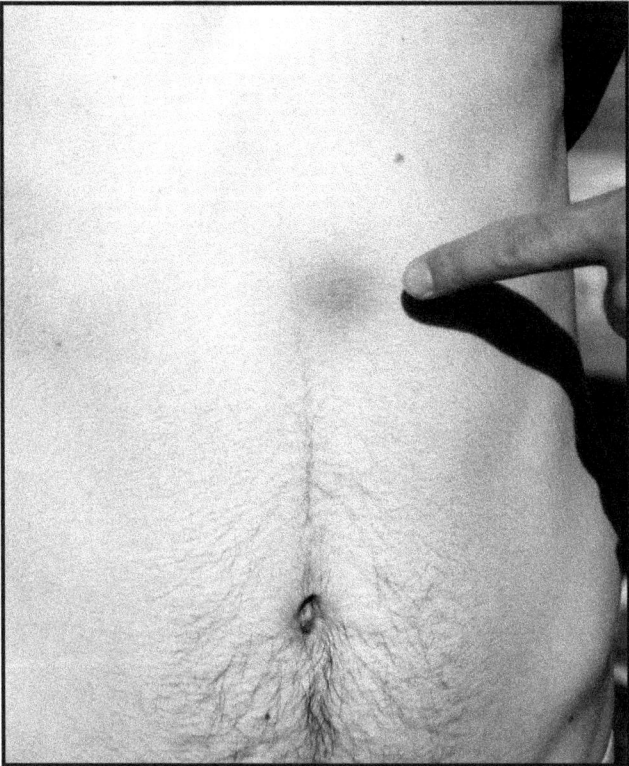

Spine Shot.

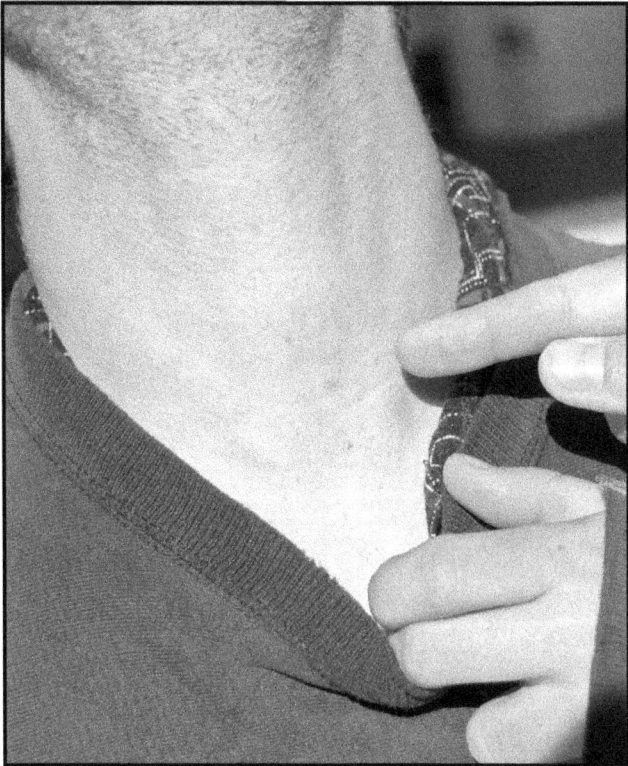

Neck shot.

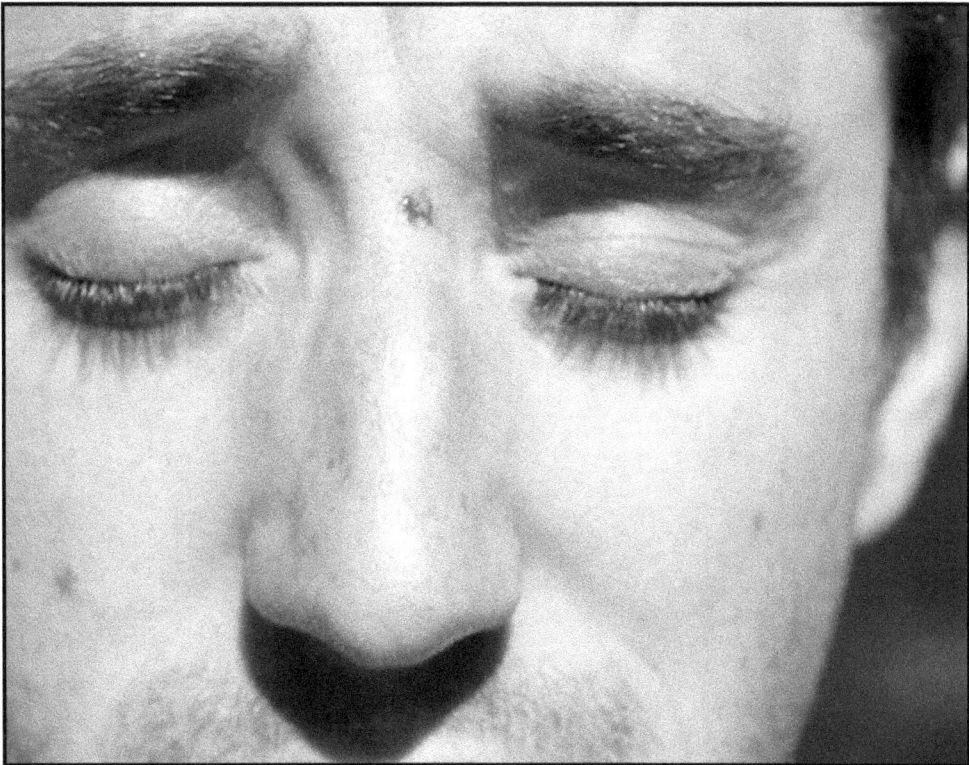

Perfect head shot: right between the eyes.

15

FORCE ON FORCE TRAINING

IN MILITARY COMBAT THERE IS THE CONSTANT FEAR OF DEATH FROM LETHAL WEAPONS EMPLOYED BY OPPONENTS WITH DEADLY INTENT. FEAR IS WITHOUT QUESTION THE MOST IMPORTANT CHARACTERISTIC OF COMBAT.

— COLONEL T.N. DUPUY, *UNDERSTANDING WAR*

WE HAVE ALREADY discussed the two primary causes of the law enforcement 1:3 hit ratio, namely (1) insufficient firearms training, and (2) the effects of Survival Stress on human performance. If you have run through the chapters on marksmanship, Point Shooting, and moving target drills, you are on your way toward overcoming the first cause. However, you still have not been inoculated against Survival Stress, which is the chief limiter of shooting performance.

To give you a sense of just how much Survival Stress affects marksmanship, consider this: There have been numerous cases of police officers and civilians *completely missing their attackers from less than 8 feet away.* To anyone who has spent much time at the range, where small targets are at least 15 feet away, missing a man-sized target from such a close distance seems unbelievable.

However, shooters at the range have not experienced Survival Stress, which pumps dozens of chemicals into the bloodstream. This potent cocktail of hormones and adrenaline has effects similar to hallucinogenic drugs: The heart rate skyrockets, and the perception of time, space, and sensory information becomes distorted.

To understand the impact of stress on accuracy, let us examine the game of pool. Like shooting, pool requires accuracy and hand-eye coordination, and even a small variation of technique can cause you to miss.

Now, have you ever played pool in a crowded bar, and missed a basic shot because everyone was watching you? Since you were not used to playing under pressure, you cracked and screwed up your technique.

Now, imagine that after that failure, you practiced enough to become a competitive pool player, capable of making amazing trick shots in front of a crowd. Then one day, in the middle of an ordinary tournament, your opponent suddenly shouts that he is going to crack your skull open with a pool cue if you don't make a basic shot in the next 1.5 seconds.

How well would all of your pool skills have prepared you for this moment? Would you be able to sink the ball as the rage-filled man charged toward you, screaming, with a pool cue raised overhead?

While this is a rather absurd fictional scenario, it highlights the differences between shooting at the range, shooting in high-stakes competition, and *shooting to survive*.

Shooting at the range is much like playing pool with your friends. With enough practice, you become skilled enough to shoot in competitions. As you improve, you become comfortable shooting on a clock in front of a crowd.

However, no matter how challenging, the stress of competition is nowhere near as stressful as someone trying to kill you at close quarters. And this overwhelming stress can negate all of your previous training, causing you to miss what would otherwise have been a very easy shot.

Just as the controlled environment of competitive pool would not have prepared you to make the shot while someone was trying to kill you with a pool cue, the static skill repetition of the shooting range does little to prepare you to shoot accurately while in fear for your life. In order to survive an attack, you must become accustomed to making shots while under life-threatening levels of Survival Stress.

My training partner Mark *(right)* is so immunized to the effects of stress that he is able to make a perfect, one-handed shot to my spine while moving under fire. What a badass.

Studies have shown that the level of Survival Stress someone experiences is dependent on how threatened he feels, how confident he is in his skills, and whether he has faced this type of threat before.

Luckily, these variables can be mitigated through training. And the training process that has proven to be the most effective at inoculating officers to the stress of combat — and surpassing the 1:3 hit ratio — is Force on Force training. Data indicates that police departments that include a comprehensive Force on Force program are achieving 80% hit ratios in lethal force encounters. That means that instead of the typical 1:3 hit ratio, these officers are hitting the suspect 4 out of 5 times.

Therefore, given the stress of a Zombie attack, and the importance of accuracy to save your life, it is essential that you engage in Force on Force (FoF) training.

WHAT IS FORCE ON FORCE?

Sometimes we see SWAT teams and special ops unit members who think they are good, but they get a rude surprise during their first force on force scenario. . . . But then they get better. Much better.
— LT. COL DAVE GROSSMAN, EXPERT ON THE STUDY OF HUMAN AGGRESSION

Force on Force (FoF) is known as "reality-based training," because the goal is to mimic real-life threats in order to trigger a Survival Stress response in the shooter. Through frequent exposure to FoF training, the shooter becomes immunized to the effects of adrenaline and hormone surges, and his shooting performance improves.

But the only way to improve your combat performance is to persevere against targets that are actively trying to hurt you. In other words: The bullseyes have to shoot back.

A FoF drill that could have prepared the pool player in our fictitious scenario could go something like this: The pool player would have a basic shot lined up for him. Then, his training partner would pretend to be the psychotic opponent. But instead of a pool cue, his opponent would be armed with a stun gun.

The player now has to make a basic corner pocket shot in 1.5 seconds, or get zapped. Although a stun gun won't kill you like a pool cue to the head, it's still extremely painful. And this fear of pain is sufficient to induce a Survival Stress response within the pool player.

Through repeated exposure to this training, the player would become immunized to Survival Stress, and would gain confidence in his ability to make the shot under pressure. So, if he were ever to be in our "Make the Shot in 1.5 Seconds or You're Dead" scenario, he would be much more likely to make the shot and survive.

Law enforcement and military FoF drills operate on a similar stress inoculation principle, except their scenarios involve the use of simulation guns. These practice weapons fire either paintballs or plastic BBs at high velocity. Although not lethal, the shots are still painful enough to trigger the effects of Survival Stress.

In one study, members of a London SWAT team were armed with Simunition training Glock 17s. Each officer was also outfitted with a heart-rate monitor to measure his level of stress.

The team was sent to a hospital to guard a wounded robber and to prevent his escape. Suddenly, another member of the SWAT team, pretending to be the robber's brother, burst into the room with a simulation shotgun, took a woman hostage and used her as a human shield. The officers then had to respond by taking out the gunman without hitting the hostage, all in a crowded hospital with scores of innocent bystanders.

When the data was analyzed, it was shown that the officers' heart rates spiked to over 160 beats per minute, about double the normal heart rate. This result occurred with all of the officers, regardless of their physical fitness. Even though they knew it was just a drill, their Survival Stress levels were similar to that felt in real-life combat.

The London study concluded that FoF training helps acclimate officers to the stress of real-life combat, and that officers who have not had this level of training would typically do poorly in real confrontations. The study also recommended that shooters need to engage in FoF training on "a repeated, consistent, sustained basis" in order to remain inoculated to combat stress.

As the ancient Roman military historian Vegetius observed in 378 AD: "Few men are born brave. Many become so through training and force of discipline." Through repeated exposure to stressful, reality-based training, Force on Force will inoculate a shooter against the effects of fear, allowing him to perform bravely and ferociously in combat.

AUTHOR'S NOTE:
A PERSONAL STORY OF FORCE ON FORCE

I had been shooting for several years before I discovered Force on Force training. At the time, I was hitting the range at least twice a month, and had become a very proficient conventional marksman, capable of keeping all my shots in one ragged hole at 7 yards, and comfortable running the Mozambique Two-Step at the same distance. Given my level of accuracy, I assumed that as long as I had a gun in my hand, I'd be pretty much ready for anything within 7 yards.

Around 2007, an airsoft store opened near my house, and I bought a KWA G17 airsoft pistol to serve as a training aid for the days I couldn't make it to the range. My friends thought that it was pretty cool, and soon we had half a dozen guys similarly armed. I was the only one who actually shot real guns, and my accuracy was superb, so I assumed I would always win.

What I learned was that my mastery of the shooting range was of very little use fighting targets that were shooting back.

We would have battles inside my home, in houses under construction, and in this super creepy abandoned Naval hospital (which we later discovered was also where our local SWAT / K9 teams trained with Simunitions).

To my shock, 70% of the time my two-handed, sighted fire was useless. At 7 yards and beyond, or when shooting from behind cover, I made good hits. But when I would turn a corner and be confronted by a "man with a gun" at 7 feet, I was just another panicked primate with a pistol, pointing and spraying. I had never trained for this, and it showed.

I could routinely put "2 in the chest, 1 in the head" at 7 yards with my .45 at the shooting range. But now, with a toy gun, fear and adrenaline had me looking at the guy trying to shoot me, and not at my sights. The result was that I would frequently miss completely — much less make a head-shot — from just 7 feet away!

It was this experience with Force on Force that taught me that I was training in a totally unrealistic fashion. For shooting those dangerous paper targets on a sunny Sunday afternoon, standing still and using my sights worked great. But in the semi-darkness of the Naval hospital, all my attention was on the person trying to shoot me, and not the little piece of plastic on the tip of my pistol.

Now I base my live fire training on how I react in Force on Force exercises, rather than on what is cool at the shooting range.

16

IF YOU OBSERVE HIGHLY SKILLED COMBATANTS IN ANY ARENA OF CONFLICT, YOU MIGHT NOTICE THAT IN THE MIDST OF THEIR FIERCE BATTLE THEY HAVE AN AURA OF CALM ABOUT THEM. THIS CALM EMANATES FROM. . . . UTILIZING THE RESOURCES AND SKILLS THAT THEY HAVE HONED DURING TRAINING OR THROUGH PREVIOUS COMBAT. THEY HAVE BECOME MASTERS OF THE TERRAIN OF CONFLICT. . . . [AND] THIS MASTERY TRANSLATES INTO EFFECTIVE PERFORMANCE IN DANGEROUS CIRCUMSTANCES.

— KENNETH R. MURRAY, *TRAINING AT THE SPEED OF LIFE*

FORCE ON FORCE FOR ZOMBIES

FORCE ON FORCE training has proven essential for achieving a high hit-ratio under the stress of a gunfight. The question is: How do we replicate the stress of a Zombie attack so that we can prepare for the Outbreak?

The answer, I believe, lies in the the famous Tueller Drill, which I have modified to simulate the stress of a Zombie attack.

The Tueller Drill was developed in the 1980s by Salt Lake City cop Dennis Tueller as a way to train officers about the dangers of a knife attack. To this day, it is considered one of the most challenging FoF drills out there.

In the drill, a policeman is armed with a holstered simulation pistol. His training partner stands 7 yards away, armed with a rubber knife. At a time of his choosing, the knifer will suddenly charge toward the officer. In order to "survive," the officer must draw his pistol and shoot the knifer twice in the chest before he gets stabbed.

It might seem at first that a knife-wielding assailant would have no chance against a cop with a gun. But, the fact is that a reasonably fit person can cover 7 yards in 1.5 seconds. So, a person armed with a knife can frequently charge and stab a man before the victim can even get his pistol out of the holster. The Tueller Drill gave rise to the "21-Foot Rule": Any man armed with a knife is a deadly threat if he is standing within 21 feet, and so an officer should get his pistol out immediately.

A Zombie attack is not unlike a knife attack. Both require direct physical contact with the victim to cause harm. And, being basically human, a Fast Zombie can also sprint 21 feet in 1.5 seconds. However, what makes the Zombie more deadly is that — unlike a knifer, who may give up after being shot in the chest — only a precise shot to the spine or brain will stop a Zombie attack.

This led me to create the Fast Zombie Drill (FZD). It is basically the Tueller Drill from hell, and the foundation of our Force on Force training.

Like the Tueller Drill, the FZD begins with you armed with a simulation pistol in a holster, and your training partner 21 feet away. However, unlike Tueller, where two shots to the chest is an acceptable outcome, the FZD only ends if you make a shot to the spine or head.

Which brings us to the most exciting part of the FZD: the consequences of failure. In the Tueller Drill, your partner is armed with a lame little rubber training knife. In the FZD, your training partner is armed with a stun gun.

IF YOU DON'T MAKE A HEAD OR SPINE SHOT, YOU'RE GETTING TAZED.

I have found that the sickening crackle of a 3 million-volt stun gun charging toward you is an effective tool for replicating the fear of a Zombie bite.

Zombie Force on Force Gear: face masks, protective eyewear, airsoft guns, black airsoft BBs, green gas, 3 million volt stun gun, animal balloons and pump.

Although it won't kill you or turn you into a Zombie, a stun gun *hurts,* and it will trigger the Survival Stress response needed for effective training.

In addition to the FZD, there are a variety of upcoming drills that will simulate scenarios that you are likely to encounter in a Zombie Apocalypse. By mastering these drills, and repeatedly practicing them several times a year, you will become inoculated to the effects of Survival Stress, and will gain the confidence needed for optimum shooting performance when under attack.

So, grab your gear, and get ready for some intense training.

17

FORCE ON FORCE SAFETY RULES

IN CHAPTER 8, we discussed the Four Rules of Firearms Safety. Those rules also apply to Force on Force training.

Even though it's "just an airsoft gun," you can easily damage an eye or chip a tooth if accidentally shot in the face. In addition to being a necessary safety precaution, practicing safe firearms handling promotes positive safety habits that will carry over when you switch back to live weapons.

ALWAYS USE THE SAME SAFETY PRECAUTIONS WITH YOUR TRAINING WEAPON THAT YOU USE WITH YOUR REAL FIREARMS.

In addition to the Four Rules, Force on Force training has its own safety precautions that must be followed. Although a lot of fun, FoF training can be extremely dangerous, and dozens of law enforcement officers have been killed accidentally due to unsafe training practices.

It's imperative that you follow all safety precautions in order to avoid tragedy.

THE 5 RULES OF FORCE ON FORCE SAFETY

RULE #1: NO LIVE WEAPONS IN THE TRAINING AREA

RULE #2: DOUBLE-CHECK EVERYONE FOR CONCEALED WEAPONS

RULE #3: TRAINING PISTOLS MUST BE CLEARLY MARKED

RULE #4: CEASEFIRE IF THINGS BECOME UNSAFE

RULE #5: PROTECT YOUR EYES

RULE #1: NO LIVE WEAPONS IN THE TRAINING AREA

In FoF training, we will be pointing guns at each other, and going for headshots. Needless to say, we need to be damn sure that they're not real weapons loaded with real bullets. While this sounds obvious, the accidental introduction of live weapons into the training area is the primary cause of death in Force on Force training.

**DOZENS OF PEOPLE HAVE BEEN KILLED OVER
THE YEARS BECAUSE SOMEONE EITHER FORGOT
THAT THEY WERE STILL CARRYING THEIR REAL GUN,
OR A REAL GUN WAS LEFT IN THE
TRAINING AREA AND SOMEONE ASSUMED
IT WAS A TRAINING PISTOL.**

They pointed these real weapons at their training partners, pulled the trigger, and really killed them.

It is imperative that you have no live weapons or ammunition in the Force on Force training area. If you are training at home, unload all of your weapons and lock them in the safe. If you are training away from home, don't bring your real gun with you, or leave it locked in the trunk of your car.

**BEFORE TRAINING IN ANY LOCATION
(AN ABANDONED NAVAL HOSPITAL, THE WOODS,
YOUR APARTMENT, ETC.) CHECK *EVERYWHERE*
TO MAKE SURE THAT THERE ARE
NO LIVE WEAPONS ANYWHERE.**

Don't just glance around. You need to perform a thorough check.

In one famous case, two officers were practicing vehicle-based shooting tactics while using their patrol cars as the training area. They were both armed with training pistols, and had removed their firearms from the area — or so they thought. When one of the officer's training pistols malfunctioned, he spotted another gun tucked under the sun visor of his buddy's patrol car. He grabbed the gun, pointed it at his partner, and killed him. Turns out, his buddy had left his backup gun in the car.

Lesson: Perform a thorough, top-to-bottom check to confirm that there are no real weapons in the training area.

RULE #2: DOUBLE-CHECK EVERYONE FOR CONCEALED WEAPONS

AFTER YOU HAVE CLEARED THE TRAINING AREA, YOU NEED TO DOUBLE-CHECK THAT THERE ARE NO WEAPONS ON YOU, YOUR PARTNER, OR ON ANY SPECTATORS.

A search of the training area includes searching everyone for weapons. In addition to guns, you want to check for knives, tactical LED lights, pepper spray, and anything else that could injure someone if accidentally introduced into the training drill.

In Force on Force training, adrenaline will be spiking, and your heart rate will be through the roof. In the midst of this fog, it's easy to revert back to your weapons' training, and deploy a backup knife or initiate a flashlight strike to your partner's face, to say nothing of the risks of a backup gun.

Before training, I ask training partners and spectators to empty their pockets into a box, and then lift their shirts to show that they have no other concealed weapons in their waistbands. Everyone should also lift up each pant leg to show they have no ankle guns or boot knives.

While this is a mild annoyance and brings back unpleasant TSA flashbacks, it's an essential safety precaution in such a dynamic training environment. In any situation when you're going to be pointing guns at one another, it's worth the extra few minutes to double check that no one is carrying a real weapon that can be grabbed in the heat of the moment.

RULE #3: TRAINING PISTOLS
MUST BE CLEARLY MARKED

There have been many instances where [Force on Force training] has prompted actual responses by armed individuals, responding to what they believe is an actual call. People have been killed because of this.
— KENNETH R. MURRAY, *TRAINING AT THE SPEED OF LIFE*

A lot of our Force on Force training is conducted in backyards, parks, and public areas, where casual onlookers might come across us. To avoid freaking them out and having them call the police about "guys with guns wearing masks," it is absolutely essential that all airsoft pistols be clearly marked as fake training pistols.

The orange tip on the barrel is not enough. The guns must be so clearly marked that a person 25 yards away can easily tell that they are not real.

**THE BEST WAY TO IDENTIFY YOUR PISTOL AS
A TRAINING GUN IS TO TO COVER THE SLIDE AND
GRIP FRAME WITH BRIGHT BLUE PAINTER'S TAPE.**

Painter's tape is easy to see at a distance, clearly identifying the pistol as a training toy, and not a real gun. Painter's tape is made with a special adhesive, which allows it to come off easily without any sticky residue.

Some airsoft guns do not come with orange barrels in order to increase realism. That's cool for collecting, but when you're pointing these guns at people, it's essential that everyone know that they are not real. Paint those barrel tips orange, and coat your slides and grips with bright blue painter's tape.

RULE #4: CEASEFIRE IF THINGS BECOME UNSAFE

**IF AT ANY POINT YOU OR YOUR PARTNER
FEELS UNSAFE, SHOUT "CEASE FIRE!"
UNTIL THE DRILL STOPS.**

There are several reasons to call a ceasefire. A piece of safety gear comes undone. An unexpected visitor enters the area, such as a child, pet, or nosy neighbor. Finally, if the drill has becomes too intense, there's no shame in calling a ceasefire and taking a break.

It's difficult to foresee every contingency, so the rule is: If you feel uneasy, call a ceasefire. It only takes a minute to restart the drill, so better a moment's delay than a lifetime of regret.

RULE #5: PROTECT YOUR EYES

Airsoft is pretty safe, but if you get shot in the eye, it's major bad news.

**IF YOUR GOGGLES FALL OFF OR BECOME DISLODGED,
IMMEDIATELY COVER YOUR EYES, CROUCH ON
THE GROUND, AND SCREAM "CEASE FIRE!"
UNTIL THE ACTION STOPS.**

About 80% of the information your brain receives comes from your eyes. Always protect them.

18

FORCE ON FORCE DRILLS

THESE SIX DRILLS represent the core of our Zombie Preparedness, and they're also a lot of fun — as long as you train safely. You will be using your airsoft training pistols and stun gun, so it's essential that you wear your protective goggles and face masks to avoid injury.

#1: SHOWDOWN DRILL

The Showdown is a fun and straightforward gunfighting drill designed to introduce you to Force on Force. It's also a great learning opportunity because you will immediately understand how your accuracy is affected by combat stress.

You and your partner will each be armed with airsoft pistols. To make your hit percentage easy to compute, you will each load only three BBs. When we perform more complex drills your gun will be fully loaded, but for this drill three is plenty. Since the average hit ratio is 1:3, loading three rounds makes it very easy to see how you compare.

1. You and your partner will each wear a balloon spine, face mask and safety goggles.
2. Stand 7 yards apart, with your pistols tucked in your waistbands.
3. With you and your partner squared off, the drill begins whenever either of you decides to fire.
4. As soon as you decide to shoot, or you see your partner reaching for his weapon, shoot him.

Although the Showdown is a simple drill, the adrenaline it produces can lead to some very interesting results that illustrate the mishaps that can happen under stress. Fumbled draws, accidentally ejected magazines, and complete misses are surprisingly common.

The Showdown is also a classic case of why you need to *move your ass.* Had I moved off the line of attack instead of staying on the X and drawing my pistol, I might have survived. However, while I was standing in place fumbling for my gun, my opponent was able to get a solid shooting stance, raise his pistol to eye level, and kill me.

You will learn a ton about yourself from this drill, so make sure to take notes:

- Were you shot?
- Was your partner shot?
- Where did the shots land?
- Were any of them solid hits to the chest?

- Did any hit the spine? The head?
- Did you use your sights?
- Did you *move your ass?*
- How did you react to the stress of combat?

SHOWDOWN I

1. My partner *(right)* draws first, and I move to catch up.

2. Having failed to *move my ass,* I stand in place shooting, and we both end up shot.

SHOWDOWN 2

1. The adrenaline rush has caused me to screw up the draw, and I've grabbed a handful of shirt on top of my gun.

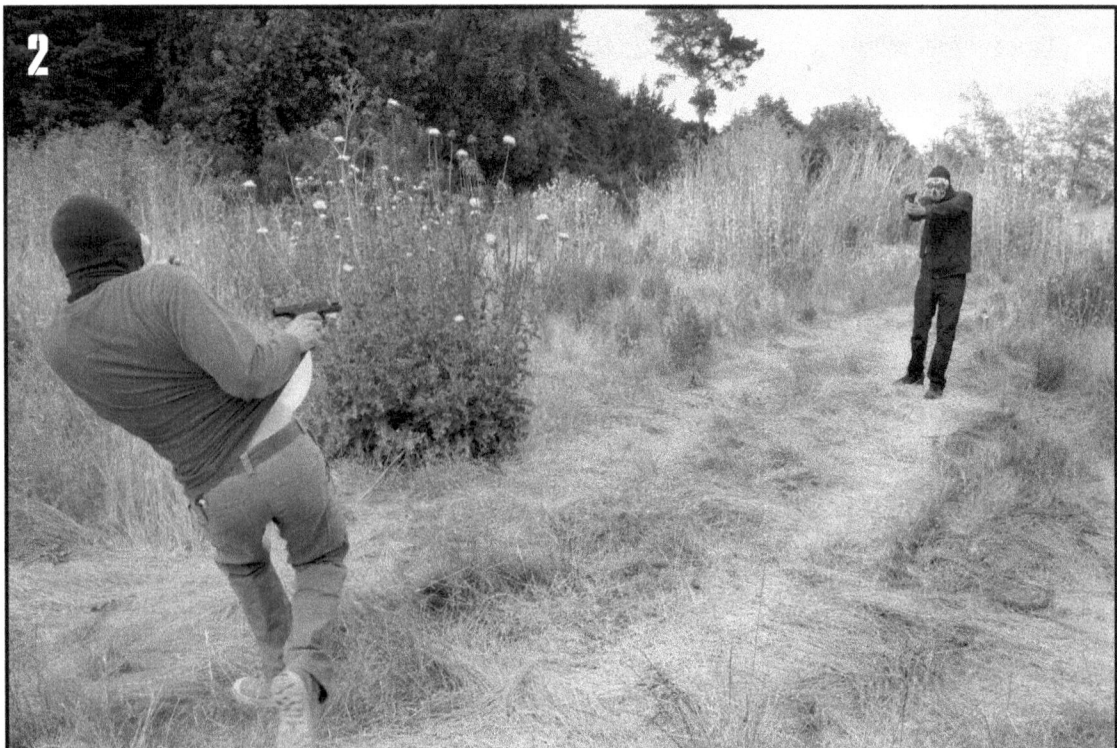

2. I desperately try to shoot from this compromised position, and end up getting shot in the face!

#2: WALKER DRILL

Now that you have experienced the simplest gunfighting drill, it's time to move on to the simplest Zombie fighting drill, which is engaging a Walker Zombie.

For this drill, your partner will be in his Zombie outfit — heavily padded with sweatshirts, face mask, safety goggles, and a balloon spine. He will also be armed with a stun gun. You should wear safety goggles and a Balaclava to protect your face from the stun gun. You will be carrying an airsoft gun loaded with three rounds. In later drills you will have a fully-loaded magazine, but we're still assessing your hit rate at this point.

You and your partner will square off at 7 yards, with your pistol in your holster. The drill begins when your partner decides to move toward you. At a time of his choosing, he will start to walk *quickly* toward you with a stun gun. Yes, the Zombies shuffle slowly in *The Walking Dead,* but he's really hungry for brains so he'll be a bit faster.

Like all Zombie drills, the Walker Drill is a fight to the finish. You must either pop his balloon spine or make a headshot to end the drill — otherwise, your ass is getting tazed. In later drills with Fast Zombies you will be able to try and run away. But due to the simplicity of the Walker Drill, if you can't hit the target you have to stand there take your punishment.

Run this drill 10 times, and then switch roles with your partner.

Record your results.

**IF YOU FEEL SICK FROM BEING TAZED,
STOP TRAINING IMMEDIATLY.**

#3: FAST ZOMBIE DRILL

The most important exercise in our FoF training is the Fast Zombie Drill (FZD), where you have to draw and make a headshot against a charging Zombie.

You are training to be able to respond to a surprise Zombie attack with your concealed carry pistol.

SINCE THE ZOMBIE OUTBREAK IS LIKELY TO ARRIVE WITHOUT WARNING, YOU MUST BE ABLE TO RECOGNIZE A SUDDEN ATTACK, AND THEN SWIFTLY RESPOND WITH PRECISION ACCURACY.

To perform the FZD, your partner will be wearing the Zombie mask, safety goggles, and balloon spine. He will be armed with a stun gun.

1. You will stand 10 yards apart, with your fully loaded airsoft gun in the holster.
2. At a time of your partner's choosing, he will charge toward you.
3. You must draw and make a spine hit or headshot. If you don't make a hit to the Central Nervous System to stop him, you get tazed.

The Fast Zombie Drill has several levels of difficulty:

Warm-up: Zombie starts 10 yards away, and your gun is in an open holster.

Basic: Zombie starts 7 yards away, you start with gun in concealment holster.

Intermediate: Zombie stands 5 yards away, you start with gun in concealment holster.

Expert: Engage three Zombie partners from concealment — with Zombies standing 7, 9, and 11 yards away, all running toward you at once.

THE FAST ZOMBIE DRILL

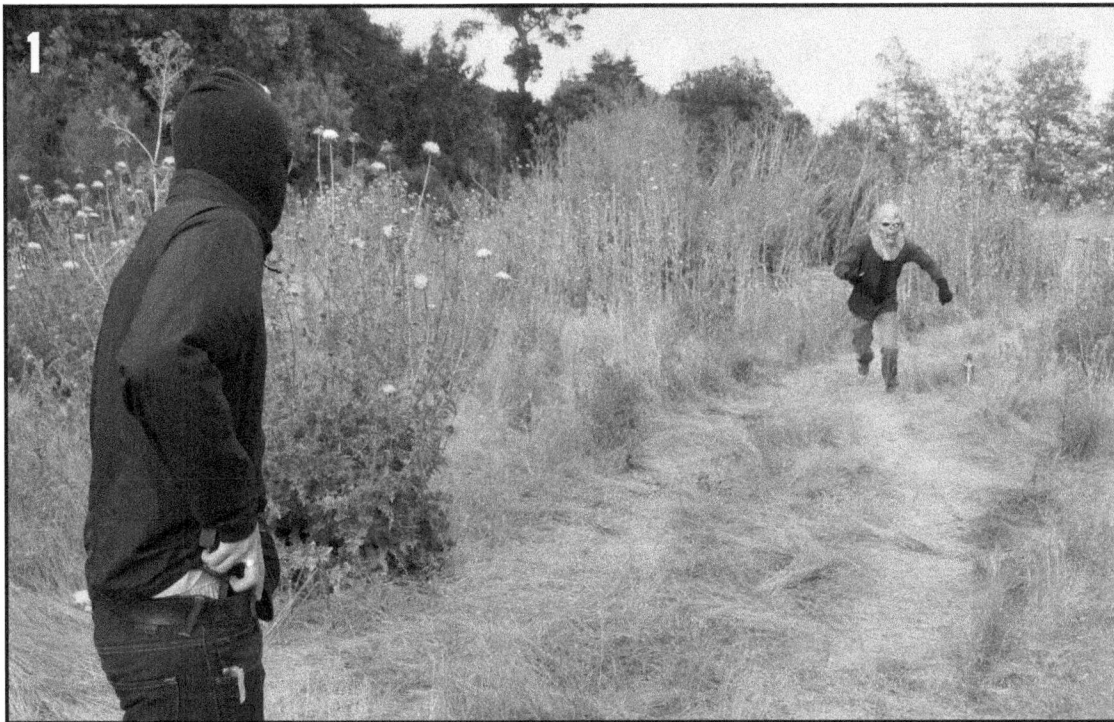

1. Brandon observes the Zombie suddenly lunge toward him, and begins to draw his pistol.

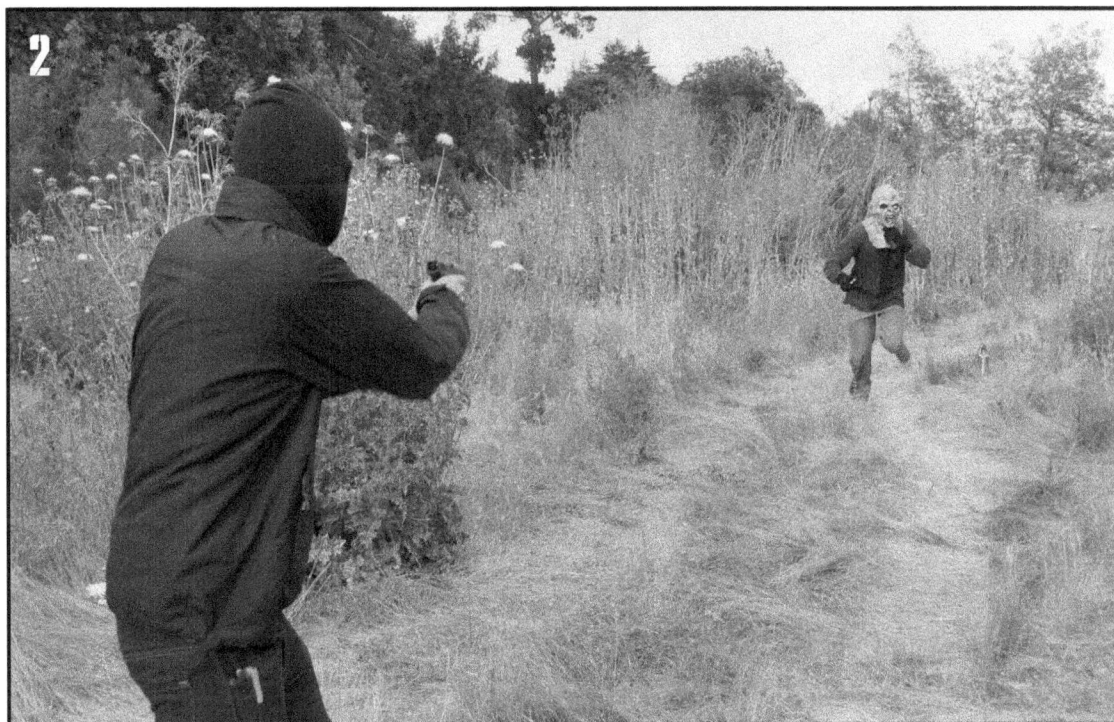

2. He gets his pistol in a two-handed grip and starts driving it toward the threat.

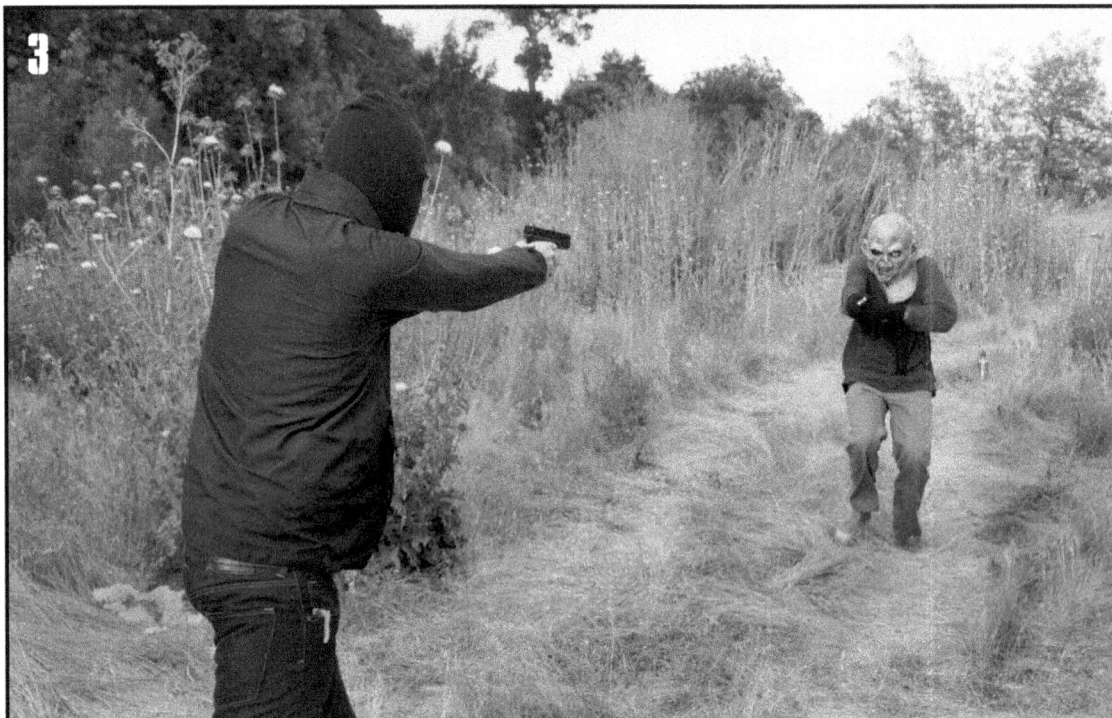

3. He begins shooting the Zombie in the chest as fast as he can pull the trigger. Note how the Zombie's left hand reflexively comes up to shield his chest.

4. The Zombie continues to charge, but he's slowing down from the pain of being shot 6 times in the chest.

5. As the Zombie makes one last desperate lunge toward him, Brandon shoots him in the head.

6. Because of the proximity to the Zombie's stun gun, Brandon reflexively resorts to shooting with one hand while drawing his support hand back for safety. He shoots the Zombie one more time in the head. The drill is now finished — and so is the Zombie.

A day after the drill, I asked Brandon whether he was shooting with one hand or two. He swore that he had shot the entire drill one-handed. Even though it was a practice drill, the adrenaline rush was so powerful that Brandon had no memory of shooting most of his shots with two hands.

#4: BUMP IN THE NIGHT DRILL

This drill should be performed in your house, as well as at your BUG-OUT location / emergency shelter if you have one. It's designed to allow you to practice responding to an intruder breaking into your home at night — whether he's a looter hungry for your supplies, or a Zombie hungry for your flesh. Break-ins will be a fact of life in a post-Apocalyptic world, so it is essential that you know how to defend your home.

The Bump in the Night Drill is performed at night, with your house set up the way it is when you go to sleep. If you turn out all the lights before bed, then all the lights should be off. If you always leave the bathroom light on, it should be left on. And so on.

If you have any expensive art or delicate things, you may wish to cover them with a towel, or remove them entirely. Although airsoft rounds are not particularly damaging or messy, they can leave small dents in plaster or pierce an unprotected painting.

Because the drill is intended to simulate you waking up to an intruder, you need to start off in bed, with your airsoft gun in the place where you keep your real firearm at night.

UNLOAD YOUR REAL FIREARM AND REMOVE IT FROM YOUR BEDROOM — DO NOT TAKE ANY CHANCES.

For maximum realism, you should also conduct this drill in the clothes you wear when you go to sleep. So, if you sleep in just your underwear, that's how you should run the drill. Obviously, you should still wear your ballistic eye protection and face mask, since there is a good chance you will be shot in the face.

Time to begin: Your training partner is somewhere in the house. He is wearing a protective face mask, goggles, and balloon spine. He will be carrying either an airsoft pistol (as a looter) or the stun gun (as a Zombie). Just like a real bump in the night, you won't know who or what is out there.

At a time of his choosing, he is to make a loud noise – kick your door, break a beer bottle in your sink to simulate a broken window, knock over a piece of furniture, rapidly open a drawer full of silverware, cough, or any other realistic noise that an intruder might make.

When you hear the noise, get out of bed, access your airsoft pistol, and investigate. Engage any intruders inside the house.

Like the Fast Zombie Drill, the Bump in the Night can be modified to various levels of difficulty:

Basic: The fight is over when the first person is shot.

Intermediate: The fight is over when either person is shot 3 times or tazed.

Advanced: The fight is only over when your partner's spine balloon has popped or he has been shot in the head, or if you are shot / tazed.

Expert: You vs. multiple intruders inside the house.

Run each level 10 times in each other's houses, and record your results. In addition to the standard hit information, take special note of:

- Which parts of your house make noise?
- Which corners of your house are particularly treacherous?
- Do you have any mirrors or framed art that allow you to see around corners?

- How can you change the layout of your home to improve your defenses?
- Is there anything else that can help or hinder your response to an intruder?

#5: BREAK-IN DRILL

In this scenario, your training partner is still the Intruder, with the same equipment as the Bump in the Night. However, this drill begins with you out-side your house, where you discover that someone — or something — has broken-in. For example, you have just fought your way home on Day 1 of the Outbreak, only to discover your front door has been smashed in.

You must enter and investigate, but you are free to use either the front door, or any other way you can enter your house. Make use of windows if possible.

If your training partner is armed with an airsoft gun, he is a looter, and three rounds to the chest, a head shot, or a popped balloon spine are suf-ficient to end the drill. However, if armed with the stun gun, he is a Zombie, and the drill only ends with a spine / headshot, or with you getting tazed.

Run this drill 10 times, and record your results. In addition to your accu-racy stats, take note of the following:

- What alternative methods are there for entering your house?
- Were you able to see the intruder through the windows, or were you forced to enter blind?
- Which hiding places did your attacker use?

These are valuable insights that may come in handy when searching your home for an intruder.

#6: ROBBERY DRILL

Typically, robberies are committed by people desperate for short-term cash, with over 27% committed by drug addicts. Because robbery is a socio-economic crime rather than a crime of passion or depravity, you greatly reduce your risk of being robbed by simply staying out of bad neighborhoods.

> **IN THE ZOMBIE APOCALYPSE, AMERICA
> WILL BECOME ONE BIG BADASS NEIGHBORHOOD,
> FILLED WITH DESPERATE AND PREDATORY PEOPLE
> WHO WILL STICK A GUN IN YOUR FACE
> AND KILL YOU TO TAKE WHAT'S YOURS.**

In a normal robbery, police advise that you should just hand over your wallet and not confront your assailant. But in the Zombie world, you need your supplies to survive: If you allow yourself to be robbed of your weapons and food, it's your death sentence. Therefore, in preparing for a post-Apocalyptic world, it is essential that you train to fight your way out of an armed robbery.

The Robbery Drill is best performed in the evening, either at dusk or at night, as this is when robberies are statistically most common. However, even practicing during the day will be of value.

Your airsoft pistol should be loaded with only 6 rounds (to prevent excessive injury to your training partner) and should be concealed in the holster. Your training partner will have an airsoft gun or a stun gun concealed in his waistband. The stun gun will represent a knife, since both require physical contact. As in a real-life robbery, you will not know ahead of time how your attacker is armed.

You will each wear a balloon spine, face mask, and goggles.

The drill begins with you walking. Your training partner will suddenly approach you while attempting to engage you in conversation. "Hey man, you got the time?" "Excuse me sir, do you know if there are Zombies this way?" And so on. You should attempt to avoid him by circling around him while telling him "Could you stop right there for me?" or "STOP!" with your hands in the fence position.

The fence position is where your hands are up at the level of your face, palms facing your assailant. Although it appears non-threatening, the fence allows you to quickly eye jab your attacker if he comes too close. It also puts your hands close to your face and neck so that you can shield yourself if attacked.

At a time of your partner's choosing, he will go for his weapon and attempt either to shoot you or taze you.

When you see him going for his waistband, draw your weapon and shoot. Because the attack is at such close range, the drill is only over when one of you has a balloon spine popped, a headshot, is tazed, or runs out of ammo.

Practice this drill 10 times, and record your results.

ROBBERY DRILL 1

1. A stranger *(left)* approaches me. He has hostile body language and a hand I can't see, so I go into the fence position.

2. I observe the stranger drawing his weapon, which means this is a robbery, so I start to draw my pistol. Simultaneously, I'm shifting my weight to my left foot so that I can *move my ass* to the right toward the 3 o'clock position.

3. By drawing his gun backwards out of his pants, the robber is giving me the fraction of a second I need to access my pistol.

4. Both of our guns are nearly up. He is moving toward me. Meanwhile, I am moving sideways to my 3 o'clock.

5. The robber's gun is poorly aligned in his grip, causing the muzzle to dip downward toward my leg. Meanwhile, my draw stroke has automatically indexed my pistol onto his chest. I continue to *move my ass* toward my 3 o'clock.

6. We're both trying to shoot each other in the head.

7. My shot strikes his left hand, which is in front of his face. If this were a real gunfight, and the round penetrated his hand, it could have been a headshot. This happens quite a bit in combat, which is why your defensive ammunition must meet FBI penetration standards.

ROBBERY DRILL 2

1. I've let this creep get too close, and now we're in a scuffle — not good.

2. The attacker *(right)* and I face off. His hand darts back for his waistband, which indicates that he has a weapon, so I go for my pistol.

3. My draw is faster and I start shooting him. But my friend Mark is highly trained, and reflexively shields his head while moving off the line of attack.

4. I foolishly remain in a fixed position, while he *moves his ass* shooting with one hand. His sudden movement to the side surprises me, and I miss the next shot.

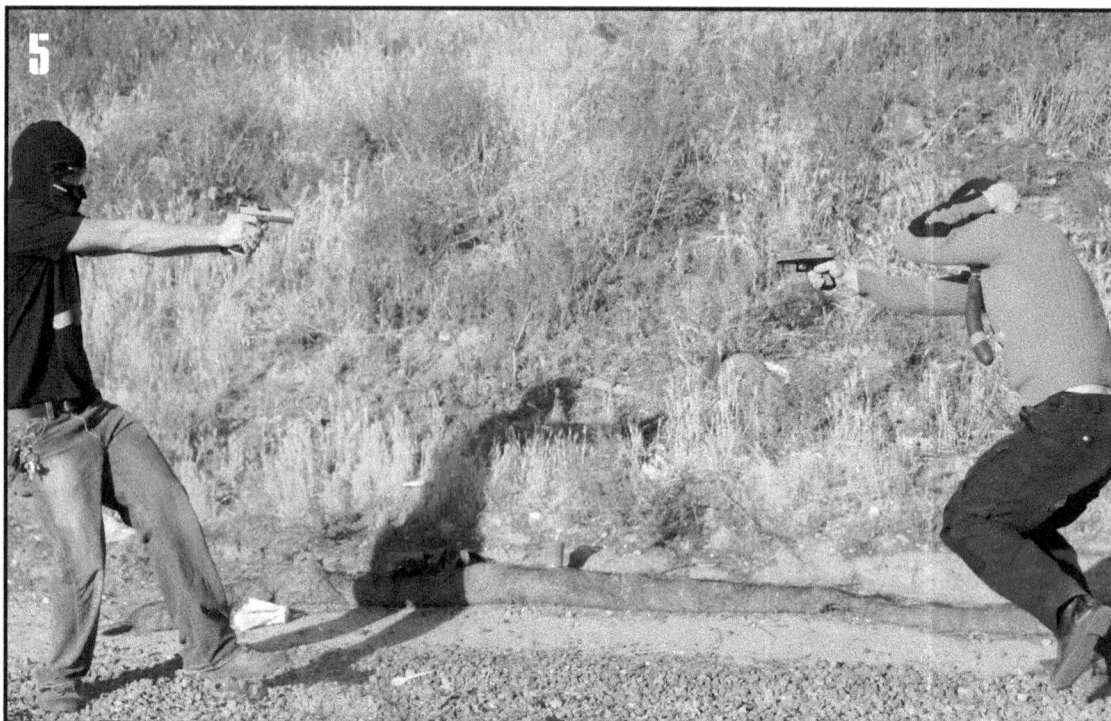

5. He's the more skilled warrior, and I end up shot in the spine. Had I been a better shot, or *moved my ass*, I might have survived — a clear case for more training.

19

ANALYZING
YOUR RESULTS

**WHAT IS THE GOOD OF EXPERIENCE
IF YOU DO NOT REFLECT?**

— FREDERICK THE GREAT

AFTER A TRAINING drill has been completed, one of the most important things you can do is analyze your results. You need to assess what is working, what could use improvement, and what is just not working at all.

Here are some things to pay attention to:

- How many shots did you fire on average?
- How many hit the target?
- How many hit the chest?
- How many hit the spine?
- How many headshots?
- How often were you shot / tazed?

- Were you able to use aimed fire with your sights, or did you point shoot?
- Which skills do you feel very confident in?
- Which do you feel you need to work on?

The goal of Force on Force training is to have you become familiar with shooting aggressive moving attackers. Eventually, with enough practice and determination, you will reliably make headshots and engage multiple attackers. Your results from this introduction to Force on Force are not a reflection of your overall worth as a shooter. They are simply a benchmark for your current level of skill.

These drills are all really difficult, so do not be discouraged if you spent the majority of your time getting shot and tazed. As you run these drills more and more, you really will get better. The more you train, the less effect the adrenaline will have. Your confidence will go up, and your accuracy will improve.

So, at the end of the day, compare war wounds with your training partner, and treat yourself to a well-deserved smoke, a nice dinner, and a few drinks.

Enjoying a post-training smoke with my buddy Mark.

20
RAPID FIRE

ONE OF THE biggest differences between conventional self-defense and Zombie shooting is the need to conserve ammunition. For standard defensive shooting, the current doctrine is to "shoot to slide lock" — that is, to empty your gun as fast as possible into your assailant. This makes total sense: Bullets are cheap and your life is precious, so you should hit the bad guy with everything you've got, as fast as possible.

But this strategy won't work in the Zombie Apocalypse, when bullets will be a precious commodity necessary for survival. Just as salt was once worth its weight in gold in Africa because it was a scarce resource that people needed to live, bullets will be an essential nutrient for anyone looking to stay alive in a world overrun by the Undead.

As we all know, Zombie blood is highly infectious, so you want to kill him from as far away as possible. You don't want him getting close enough to spray his blood all over you — unavoidable with contact weapons like swords, knives, and crowbars. So the only way to kill a Zombie without infecting yourself is with a projectile weapon. That means, once the ammo runs out, so does your life — unless you have a plentiful supply of crossbow bolts or a really secure BUGOUT location.

To illustrate the need to conserve ammo: Let's say you were carrying 500 rounds in your go bag, and you averaged a 10-shot magazine per Zombie. That would be 50 Zombies. Sounds like a lot of dead Zombies — until you look up how many people are in your city.

Assuming "only" 10% of the population of my town was infected, that's over 6,000 Zombies within 8.1 square miles of suburban sprawl. And if 10% of Los Angeles County was infected, well suddenly I would have 980,000 Zombies within a day's march of my house. So the 500 rounds of 5.7x28 in my emergency bag better last as long as possible.

The common wisdom is that we should only fire one round per Zombie. Yet, as we've seen in our Force on Force Drills, all that bullshit about "one shot, one kill" is just that — bullshit. When our adrenaline is surging, and someone (or something) is attacking us, it's simply unnatural to fire a single shot.

What is natural, and what my training partners and I have experienced, is the firing of bursts. See, after a while of performing the Fast Zombie Drills, we discovered a pattern. We never shot only one round. *Ever.* But, we didn't "shoot to slide lock" either — there just isn't enough time to do that when your attacker is sprinting from 7 yards away.

Instead, what we found, time and time again, is what I call the Burst + 1 (B+1).

In a nutshell: We would dump some rounds as fast as we could into our training partner's chest, with the hope of popping his balloon spine. From there, if he was still coming at us, it felt natural to simply raise the gun up slightly and make a headshot from a close range, typically within 3 yards or less.

THE BURST + 1 IS THE IDEAL ANTI-ZOMBIE SHOOTING PATTERN: IT CAN BE PERFORMED UNDER STRESS AND HAS A HIGH ANATOMICAL PROBABILITY OF SUCCESS.

Once we started using the B+1 in our Force on Force drills, the only time we got tazed was when we were either too slow on the draw, or when we snagged our pistol on our concealment garment. Otherwise, we got the Zombie every time.

So once you have mastered the basics of sighted marksmanship and Point Shooting, it's time to move on to Rapid Fire, using the Burst + 1 pattern as a template.

YOUR UNIQUE BURST PATTERN

Before you begin training, it is very helpful to analyze your previous Force on Force results so that you find out how you shoot instinctively under Survival Stress.

When you ran the Fast Zombie Drill, how many shots did you fire on average? How about in those drills when your partner was trying to shoot you?

Let's use me for an example. When I perform the Moving Target or Fast Zombie drills, I tend to favor 4-round bursts to the chest. Sometimes I might do 3, sometimes I might do as many as 8 if I'm panicking, but when I averaged out my results, I tended to favor a 4-round burst to the chest, followed by a headshot.

When my partner was playing an armed outlaw, my shooting habits depended on how far away he was. At 5 to 7 yards, I tended to stick to that 4-round burst pattern. However, when my partner was trying to shoot me within 3 yards, I tended to "shoot to slide lock" and fire as many rounds at him as quickly as I could. I never had the presence of mind to transition to a headshot. That is because my adrenaline was much higher when he was trying to shoot me point blank than when he was 7 yards away.

So, what this tells me about my Rapid Fire training is that I need to focus on two core concepts: a 4+1 burst drill for dealing with targets 5 to 7 yards away, and a full-on magazine dump drill for closer threats.

Since these are the two Rapid Fire scenarios I most often encounter in Force on Force, it makes sense to devote my limited training resources toward mastering what my body does naturally under stress, rather than trying to make my body conform to an externally-imposed shooting drill.

So, do some Force on Force to find out what works for you under stress. Then use that knowledge to tailor your training to your own needs.

COST OF RAPID FIRE TRAINING

In the prior chapters on Marksmanship and Point Shooting, there was a strong emphasis on dryfire, laser, airsoft, and .22-conversion kit training. That's because single-shot marksmanship and Point Shooting are not recoil dependent skills: When it comes to firing a single shot into the bullseye, a laser is the same as a .22 is the same as a .45.

However, when it comes to Rapid Fire, these cost-saving tools are largely useless since they do not provide enough recoil to train effectively. Although we will be using the .22 conversion kit at the outset, the vast majority of your Rapid Fire training must involve full recoil centerfire ammunition. You should expect to expend over 1,000 rounds in Rapid Fire training, or 2,000 if you shoot a weapon with a stiff recoil. This is expensive, but if you have performed the Force on Force Drills you know how essential Rapid Fire accuracy is to survival.

21
RAPID FIRE TRAINING

WE'VE ALREADY DISCUSSED the importance of proper trigger control, and how essential it is to accuracy. The same rule applies to Rapid Fire shooting. Only now, the trigger must not only be pressed correctly, but also very quickly, over and over again.

To minimize the effects of the trigger on Rapid Fire accuracy, you want to strive to shoot to "reset." This means that when you release the trigger, only release it until it goes past the "set" — and then stop. By not allowing the trigger to go all the way forward, you minimize the movement required to fire a subsequent shot. This will improve the speed and accuracy of your shooting.

Shooting to reset is not something you can learn with dryfire, but luckily it is something you can learn with a .22 conversion kit.

RESET TRAINING DRILL

1. With your .22 conversion kit, set up a Zombie Qualification Target 7 yards away at head height. Aim at the Big Brain, and pull the trigger. *Bang!* Now, slowly let off tension on the trigger until you feel it "click" back into place. That is the trigger resetting itself. Your goal when firing rapidly is always to allow the trigger to reset, without it traveling any farther.

2. Fire 10 to 30 rounds slowly, always releasing the trigger to the re-set point, but no farther.

3. Once you are familiar with where the reset is, begin firing 1 shot per second. Maintain your reset discipline and keep all rounds in the Big Brain.

4. Once you can shoot with proper reset discipline at 1 shot per second, it's time to try firing as fast as you can.

If you can fire 4 to 5 rounds per second while keeping all rounds in the Big Brain, you're good. If your shots are hitting low, or even worse, striking the ground in front of the target, that means that you are mashing the trigger and need more practice.

You should continue .22 training until you can keep 10 rounds of Rapid Fire in the Big Brain at 7 yards. After that, it will be time to switch over to a larger caliber, since too much Rapid Fire .22 training can cause bad habits to form.

CENTERFIRE TRAINING DRILL

Once you are comfortable firing rapidly with your .22 conversion kit, you're ready to step it up to full power, centerfire ammunition. You should make sure that your target ammunition has the same recoil characteristics as your defensive ammo. For example, if your defensive load is 9mm 124gr +P Gold Dot, your target ammunition should be a 124gr FMJ loaded to 1220 fps.

Remember: Although Rapid Fire is the skill we are learning, the most important thing of all is accuracy.

**THERE'S NO USE TRAINING TO SHOOT
AS FAST AS POSSIBLE IF YOUR SHOTS
ARE MISSING THE TARGET.**

So start slow, and progress to faster speeds only after you have mastered the basics with perfect accuracy.

1. Begin with a Zombie Qualification Target 3 yards away. Put 2 rounds into the Big Brain. Start off at one shot per second, and then increase speed as much as you can. If you start to miss, slow down.

2. When you can accurately fire a *fast* 2-round burst into the Big Brain from 3 yards away, move up to a 3-round burst.

3. Move up to 4 rounds.

4. Continue until you can empty the magazine into the Big Brain while firing as fast as you can at a distance of 3 yards.

5. Move the target back to 5 yards, and start again from the top. Then repeat, with the target at 7 yards.

BURST +1 TRAINING

After you have mastered the ability to shoot fast and accurately, it's time to focus on honing your B+1 skills at various distances. Remember, everyone is different, so find out which burst pattern works for you, rather than trying to impose someone else's preferences on your own training.

For the purpose of this example, we'll use my personal 4+1 pattern:

1. Begin with the Zombie Qualification Target 3 yards away, with a piece of printer paper taped below it to represent the upper chest.

2. With your gun in hand, fire 4 shots into the center of the piece of paper. As soon as you have fired the burst, raise the pistol and fire 1 round into the Big Brain. Start slowly, and steadily increase speed until you can do it in less than 2 seconds.

3. Repeat, from 5 yards.

4. Master the drill at 7 yards.

5. Now you're ready to pump up the realism and "train like you fight." If you have a Concealed Carry Permit, start drawing from concealment. Otherwise, you should draw from an open holster. Master at 3 yards, 5 yards, then 7 yards.

Goal: In the time it takes your partner to say, "Look Out! It's a Zombie!" you should be able to draw from concealment, and make an accurate B+ 1 against a target 7 yards away.

22
RAPID FIRE TESTING

ONCE YOU HAVE become proficient at Rapid Fire shooting and the Burst +1 principle, it's time to start performing these drills under stress.

Do not start Rapid Fire training with airsoft, and then try to use these tactics with centerfire ammunition. That is because the low recoil and excellent trigger of the airsoft gun can spoil you and cause bad habits. However, once you have mastered Rapid Fire using your centerfire handgun, it's perfectly acceptable to use airsoft since you already have the proper skillset ingrained in your muscle memory.

B+I MOVING TARGET DRILL

You should begin by practicing your B+1 skills using the Backyard Moving Target (BMT.) This is an advanced variation of drills that you have already performed.

As always, the person holding the BMT must **wear protective safety goggles.**

1. With your airsoft gun concealed in a holster, your partner will hold the BMT and begin running at you at full speed from 7 yards away. You must *move your ass* out of the line of attack, draw from concealment, and perform a B+1 on the target.

2. When you are consistently keeping your burst in the chest and making the headshot, repeat the drill starting at 5 yards.

3. Now, try it out at 3 yards. (This one's tough!)

B+1 FAST ZOMBIE DRILL

This is the same Fast Zombie Drill as before, but instead of making a spine or headshot, you need to perform a B+1.

1. Master the B+1 FZD at 7 yards.

2. When you can consistently make a B+1 against a Fast Zombie at 7 yards, try it starting from 5 yards away.

3. If you can, try it out at 3 yards — but you will probably need to go directly to a headshot at this distance.

We videotaped this drill, and upon playback we realized that the entire exercise had taken less than 2 seconds. In that time, I had fired 12 shots — 8 rounds to the chest, and 4 headshots. When I asked Brandon why he didn't stop after the first shot, he explained that he really wanted to taze me!

1. I observe the Zombie's feet begin to move, a threat stimulus that indicates he is going to charge. I grab my shirt with my left hand so I can access my pistol.

2. The Zombie is now 6 yards away, and my pistol is in hand.

3. He is now 5 yards away, and my pistol is out and on target.

4. I start shooting the Zombie in the chest as fast as I can pull the trigger. Note his arms pulling toward his chest from the pain of impact.

5. He is now 3 yards away, and I have already put 8 rounds to his chest. Yet, none has been a spine shot — likely because his balloon spine has come undone.

6. With the Zombie within 3 yards, I transition to a headshot.

7. I shoot him again in the head. Notice how my eyes are locked on his face, and that I am looking through my pistol sights.

8. His stun gun is dangerously close to me, so I transition to one-handed fire while moving backward to my 8 o'clock. This was not a conscious decision — my body did it instinctively.

9. He lunges at me, and I shoot him in the face while stepping off the line of attack.

10. His attack has been stopped, but I keep my gun indexed on him while continuing to *move my ass*. Can never be too sure with those Zombies.

23
LONG RANGE PISTOL SHOOTING

A PISTOL IS A WEAPON OF ASTONISHING EFFICIENCY AND VERSATILITY WHEN SKILLFULLY USED. . . . A REALLY GOOD MAN, WEARING A REALLY GOOD SIDEARM, IS A SERIOUS, ALMOST INSURMOUNTABLE, PROBLEM FOR ANY PERSON OR GROUP WHICH CONTEMPLATES HIS FORCIBLE COERCION.

— JEFF COOPER, LEGENDARY FIREARMS INSTRUCTOR

ALTHOUGH THE HANDGUN is first and foremost a close quarters combat tool, in the right hands it can be surprisingly effective at longer ranges.

During the Vietnam War, Navy SEAL R.J. Thomas and his team were shot down in enemy territory. Most of his crew was killed. R.J. was badly injured, and his Stoner 63A machine gun was destroyed.

Making a bad day even worse, his position was instantly set upon by dozens of North Vietnamese Army (NVA) soldiers armed with AK47s.

With only a Colt 1911 pistol in hand and his unconscious comrade as a firing rest, R.J. Thomas was able to hold off the NVA for over 40 minutes. By the time he was rescued, he had killed a dozen men armed with assault rifles from a distance of over 100 yards.

In R.J.'s own words:

"In order to get into our rice paddy, the NVA had to come over the dike. They lined up behind the dike about 100 yards away. They'd stick their AK's up over it and spray us with full auto fire, and then they'd stick their heads up to see if they hit anything. I'd shoot at them and every once in a while a round would go *thunk* and a head would disappear."

Due to his Long Range pistol skills and general badassery, R.J. was awarded the Navy Cross. He went on to become a founder of the Naval Special Warfare sniper program, a fact he considered ironic because most of his kills were with a pistol.

Although this is an incredible situation handled by an incredible marksman, it does illustrate the point that Jeff Cooper makes about a pistol's "astonishing efficiency and versatility" when used by a "really good man." Although the vast majority of our training is devoted to close range shooting, the handgun is more than capable of being effective at 100 yards and beyond — if the shooter is skillful enough.

To further illustrate this point, let's look at the ballistics of some of Speer's Gold Dot defensive hollow points when fired from a pistol.

CALIBER	VELOCITY	ENERGY AT MUZZLE	50 YDS	100 YDS
9mm 124gr +P	1220fps	410 ft/lb	324 ft/lb	273 ft/lb
.357 SIG 125gr	1350fps	506 ft/lb	389 ft/lb	316 ft/lb
.40 S&W 165gr	1150fps	484 ft/lb	398 ft/lb	342 ft/lb
.45 ACP 230gr	890fps	404 ft/lb	365 ft/lb	316 ft/lb

To give a sense of power here, a 135gr .38 special +P has 220 ft/lbs of energy at the *muzzle*. Even 100 yards away, handgun rounds still retain more than enough energy to be effective — as long as they hit their target.

The moral of this story is not that we should all sell our rifles to buy sniper Glocks. Rifles will always be far more effective at long range than any handgun. But a pistol will do in a pinch.

> **IN THE POST-APOCALYPTIC WORLD —**
> **WHERE THERE WILL BE HERDS OF ZOMBIES ON THE**
> **HORIZON OR LONE WOLVES ARMED WITH**
> **LONG GUNS — THERE MAY COME A TIME WHEN**
> **WE NEED TO DEFEND OURSELVES AT LONG DISTANCE,**
> **ARMED ONLY WITH A PISTOL.**

It's a lousy situation to be in, but if we're skillful enough to make the shot, our handguns have enough power to get the job done.

Luckily, you don't have to be a Navy SEAL like R.J. Thomas to shoot your pistol accurately out to 100 yards and beyond. All you need is practice.

LONG RANGE PISTOL PREREQUISITES

Before you can shoot targets at long range, you have to be able to shoot *really well* up close.

There is no official standard that says "You must shoot this well to ride the ride." But I would say that you should be able to hit a 1-inch wide target at 7 yards, on command.

If you can consistently hit a target that small, it's reasonable to believe that with practice you will be able to keep your shots on a 10-inch target at 70 yards. And then you're ready for some Long Range pistol training.

LONG RANGE DRYFIRE DRILL

If you haven't noticed by now, I'm a big believer in dryfire training, and now is no exception. The most important thing needed for Long Range accuracy is a steady hand and a perfect trigger press, and both of these skills can be learned for free using Long Range dryfire. It's the same as regular dryfire — only the targets are much farther away.

1. I recommend starting with a 4-inch target 25 yards away, an 8-inch target 50 yards away, and a 16-inch target at 100 yards. Adjust the size of the targets depending on your vision, and how precise your sights are.
2. Stand in your best shooting stance, hold steady, and commence dryfire practice. Keep your sights perfectly aligned on the target, and try and keep your arms steady as you ever so smoothly press the trigger.
3. Fire five shots and rest a minute, then repeat until you feel that you would have been able to hit the target if the gun were loaded.
4. Master this at 25, 50, and 100 yards before moving on to live fire.

LONG RANGE .22 PRACTICE DRILL

One of my favorite uses for the .22 conversion kit is to practice my Long Range shooting skills. The .22 is cheap to shoot and surprisingly accurate, making it the ideal round for honing your Long Range shooting skills.

Before you begin shooting, you need a reactive target that lets you know that you've hit it — typically by splattering paint, making noise, or exploding. The most practical reactive target is just a piece of steel, as the loud *clang!* of the bullet striking metal will let you know whether you made the shot. By comparison, if you're shooting at a paper target from 100 yards away, you will only know if you're on target by peering through binoculars. Which is lame.

Ideally you want a professional steel target, but if you don't have one, **empty** propane cans make a satisfying noise when you hit them. Standard 20lb cans used for BBQ's are the rough anatomical size of a Zombie's upper torso.

1. Set up your reactive target at 25 yards.
2. Using your .22 conversion kit, continue shooting until you can hit the target 100% of the time while firing from a standing position.
3. Now, move the target out to 50 yards. Keep shooting until you can hit the target at least 75% of the time from a standing position.
4. Repeat at 75 yards, until you can hit the target at least 50% of the time from a standing position.
5. Set up the target at 100 yards. The goal is to be able to hit the target 25% of the time or better from a standing position.

From 25 to 50 yards, shooting is pretty much the same as it is at 7 yards, only more difficult. However, beyond 75 yards, pistol shooting begins to resemble firing artillery, where shots must be "walked into" the target.

Known as "Kentucky Windage," the trick is to observe where the bullet struck, and adjust the shot from there. So if you are aiming at the center of the target, but the shots keep hitting low and to the right, adjust your aim a bit high and left of center.

When you get good at this, you will be able to hit targets out to 100 yards within 3 shots, as long as there is a good backdrop for the shots to impact. If you can't see where your bullets are hitting, it will be impossible to correct your aim, so I recommend setting up your target on a dirt berm or a hill.

Once you learn the right "hold over" for your pistol at different ranges, you will no longer need the dirt berm. The "hold over" is when the sights are aligned normally, but the aim is slightly above or to the side of the target in order to compensate for the unusual distance.

LONG RANGE CENTERFIRE DRILL

Unfortunately, the "hold over" for .22's will be different than the hold over for your centerfire calibers. Therefore, it is essential that you practice your Long Range marksmanship using full caliber ammunition loaded to the same velocity as your defensive caliber. Once you get good at it, you should fire at least 10 rounds of your defensive hollow points at Long Range to confirm that they have the same point of impact as your practice ammo.

Repeat Steps 1 to 5 from the earlier .22 Practice Drill, and remember where the hold over is for each distance.

Your goal is to be able to hit a torso-sized object out to 100 yards within 3 shots.

24

**YOU CANNOT CLAIM TO BE A PISTOL SHOT
UNLESS YOU ARE A FAST SHOT.**

— CAPTAIN NOEL, *THE MAXIMS OF PISTOL SHOOTING*

THE FAST DRAW

SHIT HAPPENS — *FAST* — and you need to be able to respond just as quickly. A Fast Zombie can cover 7 yards in less than 1.5 seconds. Meanwhile, a skilled outlaw can grab his gun and put a hole in your chest even faster.

Speed on the draw is a vital skill you need to survive.

**ALL YOUR SHOOTING PROFICIENCY IS
WORTHLESS IF YOU CAN'T GET YOUR GUN
OUT IN ONE HELL OF A HURRY.**

Yet being fast is the skill you should learn last, because an overemphasis on speed can ruin your ability to perform the single most important skill of all: Hitting the target accurately on your first shot, every time. As legendary pistol shot Bill Jordan was fond of saying: "Speed's fine, but accuracy is final."

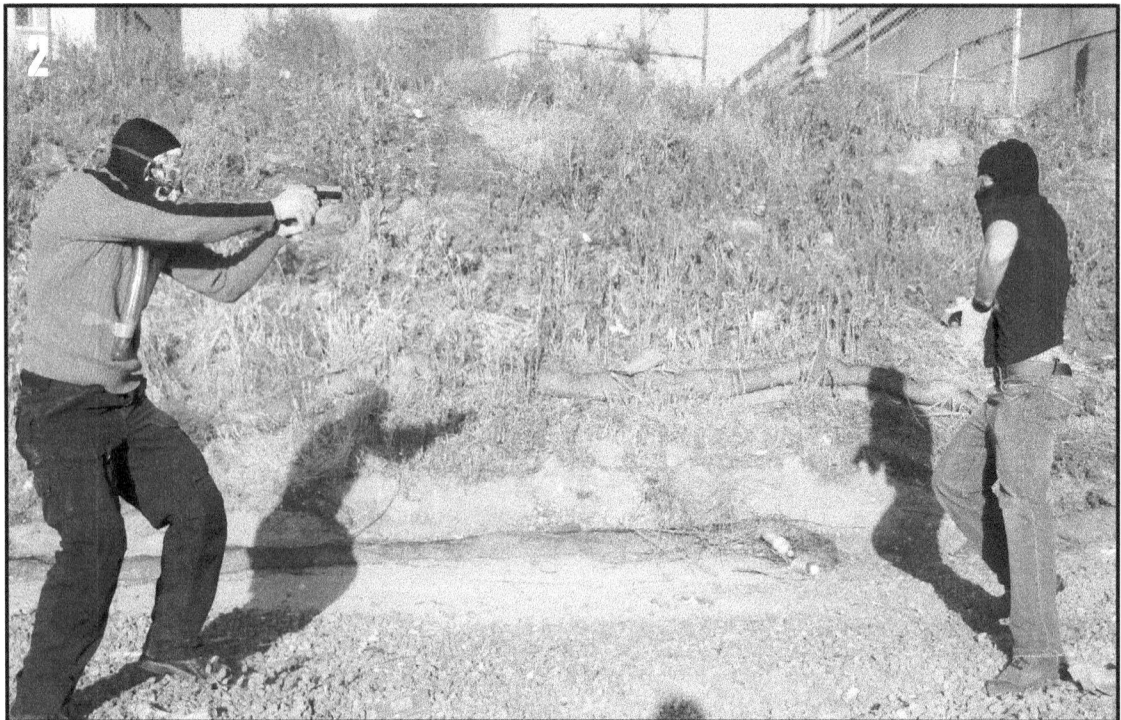

I was too slow on the draw, and ended up shot multiple times in the face. Not good.

I have placed the Fast Draw at the end of *The ZSG* because I wanted you first to master every component of accuracy, and to have it drilled into your muscle memory. Only then should you practice shooting for speed. Mastery is the basics sped up. So before you can shoot quickly, you need to be able to shoot very well slowly.

Hopefully, by the time you've made it this far, you can.

HOW FAST IS "FAST"?

The fastest draw is having the gun already in your hand when the fight starts. If you suspect that Zombies are in the area, you should absolutely draw your pistol and have it ready.

There's no time for a slow draw when attacked by Fast Zombies.

However, this is not always practical, especially on Day 1 of the Zombie Outbreak. On Day 1, you will have no hint of danger until you hear the screams of those around you being set upon by the Infected. You'll turn the corner to find out what's going on, and a Fast Zombie will be sprinting toward you. He'll be biting your face off in less than two seconds — unless you can react, draw your pistol from concealment, and put a burst in his chest and one in his brain before he reaches you.

That's how fast you need to be.

Let's be more precise: If the average human reaction time — from perceiving a stimulus to acting upon it — is .25 of a second, and a Fast Zombie can cover 7 yards in 1.5 seconds, that only leaves you with 1.25 seconds to draw your pistol from concealment and perform a B+1 drill.

That's the best-case scenario.

Now, if we consider that the Zombie may be closer than 7 yards, and that our reaction time is likely to be slower due to the sheer surprise of encountering a Zombie for the first time, it becomes clear that we will need to be even faster on the draw.

Our ultimate goal is to be able to draw from concealment and make a headshot from 3 yards away, in 1 second or less.

Although the Fast Draw is a tough skill to master, the good news is that the vast majority of your training can be done at home, for free. You can practice the Fast Draw using dryfire, the Laser Training Cartridge, or your airsoft trainer. Whichever you choose, the basic formula is the same.

FAST DRAW DRILL

1. **With your centerfire firearm unloaded, and your ammunition in a different room,** place your pistol in you concealment holster, and cover it with your concealment garment.

2. Practice clearing your concealment garment without drawing your pistol. For example, lift up your shirt with your left hand, or sweep your jacket back with your right. Perform this at least 25 times, slowly. Repeat, 25 times fast. Keep practicing until you can do it perfectly at full speed.

3. Now lift or remove your concealment garment, and practice drawing the pistol. Take your time, making sure you have a perfect grip on the gun. Now draw into a two-handed grip, with the pistol raised to eye level. Repeat 25 times slow, and then 25 times fast. Keep practicing until you always get a secure grip on the pistol when you draw.

4. Now it's time to combine these two skills. Starting slow, clear your concealment garment with your left hand, while drawing your pistol with your right. Assume a two-handed grip, and extend the pistol out to eye level. This should be a nice, slow, 1-2-3-4 count process:

   1– Clear concealment garment and grip pistol.

   2– Draw pistol.

   3– Establish a two-handed grip.

   4– Extend pistol to eye level.

   Do this slow and perfect 25 times.

5. Now that you can draw from concealment perfectly, it's time to steadily increase speed — from 1-2-3-4 to 1234 — until the whole process is more like a 1-4! blink of an eye. If at any time you fumble the draw, start back at the slow 1-2-3-4 cadence, and begin working back to high speed.

1. *Oh snap!* I see a Zombie and decide to access my pistol. My left hand moves toward the center of my chest to grab my t-shirt.

2. My left hand yanks up my t-shirt so I can get a solid grip on my pistol.

3. As my pistol clears my conceal-ment garment, my support hand moves to establish a two-handed grip.

4. I establish a two-handed grip, with my pistol below my dominant eye.

5. I drive my pistol toward the Zombie's head.

6. My arms are now at the full limit of extension. My pistol is indexed on the Zombie's head, and I'm looking through the sights while focusing on the threat.

FAST DRAW DRYFIRE DRILL

Once you have a fumble-free Fast Draw, you're ready to start working on shooting from the draw and the all-important first round hit.

To perform this drill, you should use your Laser Training Cartridge (LTC) to give you the realistic trigger feedback of dryfire while showing you whether you're hitting the target. If you do not have a LTC, use your airsoft gun.

1. Set up a Zombie Qualification Target 5-feet 10-inches off the ground, to mimic the height of the average American male.
2. Load the LTC into your pistol.
3. Stand 3 yards away from the target, with your pistol concealed in a holster.
4. Starting slowly, clear your concealment garment, draw your pistol, assume a two-handed grip, and extend the pistol out to eye level. Press the trigger, and fire a laser dot into the Big Brain.
5. Once you've achieved 100% accuracy, increase your speed: from 1-2-3-4 to 1234, until it's a 1-4! blink of an eye.
6. Continue until you can consistently maintain 100% accuracy while going as fast as you can.
7. Move back to 5 yards, and repeat.
8. Move back to 7 yards.

**PRACTICE YOUR FAST DRAW A FEW MINUTES A DAY
UNTIL IT IS SECOND NATURE.**

The more you practice, the faster you will be.

Famous gunslingers like Wild West outlaw John Wesley Hardin and FBI crack shot Delf A. "Jelly" Bryce were known to practice their draws a few hours each day. Jelly was so fast that he could drop a quarter, and have his .357 Magnum out and a bullet in the target before the coin hit the ground. So take a lesson from the pros: Practice.

AIRSOFT SAFETY CHECK DRILL

The Fast Draw is one of the most useful skills you can have, but it is also one of the most dangerous to practice.

**IF YOU DRAW IN TOO MUCH OF A HURRY,
AND HAVE BAD TRIGGER DISCIPLINE,
YOU COULD EASILY END UP SHOOTING YOURSELF
IN THE ASS, FOOT, OR DICK, DEPENDING ON WHERE
YOU CARRY YOUR PISTOL. NOT GREAT.**

So, before you progress to working on your quick draw with live ammunition, you should practice with a non-lethal projectile.

In the 1960s, famously fast shot Bill Jordan practiced with wax bullets. He would press paraffin wax into empty cartridges that were loaded only with a primer. Out to 7 yards, they were just as accurate as his .357, with the added advantage of being a whole lot safer in case of an accident.

Now that we're in the 21st Century, we can use our airsoft trainers, since they are safer and easier to work with. However, the real advantage to using airsoft for safety practice is the trigger. An airsoft gun has a very light trigger, which makes it very easy to accidentally shoot yourself. For example, I would say my KWA G17 airsoft pistol has a 1lb trigger, while my real steel Glock 21 has a 5.5lb trigger.

That means that if you can Fast Draw safely with the hair trigger of an airsoft gun without shooting yourself, you have enough trigger discipline to move on to live fire training.

Do not skip this drill. The Fast Draw can be dangerous. Do not take any chances.

1. Set up a box with a Z-Qualification Target on it, lifted 5-feet 10-inches off the ground.

2. With your loaded airsoft gun concealed in a holster, try out your Fast Draw. Start slow and work up to full speed.

3. Practice 500+ Fast Draws with your airsoft pistol without shooting yourself. Only then should you move onto live fire.

LIVE FIRE FAST DRAW DRILL

Once you have mastered the Airsoft Safety Check at full speed, it's time to start working on your Fast Draw using live fire. This drill will focus on making the headshot — fast.

1. Begin with your .22lr conversion kit concealed in a holster, and the target at 3 yards. Start slow, at the original 1-2-3-4 cadence, and go for headshots.

2. Slowly increase your speed until you are making headshots at full speed at 3 yards.

3. When you can make 25 Fast Draw headshots in a row at 3 yards, set the target up at 5 yards and repeat.

4. When mastered at 5 yards, move back to 7 yards.

5. Once you have mastered the Fast Draw headshot out to 7 yards with your .22 conversion kit, it's time to switch to full caliber ammunition. Begin slowly at 3 yards, and repeat the above steps until you can make a Fast Draw headshot out to 7 yards with centerfire ammunition.

B+1 FAST DRAW DRILL

Once you have mastered the basic Fast Draw headshot, it's time to start integrating the B+1 concept.

1. With your centerfire handgun concealed in a holster, set up a Zombie Qualification Target, with a piece of printer paper taped below it to simulate the upper torso.

2. Clear your cover garment, draw, and fire a burst to the upper chest, followed by a headshot. Start slow, and steadily increase your speed.

3. When you feel you have mastered the Fast Draw B+1 at 3 yards, move back to 5 yards.

4. Now try it out at 7 yards.

25
FINAL EXAM

WHEN WE THINK of Zombies, we think *Zombies* — like more than one. So chances are there will be a time when you need to fight off a pack by yourself. To survive such terrible odds, you will need to be extremely fast, accurate, and ruthless.

It's taken a lot of work for you to reach this level, but now that you're here: Zombies Beware.

LIVE FIRE MULTIPLE TARGETS TEST

In this part of the final exam, you will be integrating your whole live fire skill set against multiple stationary targets. That means you will need to Fast Draw from concealment, and then B+1 each target using full power centerfire ammunition.

1. Set up 2 Zombie Qualification Targets, with a piece of printer paper taped beneath them as the torso. They should be 3 yards away, and 3 yards apart.

2. Fast Draw from concealment and B+1 each target until it becomes easy.

3. Move the Zombies out to 5 yards, 3 yards apart.

4. Repeat from 7 yards away, 3 yards apart.

5. Now, start staggering the Zombies. For example: One target 3 yards away and another at 7 yards, with 5 yards between them.

6. Every 10 rounds, switch the targets' locations and distances apart.

7. Use three targets spaced 3, 5, and 7 yards away. Practice until you can draw from concealment and B+1 each target in under 5 seconds.

FORCE ON FORCE MULTIPLE ZOMBIES TEST

For this test, you will need a few training partners to play the roles of a small pack of Zombies. Each Zombie will be equipped with his own face mask, goggles, balloon spine, and stun gun. You will wear your protective goggles and face mask, and will be armed with your airsoft training pistol.

1. Load as many rounds as your real pistol holds. For example, if your gun has a 10-round magazine, only load 10 airsoft BBs.

2. Your partners will stand 7, 9, and 11 yards away, and you will have your airsoft concealed.

3. At a time of any partner's choosing, they will all suddenly sprint toward you.

4. You must B+1 each Zombie before he tazes you.

Goal: Survive!

CONCLUSION

IF YOU'RE READING this, I salute you. Statistics show that most people who buy books don't end up finishing them. So thanks for putting up with me.

But your work is not over. In fact, it's just beginning. Much like reading a book on fitness won't make you slim, *The Zombie Shooting Guide* is only useful if you go out and apply the training techniques — over and over again.

The road to mastery can be frustrating at times. I know from my own experience that there are certain things that I excel at, like Long Range pistol shooting, and some skills that I still struggle with, like Rapid Fire accuracy.

In order to succeed, we have to step out of our comfort zone. We have to find our weak spots, and make them strong. That's the only way to grow, both as a shooter and as a man.

So go out there and push yourself. Good luck. Be safe. And stay alive.

EPILOGUE: 30 CITIES
A NOT-SO-FICTIONAL SHORT STORY

KIM JONG-UN HAD LONG lamented his father's obsession with nuclear weapons. To the freshly anointed leader of North Korea, atomic bombs were a wasteful indulgence, billion dollar toys that did nothing to further his grandfather's dream of uniting Korea under the Kim dynasty.

At 28, the baby-faced Kim became the World's youngest head of state. In order to maintain power he had to appear as ruthless as his father Kim Jong-il. To burnish his martial credibility, he ordered in 2010 the torpedoing of the *Cheonan* battleship in South Korean waters, killing 46 sailors. A few months later he went after South Korea again, ordering the bombardment of Yeonpyeong island and sparking international outrage.

Despite these provocative acts, his top generals still thought him a weak, fat playboy unfit to rule the World's most militarized nation. They began scheming after his father's stroke in 2008, and now that the "Dear Leader" was dearly departed, rumors swirled of a possible coup. Kim Jong-un needed to prove his mettle to his staff, and to the World, before it was too late.

Some of the generals had served as foot soldiers in the 1950s during the failed Korean War for national unification, and were eager to try again. Yet if they invaded South Korea, with its 28,000 American troops at the DMZ, they would be locked into another hopeless war with the technologically superior US military. Meanwhile, the nuclear option was tantamount to national suicide: His father's six atomic firecrackers were no match for America's thousands of thermonuclear bombs.

Faced between losing power or losing a war, Kim Jong-un would devise a third option, a way that would allow him to retain power and reunify Korea.

In the process, he would unleash the Zombie Apocalypse.

■   ■   ■

In October 2011, Kim read an article in *The New York Times* detailing America's lack of preparation for a biological attack. Despite ten years and trillions of dollars spent on protecting the homeland from terrorism, the US continued to pay little more than lip service to biodefense, preferring to focus on airline security and nuclear proliferation.

Kim was particularly intrigued by the results of "Dark Winter," a government exercise in which a small band of terrorists armed with smallpox were able to cripple large parts of the nation.

A few nights later, while smoking opium-laced hash in an underground whorehouse outside of Pyongyang, Kim saw the film *28 Days Later* that was playing on the TV behind the bar. In the film, an incurable virus turns people into bloodthirsty maniacs and devastates England. Despite the lack of electrical infrastructure in the North, a light bulb went off in Kim's brain. He quickly finished with his 14-year old attendant, and returned to his subterranean bunker to think.

The next morning, he called a meeting of his generals and laid out his plan. First, he distributed copies of the "Dark Winter" report, pointing out America's vulnerability to biological weapons. Then he made his proposal:

If the DPRK could create an even more devastating virus, one that truly ravaged the United States, the Pentagon would be forced to withdraw all of its forces from overseas to help maintain order at home. Then, with the US troops removed from the DMZ, North Korea would be free to invade South Korea in a ruthless lightning campaign. By the time the Americans recovered, if they ever did recover, Korea would be unified under Kim and it would be a *fait accompli.*

The generals were impressed. And so the project began.

■   ■   ■

Over the next three months, Kim commanded his elite Special Forces units, which specialized in cross-border infiltration, to kidnap the top genetic scientists working on cloning programs in South Korea. Meanwhile, experts in viral research and neurology were taken from other nations and spirited back to Pyongyang via midget submarine.

Upon arrival, Kim made the prisoners' choice clear. They could work on one of the most cutting-edge and stimulating scientific programs in history while enjoying a bottomless pit of conscripted Korean virgins. Or, they could have their eyelids excised with a scalpel before being lowered head first into his father's piranha tank.

Only one principled female scientist chose the piranhas.

Using a state-of-the-art lab Kim had purchased piecemeal from the Triads with counterfeit $100 bills, the scientists set out on the deadliest scientific endeavor since the Manhattan Project.

Their mission was to create a highly contagious disease that would turn ordinary people into super fast, super strong lunatics who would relentlessly attack and infect everyone they came across. Because of their violent nature, it would be impossible to corral the infected to impose a quarantine. Unable to prevent the spread of the disease, the outbreak would spiral out of control.

When asked to elaborate, Kim had the scientists watch *28 Days Later.*

Initially skeptical, the scientists soon became engrossed in the project. Much like Los Alamos in the 1940s, the scintillating scientific research in Pyongyang outweighed the moral concerns. Ethics would be dealt with later. For now the scientists thought only of the intellectual challenge.

They began by isolating a particularly aggressive form of rabies from feral dogs that had taken to mauling unattended children in the Korean countryside. Using pyrosequencing tests, the scientists compared the DNA of this rabies with milder samples, so that they could isolate the aggressor genes.

They then modified the rabies virus to have even more of these aggressive genes. Breeding and crossbreeding, through multiple generations, the scientists created a strain of rabies that would turn a domesticated lap dog into a blood-mad wolf.

To give the infected inexhaustible drive and endurance, scientists tweaked the virus to boost the production of adrenaline, epinephrine and testosterone into overdrive. Then they spliced in sequences that would activate the same parts of the brain as the drug PCP, which was known to give its users resistance to pain, fearlessness and superhuman strength.

Using research published in the journals *Nature* and *Science* on increasing the human infection rate of the H1N1 virus, the team modified the new rabies with strains of the flu, to allow the virus to be spread through the air, rather than just through biting and other direct physical contact. Then as a finishing touch, to increase the amount of exposed bodily fluids — and the psychological horror — strains of the Ebola virus were added to cause the infected to bleed profusely from the mouth and nose.

In the lab, it was known as The Kimchi Virus, after Korea's national dish of fermented cabbage. The rest of the world would soon know it as The Zombie Virus.

*   *   *

When Kimchi was tested in one of North Korea's underground political prisons, the results were nightmarishly effective. Using only a few grams of dried viral powder, the disease spread through the prison like sparks in a fire-cracker factory.

After a 24-hour incubation period, the prison exploded into shocking scenes of violence. Incoherent humans attacked each other, ripping off cellmates' flesh and twisting limbs with bare hands. Primal screams echoed through the metal halls. Some of the prisoners burst down the doors to the outside and sprinted across the exercise yard, immune to barbed wire and bullets. They continued to maul the guards until they bled to death from dozens of gunshot wounds.

Within 48 hours there were 17,000 infected prisoners and guards. The experiment was a success.

No longer needing them, and terrified that they might escape and infect the rest of the country, Kim ordered that the prison be incinerated.

This was the secret reason behind North Korea's controversial underground nuclear test in 2013.

*   *   *

Meanwhile, the myopic focus on nuclear proliferation continued to blind Western intelligence agencies to the threat of biological attack.

Despite the a virtual Dream Team of scientists had gone missing under mysterious circumstances, despite the warnings of the CDC to prepare for a Zombie Apocalypse, despite that numerous books and films that continued to trumpet the existential threat posed by Zombies, the intelligence agencies were ordered by their higher-ups to keep their eyes on the "big picture" of nuclear proliferation.

Even though entire nations had to struggle for decades to acquire nuclear weapons, American politicians continued to believe that a handful of dastardly terrorists could easily purchase them on the black market. . . .

It is said that generals are always preparing to win the last war, and that was never more in evidence than right before the Outbreak. Although the assassination of Osama Bin Laden and the success of the Arab Spring had rendered Al Qaeda's jihadist campaigns largely irrelevant, US defense continued to focus on preventing Islamist terrorist attacks.

This would prove to be a fatal error.

■   ■   ■

While Homeland Security was data-mining passenger manifests against the 1 million names on the "Terrorist Watch List," and dutifully scanning every 15- to 55-year old Arab male for underwear bombs, 32 North Korean female commandos, disguised as sexy young tourists on summer vacation, entered the United States with the deadliest biological weapons in history. The airport scanners, trained to detect nail clippers and liquid explosives, were blind to the viral nature of the "baby powder" in the women's luggage.

Selected for their beauty, "the girls" had begun their training as concubines. They then advanced to commando school, where they studied foreign languages, urban fieldcraft, and close-quarters killing techniques. Though they each looked like an innocent schoolgirl, they had already conducted several missions against the West, and it was their spotless military record that had earned them the honor of this final assignment.

Pre-positioning themselves in 30 cities across America, the girls informed their "relatives back home" of their new addresses in "the land of opportunity."

A week later, they each received in the mail a camera with a large zoom lens to use on their "adventures."

Inside the camera body was a small tank of compressed nitrogen gas connected to a regulated valve. The lens assembly was designed to be removed and filled with the powdered Kimchi virus. When the camera shutter was activated, a small burst of nitrogen gas would eject an undetectable viral cloud into the air. Each shot would infect dozens of people within the target area, and each commando had enough Kimchi to take 50 "photos" of crowded locations throughout their target city.

The camera dispersal system was fabricated using Iranian milling machines, which the Korean government had quietly acquired in exchange for technology to improve the Persian Shabab-3 MRBM that the West was currently so worried about.

There was nothing special about the milling machines — except that they produced an Iranian signature on every fabricated part. Due to pervasive sanctions, Iran was forced to produce the majority of its machinery domestically, rather than importing it from abroad. The result was that the subtle scratch pattern produced by their milling machines could be identified by a skilled forensics expert — a veritable metallic fingerprint pointing straight back to Iran.

Because these milling machines produced many of the IEDs used to kill US forces in Iraq, the scratch pattern was well known to the US. And this fact was well known to North Korea, which is why they built their Weapons of Mass Destruction using Iranian, and not North Korean, milling machines. If the operation was compromised and the cameras were discovered, the fallout would be in Tehran.

In the lead up to the attack, Kim Jong-un announced to the World that he was renouncing his nuclear program in favor of peace. To prove his sincerity, he had his uranium enrichment facility in Yongbyon demolished in front of the TV cameras.

It seemed to the World that the Korean threat would soon be over.

In fact, the speech was a signal for his girls to attack.

■　　■　　■

Precisely one week later, the Korean commandos, dressed in short skirts with high socks and thick glasses, began their tours of America. Like many tourists, they carried obnoxiously large cameras around their necks.

In each city, they found the most crowded tourist attractions and busiest workplaces, and began snapping photos.

Each click of the shutter ejected a small puff of 600-micron death through a pinhole in the camera lens. Mixing with the currents of the air, the virus quickly lodged itself in dozens of lungs. With 32 operatives each taking 50 photos, over 28,000 people were infected within hours. Because many of the infected were tourists, they would bring the disease back to their hometowns.

Because of its size, population and importance, three girls were assigned to New York City while the other 29 cities had only one operative. In New York, the girls spread out: Grand Central and Penn Station during rush hour. Times Square. Rockefeller Center, St. Patrick's Cathedral, and the shops along Fifth Avenue. Greenwich Village. City Hall. Wall Street and the Staten Island Ferry. The Bronx Zoo. JFK Airport. Coney Island. And to get from place to place, the crowded subway stations and trains. . . .

In San Francisco, there were snapshots of tourists waiting for the cable cars, eating at Fisherman's Wharf, exploring Chinatown, and shopping at Union Square. . . . In Philadelphia, Independence Hall and the Liberty Bell were immortalized anew. . . . Chicago's girl got the hometown crowd at Wrigley Field rooting for its beloved Cubs. . . . In Los Angeles, there were photos galore at Grauman's Chinese Theater in Hollywood, the movie studios, and Disneyland. . . . In Boston, there was quite a bit of time spent at the campuses of Harvard, MIT, and Boston University. . . . In Washington DC, there were candid shots of the Lincoln Memorial and the lines of people waiting to get inside Congress. . . .

Each snapshot was a portrait of America: In Miami, the working-class diners in Little Havana, the rich bankers and condo owners along the Brickell Avenue towers, and the glitterati at South Beach nightclubs. . . . The hedonists in Las Vegas casinos. . . . The hungry at the Seattle Farmer's Market and the tourists at the Space Needle. . . . The revelers at the French Quarter in New Orleans. . . . The cattlemen and butchers at the Oklahoma City stockyards. . . . The shoppers in Minneapolis and the Mall of America, the world's biggest. . . . The devoted at the world headquarters for the Mormon Church in Salt Lake City. . . . Middle America at the Iowa State Fair in Des Moines . . . .

Atlanta. . . . Dallas. . . . Houston. . . . Baltimore. . . . Phoenix. . . . Denver . . . . Detroit. . . . Indianapolis. . . . Portland. . . . Memphis. . . . Milwaukee . . . . Charlotte. . . . Albuquerque. . . . Columbus, Ohio. . . . And Kansas City, Missouri.

Within a day, the girls had photographed the best of what America had to offer.

Their mission completed, the girls returned to their hotels, tossing the empty cameras in trashcans and dumpsters along the way. Back in their rooms, they destroyed any evidence that could lead back to Pyongyang, and wiped down every surface in the room with bleach to kill any trace of the virus. They put a Do Not Disturb sign on the door. Then they drew a nice hot bath, with a razor blade on the edge of the tub.

It would be better this way. They knew what Kimchi would do.

■ ■ ■

For the next 24 hours, America remained unaware of the attack, and the petty partisan politics and inane reality TV shows continued unabated. Without the shock and awe, the fiery immediacy of previous operations, the deadliest crime in the history of the world had gone unnoticed.

Instead of feeling ill, many of the infected at first felt a slow but rising sense of euphoria and energy. This was from the PCP receptors in their brains beginning to activate. It would be a while before the rabies kicked in.

Unbeknownst to them, the infected were already spreading the Kimchi virus. The highly contagious nature of the flu / Ebola genetic ingredients allowed the virus to be contracted through basic human contact. As they handled money at coffee shops and grocery stores, gripped staircase handrails and flushed public toilets, coughed on elevators, bumped into people on the street, shook hands with strangers, kissed their children, and made love to their wives, they infected thousands more.

■ ■ ■

The 30 cities woke up to the sound of sirens. In some neighborhoods, the sirens were drowned out by the screams.

It was the Zombie Apocalypse, and it was not nearly as fun as so many had hoped. Rather than a slow, shambling horde of Walking Dead, the infected were very much alive. And fast. Shockingly fast.

The Outbreak began with individual attackers, blood dripping from their eyes and mouths, chasing down their neighbors with the speed of a Nigerian sprinter. They burst through glass windows and hollow core doors like they weren't even there, attacking anyone they found within.

And they didn't just grab and bite. They assaulted with a berserk fury, punching, clawing, kicking, and hammer-fisting their victims into the ground while spraying infected blood into the open wounds. The virus had jammed the pain receptors in their brains — a Zombie could break every bone in his hand pounding a woman's face into hamburger meat, then immediately set upon her children without delay.

Drivers rubbernecked at the madness before them, only to plow into oncoming traffic. The sounds of the car crashes drew the infected toward them, and they were ripped apart while trapped in the wreckage. . . .

The monotony of office life was pierced by the screams of drones succumbing to the effects of the virus and attacking their co-workers. For many, the last thing they saw was their blood spraying on the cubicle walls. . . .

Thousands were mauled to death in the first hours of the attack. Thousands more survived long enough to be sent to hospitals — where they infected the hospital staff. . . .

■   ■   ■

The police were instantly overwhelmed. They were equipped to handle only handfuls of violent crimes a day — not thousands of savage killers rampaging through dozens of neighborhoods simultaneously. And due to the shortsighted budget cuts brought on by the Great Recession, many police departments were already undermanned and undertrained.

On Day 1 of the Outbreak, half the police force was wiped out within the first few hours. Responding to vague and confusing calls categorized by dispatchers as "assaults in progress," the first officers had no idea what they were walking into. Rolling up to the scene, many were barely out of their patrol cars before men, women, and children, soaked in blood and screaming in rage, began charging them at full speed. . . .

The national average for police shootings is 1 in 3, meaning that only one in three bullets even hit the target. While this had proven adequate for dealing with conventional criminals in the past, the Zombies were so pumped full of rabies, adrenaline and PCP that they could only be stopped by a bullet striking their skulls or severing their spines. Attacked by surprise, and only trained to shoot paper targets instead of aggressive, moving humans, most officers were quickly mauled and infected.

Through a mixture of luck and superior training, some officers managed to put down their initial attackers and fight their way to the shotguns and carbines in their patrol cars. A stock Remington 870 holds 4 rounds of 00 buckshot. An AR15 holds 30 rounds of 5.56. A Glock 22 holds 15 .40 S&W hollow points, plus two spare magazines on the belt. This too proved woefully inadequate.

Ammunition ran low while the ranks of the infected continued to grow. Officers fought to the last bullet, then switched to hand-to-hand combat with Maglites and batons. Only the flashlights were capable of shattering the skull in a single blow — and in the process, many officers were infected by bits of brain and blood flying into their eyes. With 9/11 over a decade in the past, most officers did not have gas masks in their patrol bags.

☰   ☰   ☰

With entire cities trying to dial 911 simultaneously, the police emergency dispatch became little more than a perpetual busy signal. Without these incoming calls, local governments couldn't track the spread of the outbreak. In a panic, people attempted to reach their loved ones, who were simultaneously attempting to contact them. . . . By 1pm of Day One, it was virtually impossible to make or receive a phone call in any of the infected cities.

Although phones no longer functioned, the cameras on the phones did, and many survivors began uploading raw video of the attacks onto the Internet, which had proven more resilient than the phone network. Within hours, the shaky, grainy images of Zombie attacks began to play on every television station in the world.

The "News," having revamped itself as a source of entertainment rather than a source of information, only made matters worse. Instead of calmly disseminating the advice pouring in over the Internet from legions of anti-Zombie and Civil Defense experts, the News continued to play the videos of the attacks while commenting on "the horror." The headline beneath the videos, in blood red, all caps, proclaimed it THE ZOMBIE APOCALYPSE. Although the infection was only in 30 of America's 20,000 cities, the talking heads repeated over and over again that there were Zombie Outbreaks "everywhere."

Convinced that it was The End of the World, people acted accordingly. Since most Americans had equated preparing for emergencies with being a survivalist nut job or "doomsday prepper," only a small fraction of the population had even the most basic survival supplies.

Had every household maintained a month's worth of food and water, people could have barricaded themselves inside their homes and let the infected starve to death — and the Outbreak would have been stopped.

Instead, the only things in abundance were fear and ignorance. In cities that were still uninfected, there was an orgy of arson, looting, rape and murder. People attempted to storm the Oakland Costco, only to be cut down by the street gangs that had already seized it. . . . The Albany Walmart burned to the ground, with thousands trapped inside. . . .

In every city, town and village, grocery stores were stripped bare, gun shops looted, gas stations sucked dry. The roads were clogged with people desperate to flee, heading for rural outposts and the false perception of safety. Obese Americans, whose only daily exercise was walking between their computer and kitchen, were collapsing from heart attacks after running from attackers, real or imagined.

More than half of America's precious supplies of food, fuel, and ammunition were exhausted in 48 hours of pointless primal panic. . . .

Over the next few days, the situation only grew more desperate. The 30 cities were overrun by Zombies, and there were growing outbreaks across the country from the infected tourists who had returned home, and from those who had managed to escape the infected cities.

■   ■   ■

In an attempt to prevent the spread of "The Zombie Virus," as it was now called, all flights were grounded. Canada and Mexico sealed their borders with the US — the Canadians deployed the Mounties, while the Mexicans enlisted the help of the cartels that controlled the border towns. Hundreds of Miami-based yachts and sailboats were sunk by Cuba after attempting to land there, and other nearby island nations followed suit, forcing the survivors to remain adrift at sea, living off fish and rainwater.

Abroad, the Zombie outbreaks caused by infected foreign tourists were brutally suppressed by the indiscriminate firebombing of any area that reported an outbreak. These cauterized cities spared the rest of the world the nightmare that had befallen the US.

Unfortunately, America's NATO allies had allowed their military capabilities, especially their Navies, to atrophy after the Cold War, and they lacked the ability (to say nothing of the will) to deploy forces across the Atlantic to aid the United States in its darkest hour. Only Britain sent troops, deploying 300 SBS commandos to liaise with the US military and formulate a joint response.

As a goodwill gesture, the Russians sent a container ship of AK-47's and ammunition to the port of New York to help alleviate the city's critical lack of firearms. The Chinese agreed to write down some US debt, but that proved a worthless gesture, as the value of the post-Zombie dollar was already at Weimar levels of hyperinflation.

In short: America stood alone.

■ ■ ■

With law enforcement dead, infected, or overwhelmed by Zombies and panicked civilians, the military was called in to restore order. This proved easier said than done. It had taken over 140,000 combat troops to come even close to pacifying Iraq, a small country of 32 million — less than the population of California. There were over 314 million Americans spread across 3.79 million square miles, and between the Zombie Outbreak and the looting, America made Fallujah look like Disneyland.

Further complicating the troop deployment was the lack of leadership in Washington. The DC operative had managed to infect several dozen Congressmen and Senators, and many of the rest refused to expose themselves by attending public meetings in the chambers.

Those brave enough to show up became ensnarled in bureaucratic pissing matches over who was in control, what tactics to use against the infected, and, most pressing of all, where should the forces be sent? To the infected cities to liquidate the Zombies, or to the non-infected cities to restore order? Should the military forces be spread evenly across the country, or concentrated in major population centers? No one was sure, and the indecision and delay brought only more death and chaos.

The Pentagon, which boasts of preparing for every military contingency, had an inadequate plan for dealing with a Zombie Outbreak. Largely drafted to humor the former President, the plan was based on the assumption that the Zombies would be of the slow, "walking dead" variety of pop culture, and not the high-speed infected psychos unleashed by the Kimchi Virus.

Worse still, *Plan Z*, as it was called, assumed that the Outbreak would begin in a single location. Due to the supernatural / implausible prospect of reanimated corpses feasting on the living, it was assumed that this outbreak would be caused by a spill of "material" from Area 51 or the Dugway Proving Grounds.

Because these were classified military bases, Plan Z assumed that the Outbreak would be easily contained, and that word would not leak to the media.

In short, the Pentagon had not prepared for the coordinated, nation-wide Zombie attack and the media-fueled panic that ensued.

■   ■   ■

Perhaps even more than the Zombies, it was the corrosive effects of national hysteria that would hamper the military rescue effort.

American society was held together by an intricate web of interconnecting supply lines and digital communications. Using the Internet to coordinate shipments down to the hour, major business now relied on "Just in Time Deliveries," rather than the large warehouses of goods used by previous generations. When the delivery of goods broke down, the stores' limited stocks were bought or looted within the first few hours.

There were widespread blackouts caused by fires, employee attrition at the power plants, and most crippling of all, severe shortages of the coal, oil, and natural gas needed to keep the turbines spinning. Despite inventing nuclear power, only 20% of the country's electricity was produced by this reliable, low maintenance resource. Without electricity, all of the technological wizardry that allowed American society to function became a series of inert glass boxes, making it impossible to coordinate a nationwide resupply.

Meanwhile, America's roads and highways, the arteries of its economy, were clogged by car crashes, refugees, and marauding Zombie herds. Traffic backed up for tens of miles, and when people's gasoline ran out, the highways became parking lots. In the infected cities, they became graveyards.

The cumulative effect of this supply break-down was that, a week into the Zombie Outbreak, the world's largest exporter of food had begun to starve.

Without electricity and gasoline, with the roads closed and the railroads neglected, it was impossible to transport America's huge surpluses more than a few miles from the point of production. Because most homes' refrigerators held more condiments than food, it wouldn't be long before it wasn't just the Zombies eating people. . . .

■ ■ ■

Faced with a rapidly deteriorating situation, the military resorted to a two-pronged approach. Domestic US forces would create "safe zones" on the military bases scattered around the country to provide food, shelter and security to any refugees who could make it there. Meanwhile, all US forces stationed abroad would be recalled to fight the war at home. . . .

With law enforcement gone, and the military dispersed on isolated bases, the only force capable of stemming the rising tide of infected were civilian gun owners.

Due to the unique protections of the 2nd Amendment of the US Constitution, American citizens were the most heavily-armed force in the world, with over 270 million firearms dispersed in over 52 million homes. With this many men and women under arms, it should have been easy to put down the Zombies, whose population still numbered less than a million.

Alas, although a high percentage of Zombie movie fans were gun owners, the majority of armed Americans were grossly unprepared for the Zombie Apocalypse.

To begin with, the majority of Americans purchased their ammunition in small boxes at the shooting range, and only kept limited quantities of ammo at home. This ammunition quickly ran out.

To top it off, over half the civilian firearms were low-capacity hunting weapons. These bolt-action rifles and long-barreled shotguns were suitable for dispatching one or two Zombies from a distance, but too slow and unwieldy for dealing with Fast Zombies at close range, which is where most attacks occurred.

On the other end of the pendulum were Americans who had spent their money acquiring multiple semi-automatic rifles and handguns — but had spent almost no time training to use these tools in realistic combat scenarios. They survived the initial attacks through sheer firepower, only to have the dozens of shots from their "spray and pray" tactics attract hundreds of Zombies to their homes.

Once a nation of riflemen famed for their marksmanship in the field, the majority of modern shooters could only shoot accurately with a rifle, from a bench, against a stationary paper target on a bright sunny day. Forced to fight standing up against moving targets that were trying to kill them, shooters armed with these superbly accurate weapons missed, time and time again.

Few, if any, had trained for making head shots against moving targets, the skill required to survive a close-quarters Zombie attack. Lacking sufficient training and accuracy, they sprayed away their precious ammunition before being killed or infected, their empty guns still clutched in their warm dead hands.

America, with its vast supplies of food and firearms, had the infrastructure necessary to survive the Zombie Apocalypse. But when the government broke down, the civilian population lacked the training and preparation needed to step up and put down the Outbreak. . . . .

■   ■   ■

Meanwhile, back in North Korea, Kim Jong-un watched the news, laughing and laughing. With no antidote or cure for the Zombie Virus, it would only be a matter of time before Korea was one nation, and America was destroyed.

It had all been so easy.

NOTES

Introduction

The police and military will...: *NRA: The Untold Story of Gun Confiscation After Katrina. YouTube.* YouTube, 07 Mar. 2007. Web. 19 Apr. 2013.
http://www.youtube.com/watch?v=-taU9d26wT4

In reality, police statistics...: Aveni, Thomas J., MS. "Officer-Involved Shootings: What We Didn't Know Has Hurt Us." The Police Policy Studies Council, Aug. 2003. Web. 18 May 2013.
http://www.theppsc.org/Staff_Views/Aveni/OIS.pdf.

However, in my research...: Murray, Kenneth R. *Training at the Speed of Life, pg 2* Gotha (FL.): Armiger Publications, 2006. Print.

1. Know Your Enemy

It is said that if you know your enemies ...: "Sun Tzu Quotes." *Wikiquote.* Wikipedia, n.d. Web. 19 Apr. 2013.
http://en.wikiquote.org/wiki/Sun_Tzu.

When most of us think about Zombies...: "Definition of the Modern Zombie." *Zombie Research Society. Definition of the Modern Zombie Comments.* N.p., n.d. Web. 19 Apr. 2013. http://zombieresearchsociety.com/archives/9340.

And they cannot be killed with ...: Brooks, Max. *World War Z: An Oral History of the Zombie War.* Pg 97 New York: Crown, 2006. Print.

Some Zombie purists have ...: Zombie Research Society. "Definition of the Modern Zombie."

"Mix rabies with a flu virus ...": Than, Ker. ""Zombie Virus" Possible via Rabies-Flu Hybrid?" *National Geographic.* National Geographic Society, 27 Oct. 2010. Web. 18 May 2013. http://news.nationalgeographic.com/news/2010/10/1001027-rabies-influenza-zombie-virus-science/.

"What took me three weeks in...": Hylton, Wil S. "How Ready Are We For Bioterrorism?" *The New York Times.* The New York Times, 30 Oct. 2011. Web. 19 Apr. 2013. http://www.nytimes.com/2011/10/30/magazine/how-ready-are-we-for-bioterrorism.html?pagewanted=all.

In addition to speed and strength...: "Rage Virus." Zombiepedia, n.d. Web. 20 Apr. 2013. http://zombie.wikia.com/wiki/Rage_virus.

Even minor disasters...: Barnard, Anne. "Cleaning Up After Nature Plays a Trick." *The New York Times.* The New York Times, 31 Oct. 2011. Web. 19 Apr. 2013. http://www.nytimes.com/2011/10/31/nyregion/october-snowstorm-sows-havoc-on-northeastern-states.html?pagewanted=all.

The problem will only cascade...: "Just in Time (business)." *Wikipedia.* Wikimedia Foundation, 19 Apr. 2013. Web. 19 Apr. 2013. http://en.wikipedia.org/wiki/Just_in_time_%28business%29.

Meanwhile, 1 in 3 American households has a gun...: Tavernise, Sarah, and Gebeloff, Robert. "Share of Homes With Guns Shows 4-Decade Decline." *The New York Times.* The New York Times, 10 Mar. 2013. Web. 19 Apr. 2013. http://www.nytimes.com/2013/03/10/us/rate-of-gun-ownership-is-down-survey-shows.html?pagewanted=2.

By 2009, a survey by *La Nacion* ...: Aguirre, Fernando. *The Modern Survival Manual: Surviving the Economic Collapse: Based on Personal First Hand Experience of the 2001 Economic Collapse in Argentina.* N.l.: Fernando Aguirre, 2009. Print.

2. Choosing the Right Weapon

"After God, we should place...": Dennis, George T. "Maurice's Stratégikon." *Google Books.* Google, n.d. Web. 20 Apr. 2013.
http://books.google.com/books?id=ihDmbG-BhXsC.

ocular herpes is the leading cause...: "Herpes of the Eye." *Wikipedia.* Wikimedia Foundation, 04 Feb. 2013. Web. 20 Apr. 2013.
http://en.wikipedia.org/wiki/Herpes_of_the_eye

The average amount of semen...: Kennard, Jerry. "Facts About Ejaculation & Ejaculate." *About.com Men's Health.* About.com, 06 Aug. 2006. Web. 20 Apr. 2013.
http://menshealth.about.com/od/sexualhealth/a/ejaculation.htm.

The human body contains... : "How Much Blood Is in the Average Human Body? — Question #289065 - Homework Help." *Enotes.com.* Enotes.com, 09 Oct. 2011. Web. 20 Apr. 2013.
http://www.enotes.com/homework-help/how-much-blood-average-human-body-289065.

However, opponents point out...: Quinnett, Paul, PHD. "Suicide: The Forever Decision." *QPR Triage Training for Law Enforcement.* QPR Institute, 2011. Web. 20 Apr. 2013.
http://www.qprinstitute.com/Chapter15.htm.

By comparison, if a Walther p22...: Admin. "Ruger SR22 Pistol vs. Walther P22." *The Shooters Depot.* The Shooters Depot, 13 Jan. 2012. Web. 20 Apr. 2013.
http://www.theshootersdepot.com/ruger-sr22-pistol-vs-walther-p22/.

And considering that the average workday ...: Anthony, Jillian. "Americans Receive Less Vacation Time in 2012." *CNNMoney.* Cable News Network, 16 Nov. 2012. Web. 20 Apr. 2013.
http://money.cnn.com/2012/11/16/pf/americans-vacation-time/index.html.

Conversely, 39 of the 50 states ...: "Concealed Carry in the United States." *Wikipedia.* Wikimedia Foundation, 19 Apr. 2013. Web. 20 Apr. 2013.
http://en.wikipedia.org/wiki/Concealed_carry_in_the_United_States.

They will either attempt to confiscate ...: *NRA: The Untold Story of Gun Confiscation After Katrina. YouTube.* YouTube, 07 Mar. 2007. Web. 19 Apr. 2013.
http://www.youtube.com/watch?v=-taU9d26wT4.

4. Gun Myths

With the exception of hits to the brain …: Patrick, Urey W., Special Agent. "Handgun Wounding Factors and Effectiveness." Firearms Tactical, 14 July 1989. Web. 20 Apr. 2103. http://firearmstactical.com/pdf/fbi-hwfe.pdf.

According to FBI tests…: Ibid.

To put it more succinctly…: Ibid.

According to statistics compiled by …: Beaman V, Annest JL, Mercy JA, Kresnow Mj, Pollock DA. "Lethality of Firearm-Related Injuries in the United States Population." *National Center for Biotechnology Information.* U.S. National Library of Medicine, n.d. Web. 19 Apr. 2013. http://www.ncbi.nlm.nih.gov/pubmed/10692193.

For example, in the infamous 1986 …: "1986 FBI Miami Shootout." *Wikipedia.* Wikimedia Foundation, 19 Apr. 2013. Web. 19 Apr. 2013. http://en.wikipedia.org/wiki/1986_FBI_Miami_shootout.

In 2009, a 37-year-old Gangster Disciple ….: Remsberg, Charles. "Why One Cop Carries 145 Rounds of Ammo on the Job." PoliceOne.com, 17 Apr. 2013. Web. 23 Apr. 2013. http://www.policeone.com/police-heroes/articles/6199620-Why-one-cop-carries-145-rounds-of-ammo-on-the-job/.

5. Lessons From Law Enforcement

When thousands of red-panted…: Russ, Daniel. " 'Le Pantalon Rouge, C'est La France!' " *Civilian Military Intelligence Group.* N.p., 31 Aug. 2012. Web. 20 Apr. 2013. http://civilianmilitaryintelligencegroup.com/12521/le-pantalon-rouge-cest-la-france.

The easy-to-spot French ….: Ibid.

"You don't hurt 'em if you don't hit them.": "Famous Marine Quotes." 3rdmarines. net, n.d. Web. 20 Apr. 2013. http://www.3rdmarines.net/Marine_Quotes.htm.

Another similarity is that police shootings …: Aveni. "Officer-Involved Shootings: What We Didn't Know Has Hurt Us."

Not only were head and spine shots rare…: Dahl, Julia. "Empire State Building Shooting Sparks Questions about NYPD Shot Accuracy." *CBSNews.* CBS Interactive, 29 Aug. 2012. Web. 19 Apr. 2013. http://www.cbsnews.com/8301-504083_162-57502545-504083/empire-state-building-shooting-sparks-questions-about-nypd-shot-accuracy/.

While this is a bit of a generalization...: Baker, Al. "11 Years of Police Gunfire, in Painstaking Detail." *The New York Times.* The New York Times, 08 May 2008. Web. 20 Apr. 2013.
http://www.nytimes.com/2008/05/08/nyregion/08nypd.html?_r=0.

From 1990-2001, The Miami ...: Aveni. "Officer-Involved Shootings: What We Didn't Know Has Hurt Us."

Meanwhile, some departments ...: Murray. *Training at the Speed of Life.* pg 2

6. Understanding the 1:3 Hit Ratio

Alarmingly, "nearly 6 in 10 departments...: "Force Science News #168: New Survey Exposes 'Disturbing' Shortcomings in Firearms Training + New Document Helps Prevent Conflicts in Multi-agency OIS Probes."*Force Science News.* Force Science Institute Ltd., 14 July 2011. Web. 20 Apr. 2013.
http://www.forcescience.org/fsinews/2011/01/force-science-news-168-new-survey-exposes-%E2%80%9Cdisturbing%E2%80%9D-shortcomings-in-firearms-training-new-document-helps-prevent-conflicts-in-multi-agency-ois-probes/.

Once officers have "qualified"...: "Ibid.

The issue is a lack of realism ...: Ibid.

By relying exclusively on stationary ...: "Force Science News #44: Three Battles: Top Challenges for Deadly Force Trainers."*Force Science News RSS.* Force Science Institute Ltd., 12 May 2006. Web. 20 Apr. 2013.
http://www.forcescience.org/fsinews/2006/05/battles-top-challenges-for-deadly-force-trainers/.

Furthermore, most departments only have requalification ...: Rostker, Bernard Rostker D., Lawrence Hanser M. Hanser, William M. Hix, Carl Jensen, Andrew R. Morral, Greg Ridgeway, and Terry L. Schell. "Evaluation of the New York City Police Department Firearm Training and Firearm-Discharge Review Process." RAND Center on Quality Policing, 2008. Web. 18 May 2013.
http://www.nyc.gov/html/nypd/downloads/pdf/public_information/RAND_FirearmEvaluation.pdf.

For example, the LAPD shoots...: Baker. "11 Years of Police Gunfire, in Painstaking Detail."

When a person's life is in danger...: "Force Science News #103: Fear, Stress, and the Survival Personality." *Force Science News RSS.* Force Science Institute Ltd., 15 Aug. 2008. Web. 20 Apr. 2013.
http://www.forcescience.org/fsinews/2008/08/fear-stress-and-the-survival-personality/.

The front sight, lauded as …: Siddle, Bruce K. *Sharpening the Warrior's Edge,* pg 117. Millstadt, IL: PPCT Management Systems, 1995. Print.

Rather than standing still …: Ibid. pg 120

According to a study of officers …: "Force Science News #103: Fear, Stress, and the Survival Personality."

The largest single predictor…: "Force Science News #61: New Findings About Simulation Training and the Stress of Post-Shooting Interviews." *Force Science News RSS.* Force Science Institute Ltd., 15 Dec. 2006. Web. 20 Apr. 2013. http://www.forcescience.org/fsinews/2006/12/new-findings-about-simulation-training-and-the-stress-of-post-shooting-interviews/.

By repeatedly exposing officers …: Ibid.

Much like a person who is allergic ….: Ibid.

Instead of becoming panicked …: Ibid.

7. Training Equipment

"I've heard of one officer …: Martin, Dennis. "The Iron Hand of War." CQB Services, n.d. Web. 20 Apr. 2013. http://www.cqbservices.com/?page_id=11.

However, because the vast majority of attacks … "NYPD SOP 9 — Analysis of Police Combat." *The Virginia Coalition Police and Deputy Sheriffs.* Virginiacops.org, n.d. Web. 20 Apr. 2013. http://www.virginiacops.org/articles/shooting/combat.htm.

I was inspired to use stun guns by …. http://www.moderncombativesystems.net/index.htm

8. Firearms Safety

Bill Jordan, who accidently ….: "In the Line of Duty: Patrol Agent John A. Rector." San Diego County Law Enforcement Memorial Foundation, 2007. Web. 20 Apr. 2013. http://www.sdmemorial.org/index.php?/memorial/comments/76/.

Many "professionals" have shot themselves….: "Dumbass DEA Agent." YouTube, 20 Sept. 2006. Web. 20 Apr. 2013. http://www.youtube.com/watch?v=AmRN00KbCr8.

9. Marksmanship: From Basics to Bullseyes

"Fast is fine, but accuracy is everything.": "Wyatt Earp Quote." *BrainyQuote.* Xplore, n.d. Web. 20 Apr. 2013. http://www.brainyquote.com/quotes/quotes/w/wyattearp132804.html.

Your support hand should be angled ....: Stanford, Andy. *Surgical Speed Shooting: How to Achieve High-speed Marksmanship in a Gunfight.* Pg 28. Boulder, CO: Paladin, 2001. Print.

The thumb grip is essential ...: Ibid. Pg 28.

Think 60/40 support hand ...: Ibid. Pg 30.

"[Our natural] response, when suddenly attacked ...": Siddle. *Sharpening the Warrior's Edge.* Pg 53.

In Westmoreland's 1989 study....: Ibid. Pg 50.

At 7 yards and under....: Stanford. *Surgical Speed Shooting.* Pg 52.

"Both eyes have to be open ....": Siddle. *Sharpening the Warrior's Edge.* Pg 117

"The difference between a good marksman ....": Stanford. *Surgical Speed Shooting.* Pg 59.

Additionally, when in fear for your life...: Siddle. *Sharpening the Warrior's Edge.* Pg 115.

10. Point Shooting: The Emergency Marksmanship Skill

Research indicates ...: Aveni. "Officer-Involved Shootings: What We Didn't Know Has Hurt Us."

"The lens [of the eye] ...: Siddle. *Sharpening the Warrior's Edge.* Pg 117.

Hundreds of after-action reports ...: Aveni. "Officer-Involved Shootings: What We Didn't Know Has Hurt Us."

And rock solid confidence ...: Siddle. *Sharpening the Warrior's Edge.* Pg 15.

When engaged in an adrenaline ...: "Force Science News #61: New Findings About Simulation Training and the Stress of Post-Shooting Interviews."

However, when confronted by ...: Ibid.

This precise focus serves ...: "Sighting, Aiming, Pointing." Warrior Talk Forums, 20 Nov. 2003. Web. 20 Apr. 2013.
http://www.warriortalk.com/archive/index.php/t-547.html.

Tape a Zombie Qualification Target to the wall, 5'10" ...: "Average Height Around the World." Wikimedia Foundation, n.d. Web. 20 Apr. 2013.
https://en.wikipedia.org/wiki/Human_height#Average_height_around_the_world.

The reason for this is because a Fast Zombie can...: Hayes, Gila. "The Tueller Drill Revisited." Armed Citizens Legal Defense Network, Inc, May 2008. Web. 20 Apr. 2013.
http://armedcitizensnetwork.org/the-tueller-drill-revisited.

11. Move Your Ass

In the 1950s, a USAF Colonel named John Boyd ...: "OODA Loop." Wikimedia Foundation, 19 Apr. 2013. Web. 20 Apr. 2013.
http://en.wikipedia.org/wiki/OODA_loop.

Now the speed of Zombie brain processing ...: "Human Benchmark — Reaction Time Test." *Reaction Time Test.* Human Benchmark, 2012. Web. 20 Apr. 2013.
http://www.humanbenchmark.com/tests/reactiontime/.

12. The Backyard Moving Target

Systems like the Australian R-TMS ...: "MCSC Demonstrates Robotic Moving Target System." Marine Corps Systems Command, 16 June 2011. Web. 20 Apr. 2013.
http://www.marcorsyscom.marines.mil/News/PressReleaseArticleDisplay/tabid/8007/Article/65808/mcsc-demonstrates-robotic-moving-target-system.aspx.

13. Moving & Shooting

"To halt under fire is folly...": Tsouras, Peter. *Warrior's Words: Quotation Book — From Sesostris III to Schwarzkopf, 1871 B.C.–1991 A.D. Pg 79.* London: Arms & Armour P., 1992. Print.

14. Mental Practice

"Mental practice benefits performance ...": Siddle. *Sharpening the Warrior's Edge.* Pg 102.

What is so important about this ...: Ibid. Pg 103.

The more past experience ...: Siddle. *Sharpening the Warrior's Edge.* Pg 103.

15. Force on Force Training

"In military combat there is …": Tsouras. *Warrior's Words.* Pg 83.

Studies have shown that the amount of Survival Stress …: Siddle. *Sharpening the Warrior's Edge.* Pg 92.

In order for a shooter to be able to access …: Murray. *Training at the Speed of Life.* Pg 28.

Luckily, "stress is a matter of perception…": Siddle. *Sharpening the Warrior's Edge.* Pg 107.

However, these shooters have not experienced …: "Force Science News #103: Fear, Stress, and the Survival Personality."

To give you a sense of just how …: Aveni. "Officer-Involved Shootings: What We Didn't Know Has Hurt Us."

Much like being great at playing pool …: Siddle. *Sharpening the Warrior's Edge.* Pg 40.

Data indicates that police departments …: Murray. *Training at the Speed of Life.* Pg 25.

"Sometimes we see SWAT teams …": Ibid. Pg 3.

Force on Force (FoF) is known as …: Ibid. Pg 2.

In one Force Science study…: "Force Science News #61: New Findings About Simulation Training and the Stress of Post-Shooting Interviews."

When the data was analyzed…: Ibid.

The study also recommended…: "Force Science News #168: New Survey Exposes 'disturbing' Shortcomings in Firearms Training + New Document Helps Prevent Conflicts in Multi-agency OIS Probes."

This enhanced confidence minimizes …: Siddle. *Sharpening the Warrior's Edge.* Pg 15.

As the ancient Roman military historian …: Tsouras. *Warrior's Words.* Pg 50.

16. Force on Force for Zombies

In my research, I came across …: Hayes. "The Tueller Drill Revisited."

The Tueller drill gave …: Ibid.

17. Force on Force Safety Rules

While this sounds obvious…: Murray. *Training at the Speed of Life.* Pg 136.

Dozens of people have been killed …: Ibid. Pg 10.

19. Analyzing Your Results

"What is the good of experience…: Tsouras. *Warrior's Words.* Pg 357.

23. Long Range Pistol Shooting

"A pistol is a weapon of astonishing …": Kirchner, Paul. *More of the Deadliest Men Who Ever Lived.* Pg 381. Boulder: Paladin, 2009. Print.

In the Vietnam War, Navy SEAL R.J Thomas …: Ibid. Pg 380.

"In order to get into our rice paddy…": Ibid. Pg 380.

Using a 1911 pistol, with …: Ibid. Pg 380.

R.J. held them off long …: Ibid. Pg 383.

While this is an incredible situation…: Ibid. Pg 381.

Speer gold dot ballistics table…: "Speer Ammo — Ballistics Tables." Speer Ammo, 2013. Web. 20 Apr. 2013. http://www.speer-ammo.com/ballistics/ammo.aspx.

24. The Fast Draw

You cannot claim to be a pistol shot …: Martin. "The Iron Hand of War."

In the 1960s, Bill Jordan …: Jordan, William H. *No Second Place Winner.* Pg 83. Concord, NH. Police Bookshelf, 1965. Print.

SOURCES

"1986 FBI Miami Shootout." *Wikipedia.* Wikimedia Foundation, 19 Apr. 2013. Web. 19 Apr. 2013. http://en.wikipedia.org/wiki/1986_FBI_Miami_shootout.

28 Days Later. Dir. Danny Boyle. Perf. Alex Palmer, Cillian Murphy, Naomie Harris. 20th Century Fox, 2003. DVD.

Admin. "Ruger SR22 Pistol vs. Walther P22." *The Shooters Depot.* The Shooters Depot, 13 Jan. 2012. Web. 20 Apr. 2013. http://www.theshootersdepot.com/ruger-sr22-pistol-vs-walther-p22/.

Aguirre, Fernando. *The Modern Survival Manual: Surviving the Economic Collapse: Based on Personal First Hand Experience of the 2001 Economic Collapse in Argentina.* N.l.: Fernando Aguirre, 2009. Print.

Anthony, Jillian. "Americans Receive Less Vacation Time in 2012." *CNNMoney.* Cable News Network, 16 Nov. 2012. Web. 20 Apr. 2013. http://money.cnn.com/2012/11/16/pf/americans-vacation-time/index.html.

Applegate, Rex, and Michael D. Janich. *Bullseyes Don't Shoot Back: The Complete Textbook of Point Shooting for Close Quarters Combat.* Boulder, CO: Paladin, 1998. Print.

Aveni, Thomas J., MS. "Officer-Involved Shootings: What We Didn't Know Has Hurt Us." The Police Policy Studies Council, Aug. 2003. Web. 18 May 2013. http://www.theppsc.org/Staff_Views/Aveni/OIS.pdf.

"Average Height Around the World." Wikimedia Foundation, n.d. Web. 20 Apr. 2013. https://en.wikipedia.org/wiki/Human_height#Average_height_around_the_world.

Ayoob, Massad F. *The Truth About Self-Protection.* New York: Bantam, 1983. Print.

Ayoob, Massad. *The Gun Digest Book of Combat Handgunnery 6th Edition.* Iola: Gun Digest, 2007. Print.

Baker, Al. "11 Years of Police Gunfire, in Painstaking Detail." *The New York Times.* The New York Times. 08 May 2008. Web. 20 Apr. 2013. http://www.nytimes.com/2008/05/08/nyregion/08nypd.html?_r=0.

Barnard, Anne and Maslin, Sarah. "Cleaning Up After Nature Plays a Trick." *The New York Times.* The New York Times, 31 Oct. 2011. Web. 19 Apr. 2013. http://www.nytimes.com/2011/10/31/nyregion/october-snowstorm-sows-havoc-on-northeastern-states.html?pagewanted=all.

Beaman V, Annest JL, Mercy JA, Kresnow Mj, Pollock DA. "Lethality of Firearm-Related Injuries in the United States Population." *National Center for Biotechnology Information.* U.S. National Library of Medicine, n.d. Web. 19 Apr. 2013. http://www.ncbi.nlm.nih.gov/pubmed/10692193.

"Bird Flu - "The Single Biggest Threat to Man's Continued Dominance on the Planet Is a Virus." Bird Flu Book, 2008. Web. 16 June 2013.

Bourne, J. L. *Day by Day Armageddon.* New York: Pocket, 2009. Print.

Bourne, J. L. *Day by Day Armageddon: Shattered Hourglass.* New York: Gallery, 2012. Print.

Brooks, Max. *World War Z: An Oral History of the Zombie War.* New York: Crown, 2006. Print.

Brooks, Max. *The Zombie Survival Guide: Complete Protection From the Living Dead.* New York: Three Rivers, 2003. Print.

Catalano, Shannan M., Ph.D. "Victimization During Household Burglary." Bureau of Justice Statistics (BJS), 30 Sept. 2010. Web. 20 Apr. 2013. http://bjs.gov/index.cfm?ty=pbdetail.

"Concealed Carry in the United States." *Wikipedia.* Wikimedia Foundation, 19 Apr. 2013. Web. 20 Apr. 2013. http://en.wikipedia.org/wiki/Concealed_carry_in_the_United_States.

Dahl, Julia. "Empire State Building Shooting Sparks Questions About NYPD Shot Accuracy." *CBSNews.* CBS Interactive, 29 Aug. 2012. Web. 19 Apr. 2013. http://www.cbsnews.com/8301-504083_162-57502545-504083/empire-state-building-shooting-sparks-questions-about-nypd-shot-accuracy/.

Dawn of the Dead. Dir. Zach Snyder and James Gunn. By George A. Romero. Perf. Sarah Polley, Ving Rhames, Jake Webber. Universal Studios, 2004. Film.

"Definition of the Modern Zombie." *Zombie Research Society. Definition of the Modern Zombie Comments.* N.p., n.d. Web. 19 Apr. 2013. http://zombieresearchsociety.com/archives/9340.

Dennis, George T. "Maurice's Stratégikon." *Google Books.* Google, n.d. Web. 20 Apr. 2013. http://books.google.com/books?id=ihDmbG-BhXsC.

"Dumbass DEA Agent." YouTube, 20 Sept. 2006. Web. 20 Apr. 2013. http://www.youtube.com/watch?v=AmRN00KbCr8.

Eligon, John. "One Bullet Can Kill, but Sometimes 20 Don't, Survivors Show." *The New York Times.* The New York Times, 03 Apr. 2008. Web. 19 Apr. 2013. http://www.nytimes.com/2008/04/03/nyregion/03shot.html?_r=3&.

"Factoring Bone Into the Equation [Archive] - M4Carbine.net Forums." *Factoring Bone into the Equation [Archive] - M4Carbine.net Forums.* M4carbine.net, 04 May 2009. Web. 20 Apr. 2013. http://www.m4carbine.net/archive/index.php/t-30556.html.

"Famous Marine Quotes." 3rdmarines.net, n.d. Web. 20 Apr. 2013. http://www.3rdmarines.net/Marine_Quotes.htm.

"Force Science News #17: Is the 21-Foot Rule Still Valid When Dealing With an Edged Weapon? Part 1." *Force Science News RSS.* Force Science Institute Ltd., 22 Apr. 2005. Web. 20 Apr. 2013. http://www.forcescience.org/fsinews/2005/04/remember-to-register-for-the-upcoming-force-science-seminar/.

"Force Science News #44: Three Battles: Top Challenges for Deadly Force Trainers." *Force Science News RSS.* Force Science Institute Ltd., 12 May 2006. Web. 20 Apr. 2013. http://www.forcescience.org/fsinews/2006/05/battles-top-challenges-for-deadly-force-trainers/.

"Force Science News #61: New Findings About Simulation Training and the Stress of Post-Shooting Interviews." *Force Science News RSS.* Force Science Institute Ltd., 15 Dec. 2006. Web. 20 Apr. 2013. http://www.forcescience.org/fsinews/2006/12/new-findings-about-simulation-training-and-the-stress-of-post-shooting-interviews/.

"Force Science News #103: Fear, Stress, and the Survival Personality." *Force Science News RSS.* Force Science Institute Ltd., 15 Aug. 2008. Web. 20 Apr. 2013. http://www.forcescience.org/fsinews/2008/08/fear-stress-and-the-survival-personality/.

"Force Science News #168: New Survey Exposes 'Disturbing' Shortcomings in Firearms Training + New Document Helps Prevent Conflicts in Multi-agency OIS Probes." *Force Science News.* Force Science Institute Ltd., 14 July 2011. Web. 20 Apr. 2013. http://www.forcescience.org/fsinews/2011/01/force-science-news-168-new-sur-vey-exposes-%E2%80%9Cdisturbing%E2%80%9D-shortcomings-in-firearms-training-new-document-helps-prevent-conflicts-in-multi-agency-ois-probes/.

Grey, James. "Urban Survival: 5 Things People Say They Can or Would Do in a Survival Situation – and Why They Won't Based on Recent 3rd World Urban Survival Events." *Death Valley Magazine,* 10 May 2013. Web. 12 May 2013. http://www.deathvalleymag.com/2013/05/10/urban-survival-the-5-things/.

"Gunshot Wound Head Trauma." *American Association of Neurological Surgeons.* AANS, Mar. 2011. Web. 20 Apr. 2013. http://www.aans.org/Patient%20Information/Conditions%20and%20 Treatments/Gunshot%20Wound%20Head%20Trauma.aspx.

Hayes, Gila. "The Tueller Drill Revisited." Armed Citizens Legal Defense Network, Inc, May 2008. Web. 20 Apr. 2013. http://armedcitizensnetwork.org/the-tueller-drill-revisited.

"Herpes of the Eye." *Wikipedia.* Wikimedia Foundation, 04 Feb. 2013. Web. 20 Apr. 2013. http://en.wikipedia.org/wiki/Herpes_of_the_eye.

"How Much Blood is in the Average Human Body? - Question #289065 — Homework Help." *Enotes.com.* Enotes.com, 09 Oct. 2011. Web. 20 Apr. 2013. http://www.enotes.com/homework-help/how-much-blood-average-human-body-289065.

"How Much Blood Loss Is Fatal for a Human?" *Yahoo! Answers.* Yahoo!, 2008. Web. 19 May 2013. http://answers.yahoo.com/question/index?qid=20080122133153AAC8D4M.

"How Thick Is the Human Skull?" *WikiAnswers.* Wikimedia Foundation, n.d. Web. 20 Apr. 2013. http://wiki.answers.com/Q/How_thick_is_the_human_skull.

"Human Benchmark — Reaction Time Test." *Reaction Time Test.* Human Benchmark, 2012. Web. 20 Apr. 2013. http://www.humanbenchmark.com/tests/reactiontime/.

Hylton, Wil S. "How Ready Are We for Bioterrorism." *The New York Times.* The New York Times, 30 Oct. 2011. Web. 19 Apr. 2013. http://www.nytimes.com/2011/10/30/magazine/how-ready-are-we-for-bioterrorism. html?pagewanted=all.

"In the Line of Duty: Patrol Agent John A. Rector." San Diego County Law Enforcement Memorial Foundation, 2007. Web. 20 Apr. 2013. http://www.sdmemorial.org/index.php?/memorial/comments/76/.

Jordan, William H. *No Second Place Winner.* Concord: Police Bookshelf, 1965. Print.

"Just in Time (business)." *Wikipedia.* Wikimedia Foundation, 19 Apr. 2013. Web. 19 Apr. 2013. http://en.wikipedia.org/wiki/Just_in_time_%28business%29.

Kennard, Jerry. "Facts About Ejaculation & Ejaculate." *About.com Men's Health.* About.com, 06 Aug. 2006. Web. 20 Apr. 2013. http://menshealth.about.com/od/sexualhealth/a/ejaculation.htm.

Kirchner, Paul. *More of the Deadliest Men Who Ever Lived.* Boulder: Paladin, 2009. Print.

Kirkman, Robert, Charles Adlard, Tony Moore, and Cliff Rathburn. *The Walking Dead: Compendium One.* Berkeley, CA: Image Comics, 2009. Print.

Kirkman, Robert, and Charles Adlard. *The Walking Dead: Compendium Two.* Berkeley, CA: Image Comics, 2012. Print.

Left 4 Dead. Bellevue, WA: Valve Corp., 2008. Computer software.

Martin, Dennis. "The Iron Hand of War." CQB Services, n.d. Web. 20 Apr. 2013. http://www.cqbservices.com/?page_id=11.

"Max Brooks on the World War Z Movie." *YouTube.* YouTube, 03 Apr. 2013. Web. 12 May 2013. http://www.youtube.com/watch?feature=player_embedded.

McLaughlin, Michael. "Felon Voting Laws Disenfranchise 5.85 Million Americans With Criminal Records: The Sentencing Project." *The Huffington Post.* TheHuffingtonPost.com, 12 July 2012. Web. 20 Apr. 2013. http://www.huffingtonpost.com/2012/07/12/felon-voting-laws-disenfranchise-sentencing-project_n_1665860.html.

"MCSC Demonstrates Robotic Moving Target System." Marine Corps Systems Command, 16 June 2011. Web. 20 Apr. 2013. http://www.marcorsyscom.marines.mil/News/PressReleaseArticleDisplay/tabid/8007/Article/65808/mcsc-demonstrates-robotic-moving-target-system.aspx.

Mogk, Matt. *Everything You Ever Wanted to Know About Zombies.* New York: Gallery, 2011. Print.

Mogk, Matt. *Zombie Research Society.* N.p., 2007. Web. 16 June 2013. http://zombieresearchsociety.com/.

Murray, Kenneth R. *Training at the Speed of Life.* Gotha, FL. Armiger Publications, 2006. Print.

Night of the Living Dead. Dir. George A. Romero. By George A. Romero and John Russo. Perf. Duane Jones, Judith O'Dea, Marilyn Eastman, and Karl Hardman. Continental Distributing, Inc., 1968. DVD.

"North Hollywood Shootout." *Wikipedia.* Wikimedia Foundation, 19 Apr. 2013. Web. 19 Apr. 2013. http://en.wikipedia.org/wiki/North_Hollywood_shootout.

NRA: The Untold Story of Gun Confiscation After Katrina. YouTube. YouTube, 07 Mar. 2007. Web. 19 Apr. 2013. http://www.youtube.com/watch?v=-taU9d26wT4.

"NYPD SOP 9 — Analysis of Police Combat." *The Virginia Coalition Police and Deputy Sheriffs.* Virginiacops.org, n.d. Web. 20 Apr. 2013. http://www.virginiacops.org/articles/shooting/combat.htm.

Ogunbadejo,Gloria. "Mob Mentality, Violence and Aggression." *The Punch Nigeria's Most Widely Read Newspaper.* Punch, 26 Aug. 2012. Web. 19 Apr. 2013. http://www.punchng.com/columnists/mental-health-matters/mob-mentality-violence-and-aggression/.

"OODA loop." Wikimedia Foundation, 19 Apr. 2013. Web. 20 Apr. 2013. http://en.wikipedia.org/wiki/OODA_loop.

Patrick, Urey W., Special Agent. "Handgun Wounding Factors and Effectiveness." Firearms Tactical, 14 July 1989. Web. 20 Apr. 2103. http://firearmstactical.com/pdf/fbi-hwfe.pdf.

"Pelvic Shot — Is It Worth Considering?" *DefensiveCarry Concealed Carry Forum RSS.* DeffensiveCarry, 01 Sept. 2007. Web. 20 Apr. 2013. http://www.defensivecarry.com/forum/defensive-carry-tactical-training/31850-pelvic-shot-worth-considering.html.

Quinnett, Paul, PHD. "Suicide: The Forever Decision." *QPR Triage Training for Law Enforcement.* QPR Institute, 2011. Web. 20 Apr. 2013. http://www.qprinstitute.com/Chapter15.htm.

"Rage Virus." Zombiepedia, n.d. Web. 20 Apr. 2013. http://zombie.wikia.com/wiki/Rage_virus.

"Red Coat (British Army)." *Wikipedia.* Wikimedia Foundation, 05 Sept. 2013. Web. 19 May 2013. http://en.wikipedia.org/wiki/Red_coat_%28British_army%29.

Remsberg, Charles. "Why One Cop Carries 145 Rounds of Ammo on the Job." PoliceOne.com, 17 Apr. 2013. Web. 23 Apr. 2013. http://www.policeone.com/police-heroes/articles/6199620-Why-one-cop-carries-145-rounds-of-ammo-on-the-job/.

Resident Evil. Dir. Paul Anderson. Perf. Milla Jovovich,. Sony Pictures, 2002. Film.

Rostker, Bernard Rostker D., Lawrence Hanser M. Hanser, William M. Hix, Carl Jensen, Andrew R. Morral, Greg Ridgeway, and Terry L. Schell. "Evaluation of the New York City Police Department Firearm Training and Firearm-Discharge Review Process." RAND Center on Quality Policing, 2008. Web. 18 May 2013. http://www.nyc.gov/html/nypd/downloads/pdf/public_information/RAND_FirearmEvaluation.pdf.

Russ, Daniel. " 'Le Pantalon Rouge, C'est La France!'" *Civilian Military Intelligence Group.* N.p., 31 Aug. 2012. Web. 20 Apr. 2013. http://civilianmilitaryintelligencegroup.com/12521/le-pantalon-rouge-cest-la-france.

Siddle, Bruce K. *Sharpening the Warrior's Edge.* Millstadt, IL: PPCT Management Systems, 1995. Print.

"Sighting, Aiming, Pointing." Warrior Talk Forums, 20 Nov. 2003. Web. 20 Apr. 2013. http://www.warriortalk.com/archive/index.php/t-547.html.

"Speer Ammo — Ballistics Tables." Speer Ammo, 2013. Web. 20 Apr. 2013.
http://www.speer-ammo.com/ballistics/ammo.aspx.

Stanford, Andy. *Surgical Speed Shooting: How to Achieve High-speed Marksmanship in a Gunfight.* Boulder, CO: Paladin, 2001. Print.

"Sun Tzu Quotes." — *Wikiquote.* Wikipedia, n.d. Web. 19 Apr. 2013.
http://en.wikiquote.org/wiki/Sun_Tzu.

Tavernise, Sabrina and Gebeloff, Robert. "Share of Homes With Guns Shows 4-Decade Decline." *The New York Times.* The New York Times, 10 Mar. 2013. Web. 19 Apr. 2013.
http://www.nytimes.com/2013/03/10/us/rate-of-gun-ownership-is-down-survey-shows.html?pagewanted=1.

Taylor, Chris. "Get Your Organization to Think and Act Like a Fighter Pilot." VentureBeat, 06 Feb. 2013. Web. 20 Apr. 2013.
http://venturebeat.com/2013/02/06/helping-your-organization-move-like-a-fighter-pilot/.

Than, Ker. " 'Zombie Virus' Possible Via Rabies-Flu Hybrid?" *National Geographic.* National Geographic Society, 27 Oct. 2010. Web. 18 May 2013.
http://news.nationalgeographic.com/news/2010/10/1001027-rabies-influenza-zombie-virus-science/.

Tsouras, Peter. *Warrior's Words: Quotation Book m— From Sesostris III to Schwarzkopf, 1871 B.C.–1991 A.D.* London: Arms & Armour P., 1992. Print.

"The Walking Dead." *The Walking Dead.* Created by Frank Darabont. Perf. Andrew Lincoln, Steven Yeun, Sarah Wayne Callies. AMC. N.d. Television.

"Wyatt Earp Quote." *BrainyQuote.* Xplore, n.d. Web. 20 Apr. 2013.
http://www.brainyquote.com/quotes/quotes/w/wyattearp132804.html.

"Zombie Squad • Index Page." Zombie Squad, 2003. Web. 16 June 2013.
http://zombiehunters.org/forum/.

ACKNOWLEDGMENTS

ALTHOUGH WE THINK of writing as this solitary task, where the lone hero vanquishes one blank page after the next, that's simply not the case. Without the love and support of my friends and family, I never would have been able to complete *The Zombie Shooting Guide.*

My two best friends have had my back since middle school. Sam Goldenberg, your truly excellent photographs really make the book. I don't tell you this enough man, but you've got real talent. Thank you for all your hard work and for putting up with me.

And Brandon Finn, thanks for designing the Zombie Qualification Target, your on-point advice, and for running around in that claustrophobic Zombie mask. Most important, it was your suggestion that I live abroad after graduation that led me to become a writer. If not for you, I'd probably be living in Orange County and working at the mall.

Xing Chen, you've been a phenomenal friend and editor. You were the first person to read the book, and your encouraging words and detailed critiques were just what I needed to keep going. Congrats on the PhD, Dr. Amiga!

Thanks — and apologies — to my other training partners and guinea pigs whose photos appear here. Rex Crossen, you were the first one brave enough to run the Fast Zombie Drill. Sorry for shooting you in the face, I know that sucked. Kelsey Dyer, you were a terrific moving target. And Mark Wildman, those Robbery Drills you did ended up being some of the best photos in the book.

Laurie Young, book designer and magician: You took my raw Word document, and transformed the jumble of text and photos into a polished book that I'm proud of. Thank you for all your hard work. I'm very grateful.

It's not everyday that you get a Pulitzer Prize-winning photojournalist willing to optimize 200 Zombie photos for print. Thank you for coming to the rescue, Kim Komenich. The pictures came out great.

Alex Saskalidis of Greece, aka Mr. Brainstorm, your book cover, logo and t-shirt designs were awesome. I really appreciate your tireless enthusiasm and patience with all those revisions. . . . I found Alex when I posted the project on 99designs, a crowdsourcing site. Within a few days, nearly 50 graphic artists from around the world submitted their book cover ideas. It's amazing, the talent out there. My thanks to all the designers, especially to the other Finalists for their creativity and hard work: Andrea Bianchi of Italy, Łukasz Pomotowski of Poland, nalll of Serbia, Leslie K. of Hungary, and Betlehem Fekade of the UK.

Speaking of crowdsourcing, *The Zombie Shooting Guide* could not have gotten off the ground without financial support. Kickstarter is an awesome way to fund creative projects, and I am grateful it exists. I must also give a shout-out to Zoltan Sandors and Morgan Peterson, who so deftly taped and edited my Kickstarter video.

During the 31 nerve-wracking days of my Kickstarter campaign, 116 people, including strangers, gave up some of their hard-earned cash to make the book a reality. I want to thank all the backers for their generosity and for their patience while I finished the book, especially my biggest and most enthusiastic supporters: my grandparents, Helen and Nicolaos Costantinou; my mom, Marianne Costantinou; Sam's parents, Kathi Roisen and Howard Goldenberg; Brandon and his folks, Richard and Judith Finn; my extended family: Aunt Theodosia Katsouris, my uncles Matt Greenman and John Greenman, and my cousins Christos Toufexis, Jessica Barmack, James and Alexa Dedousis, Peter and Maria Dedousis, and Martin and Mariana Dulin.

Also, my friends who backed my project: Zach Skigen, Matt Pavlik, Xing, Marston Litvinsky, Nicholas Karas, Joe Buty, Jason Phillips, Judd Lyon, Matt Fiddler, Steven Campodonico, Brian Renslow, Garreth Hawkins, Major Marcell, Matt Matier, Elliott Block, Charles Rodriguez, Dean Guzman, Seth Gutierrez, Jonathan Biddle, Feras Maidaa, and Alex Schlenk. Thank you for your support. I won't forget it.

And my mom's friends and newspaper colleagues who gave generously include: Linda Robertson, Irene Lacher, Michael Schefer, Stu Bykofsky, Alfred Lubrano, Lois Murphy and Benjamin Eisner, Yves Colon and Melissa Moonves, Dylan Landis, Diana Yonkouski, Richard Paoli, Terry Robertson, Lynn Ludlow and Margo Freistadt, and Benjamin Gattegno and Lora Reynolds. Last but not least: Liz Schaeffer, my babysitter and training partner from my Ninja Turtles and Spiderman days, who was my first official backer.

Of course, without Zombies, there would be no *The Zombie Shooting Guide*. I am grateful to all the writers, directors, actors and artists whose work has inspired me over the years.

I also want to thank the great forums and websites that taught me so much, especially Zombie Squad and the Zombie Research Society. Also, a big thanks to the members of the Usual Suspect Network (USN) and the Spyderco forums: Your support and input on the cover design really meant a lot to me.

And to Ray at the COPYHUB print shop in Sherman Oaks, CA, where every draft of *The ZSG* cost me $10, instead of the $40 charged by the guys up the street: Your prices and friendly service made the revisions a little less painful.

In the end, though, it's all about family. I want to thank mine for being there for me.

Dad, thank you for vetting the final draft, your wise counsel and last-minute fixes. You made sure the book was safe and sound, for my readers and for me.

Mom, I really could not have done *The ZSG* without you. You hounded everyone you ever met for my Kickstarter fundraiser, edited the book from massive revisions to the final buff & polish, nitpicked the cover entries, and shepherded its publication. A Zombie doesn't stand a chance with you by my side.

Finally, I dedicate the book to my grandparents. *Yiayia and Pappou,* I am so grateful for your unconditional love and endless sacrifices for me. *Sas agapo toso poli.*

ABOUT

AUTHOR

Mark Greenman is an NRA Certified Pistol Instructor, gear nerd and Zombie fan. He is a graduate of the University of California at Santa Barbara, where he studied military history, and now lives in Los Angeles.

Photo: Skyrider Photography

PHOTOGRAPHER

Sam Goldenberg began shooting at 11 — first with a potato cannon, then a competition trap shotgun, and finally a camera. He is a graduate of the S.I. Newhouse School of Public Communications at Syracuse University and a certified bicycle mechanic. He lives in the San Francisco Bay Area, and hopes the Zombies don't like hills.

ZOMBIE QUALIFICATION TARGET

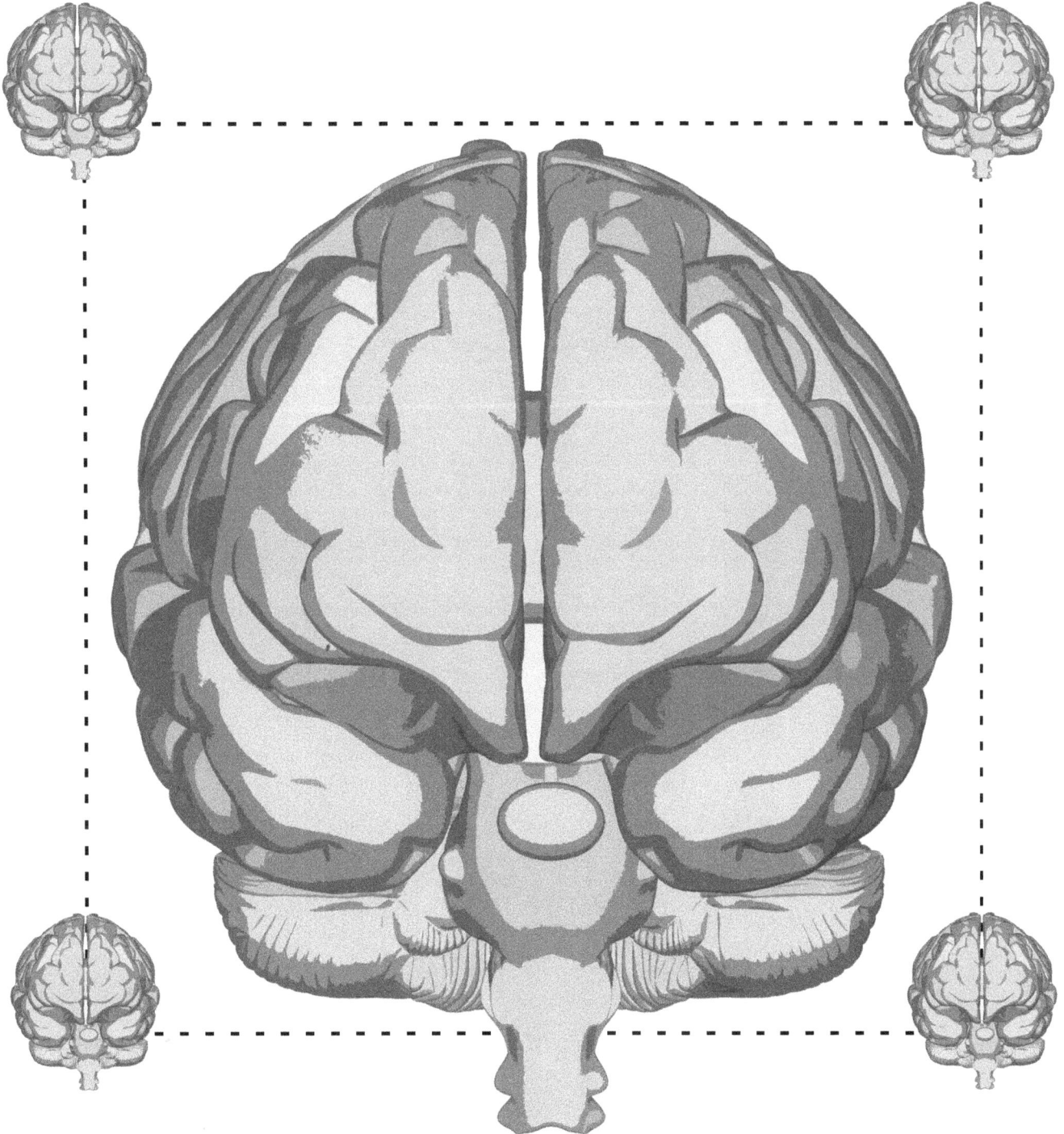

The Zombie Shooting Guide
© 2013 by Mark Greenman
Design: Brandon Finn

ZOMBIE QUALIFICATION TARGET

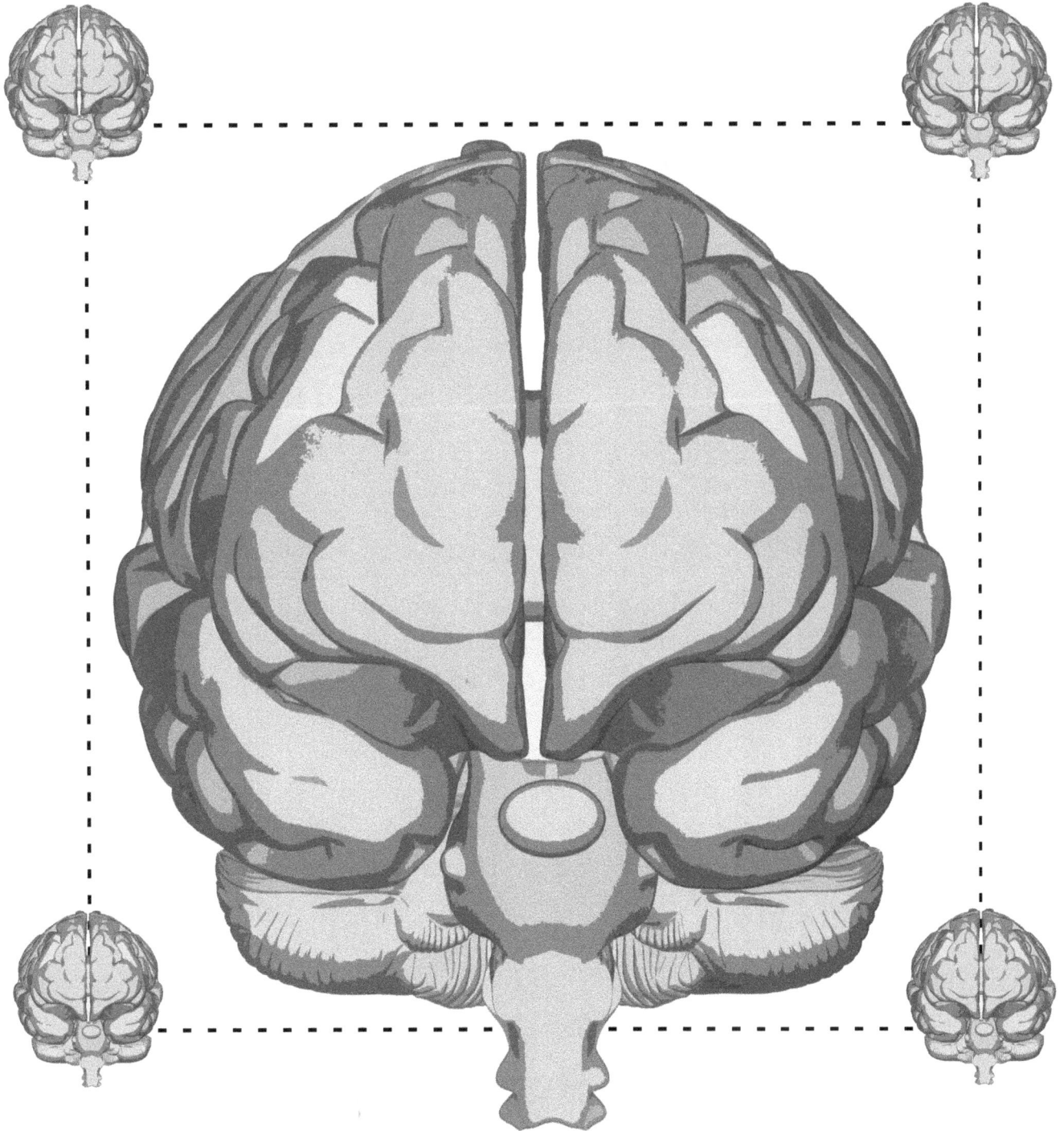

ZOMBIE QUALIFICATION TARGET

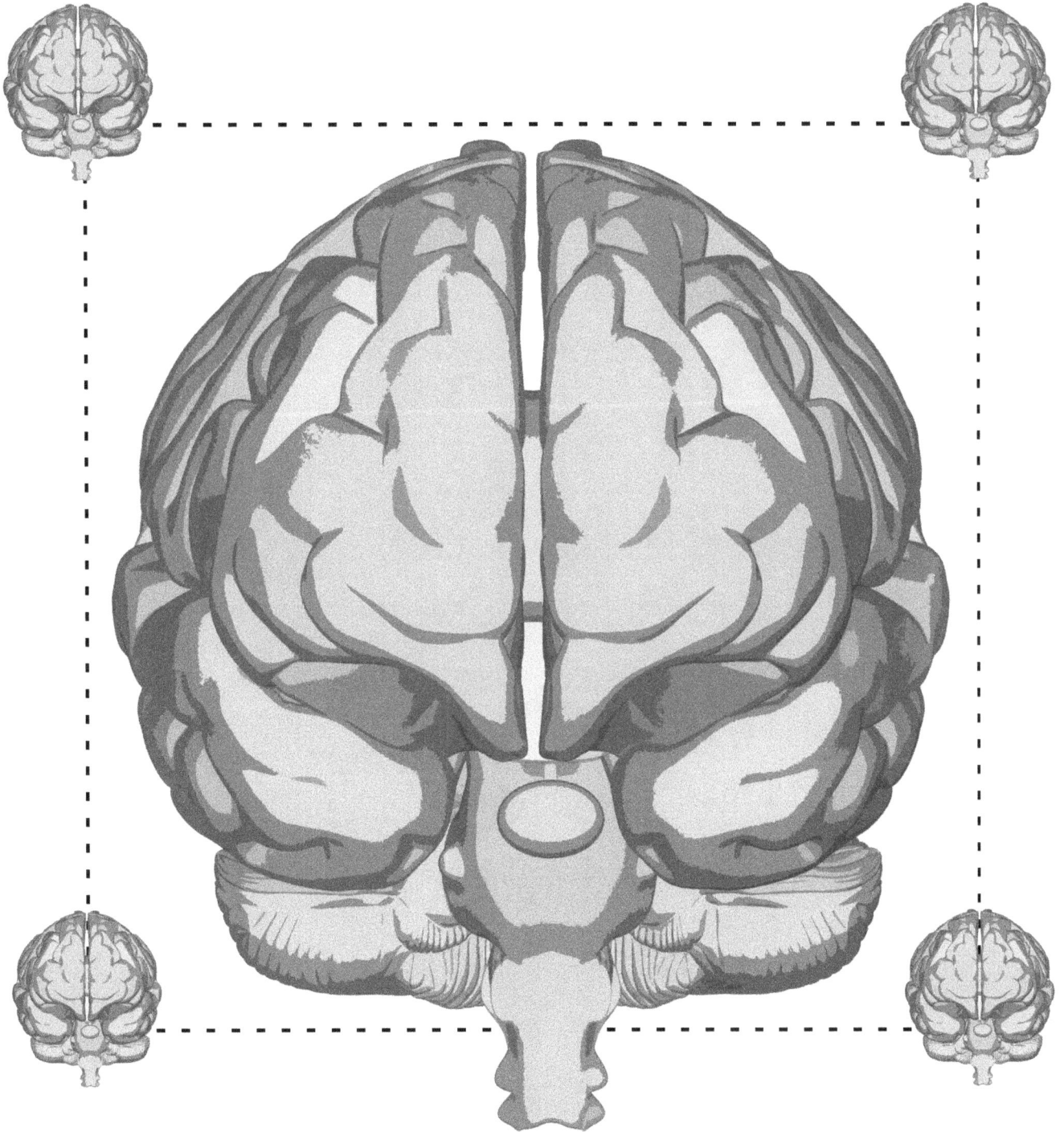

ZOMBIE QUALIFICATION TARGET

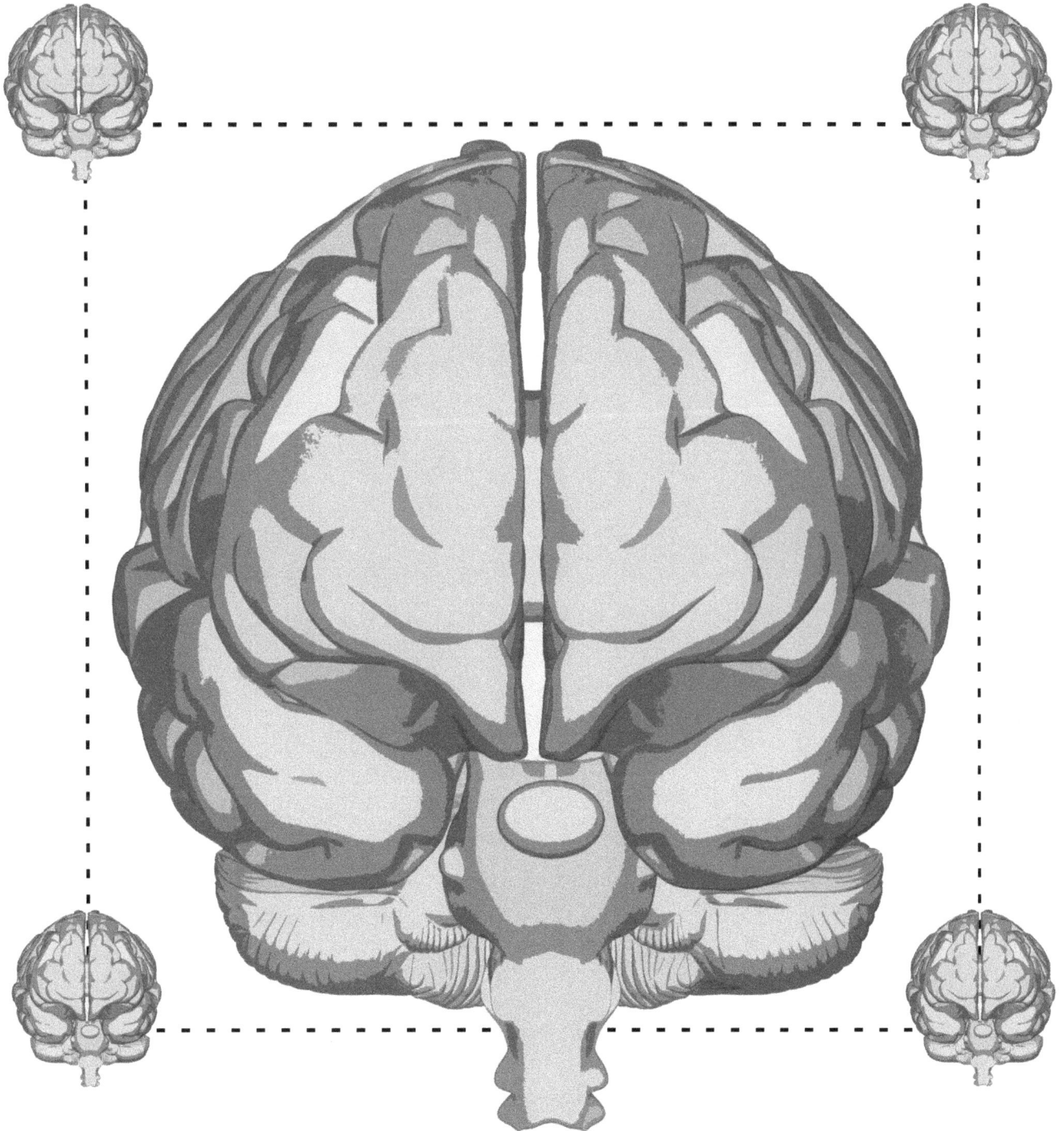

ZOMBIE QUALIFICATION TARGET

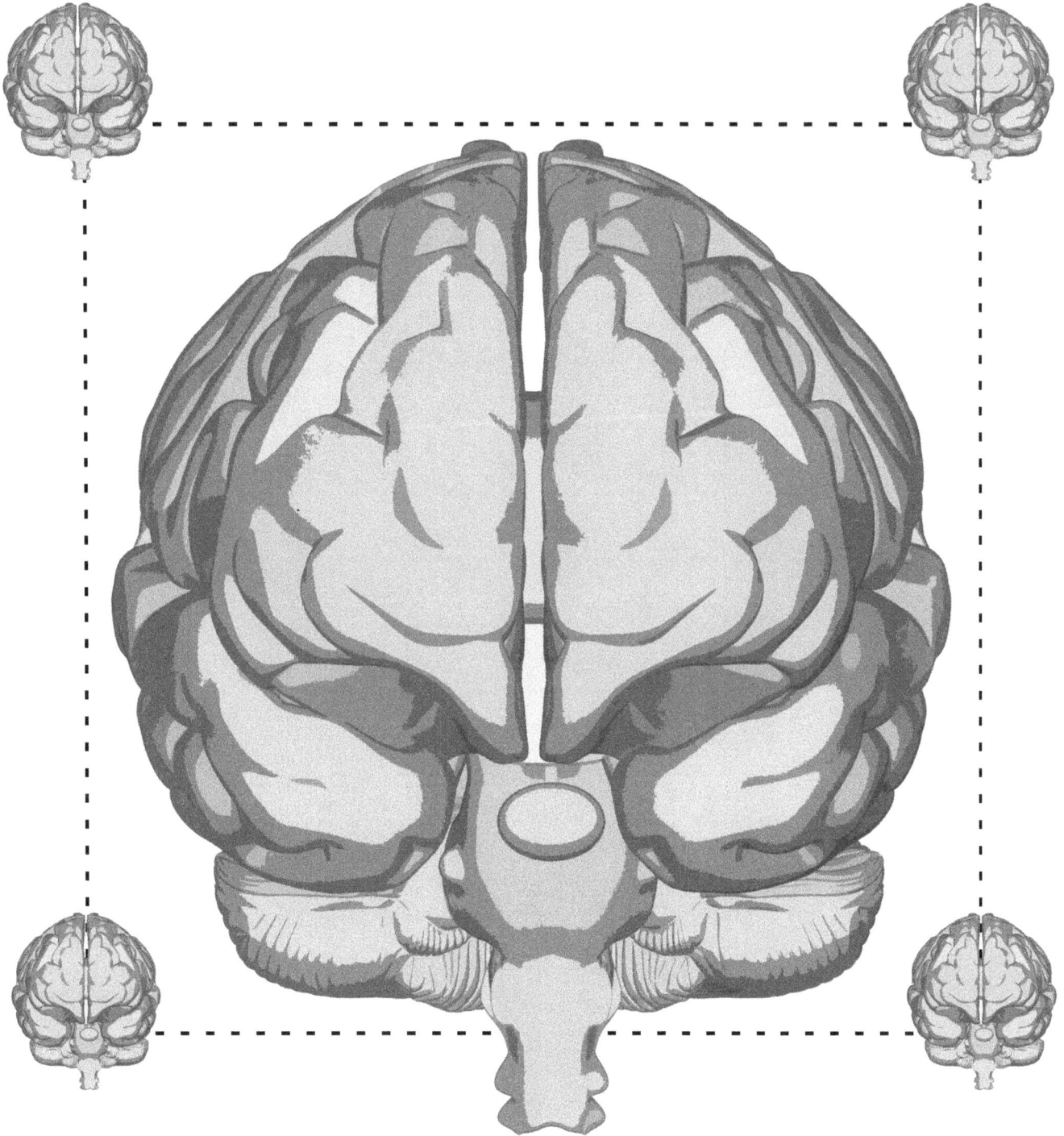

The Zombie Shooting Guide
© 2013 by Mark Greenman
Design: Brandon Finn

www.ingramcontent.com/pod-product-compliance
Lightning Source LLC
Chambersburg PA
CBHW080457110426
42742CB00017B/2910